Blantyre Mission and the Making of Modern Malawi

Copyright 2018 Andrew C. Ross

All rights reserved. No part of this publication may be reproduced, stored in a retrieval system, or transmitted in any from or by any means, electronic, mechanical, photocopying, recording or otherwise without prior permission from the publishers.

Published by
Luviri Press
P/Bag 201 Luwinga
Mzuzu 2
Malawi

ISBN   978-99960-60-56-4
eISBN   978-99960-60-55-7

Luviri Reprints no. 1

Luviri Press is represented outside Malawi by:
African Books Collective Oxford (order@africanbookscollective.com)

www.mzunipress.blogspot.com
www.africanbookscollective.com

Editorial assistance and cover: Daniel Neumann

Blantyre Mission and the Making of Modern Malawi

Andrew C. Ross

Luviri Press

Luviri Reprints no. 1
Mzuzu
2018

Luviri Reprints

Many books have been published on or in Malawi that are no longer available. While some of these books simply have run their course, others are still of interest for scholars and the general public. Some of the classics have been reprinted outside Malawi over the decades, and during the last two decades, first the Kachere Series and then other publishers have achieved "never out of stock status" by joining the African Books Collective's Print on Demand approach, but there are still a good number of books that would be of interest but are no longer in print.

The Luviri Reprint Series has taken up the task to make those books on or from Malawi, which are out of print but not out of interest, available again, through Print on Demand and therefore worldwide.

While the Luviri Reprint Series concentrates on Malawi, it is also interested in the neighbouring countries and even in those further afield.

Luviri Reprints publish the books as they originally were. Usually a new Foreword is added, and where appropriate, new information has been added. All such additions, mostly in footnotes, are marked by an asterisk (*).

The Editors

Foreword

Blantyre Mission and the Making of Modern Malawi by Andrew C. Ross is a book that should always remain in print in Malawi. It is the authoritative account of a component of Malawi's history that has been highly influential in making it the country that it is today. While other scholars will doubtless consider various aspects of the role of the Church of Scotland Blantyre Mission, no one will ever again occupy the position that Andrew Ross did in the late 1950s and early 1960s when he was able to interact with elderly people whose memories stretched back to the early beginnings of the Mission in the late 19th century. Andrew was able to talk at length, for example, with Rev Harry Kambwiri Matecheta, the first Malawian to be ordained to the ministry in 1911. By the time Andrew met him he was a very elderly man but he could remember as a 10-year old boy witnessing the arrival of the group of Scots who founded Blantyre Mission in 1876. Andrew thus had oral sources available to him that will not be accessible in the future.

He also had a particular motivation for researching the early history of Blantyre Mission. Living through the State of Emergency in 1959-60, Andrew had to face the question of what kind of country Malawi was or should be. Should it find its future in the Federation of Rhodesia and Nyasaland, under the authority of a Parliament in Salisbury dominated by white settlers or did it have a fundamentally different character and destiny? This question sent Andrew back to the late nineteenth century when the modern nation of Malawi took shape as he sought to uncover the vision that had inspired those involved at the time, particularly at the Blantyre Mission.

Another good reason for this book to remain always in print is that it contains the best available study of David Clement Scott, the head of Blantyre Mission during its most creative and ground-breaking period. In an age of many extraordinary missionaries, Scott stands out for the original and radical nature of his vision for the territory and the people among whom he was working. In particular, the tension between Scott and the fledgling British administration in the 1890s brought out the contrast between the colonialism then coming into the ascendency and the confidence in African leadership and African culture that marked Scott's leadership of the Blantyre Mission. This was a tension that came to a head in the 1950s with the movement that achieved independence for Malawi. Yet colonialism has cast a long shadow and many of the issues with which Scott was struggling are yet to be fully resolved.

The relevance of Scott's thinking is underlined also by the preoccupation of modern African theology with questions of inculturation. The first generation of African theologians who were publishing in the later part of the twentieth century were greatly concerned with the question of how to be both truly African and truly Christian. Remarkably, Scott had anticipated this concern a hundred years earlier and was far ahead of his time in grappling, in collaboration with his Malawian colleagues, with the question of what a truly African Christianity would be like. Inculturation is a perennial point of concern for mission studies and it will always be instructive to turn to the thinking of an extraordinarily creative thinker who was engaged this question during the first generation of the appropriation of the Christian faith in southern Malawian communities.

Another point that, sadly, proves to be of continuing relevance is the struggle to counter racism. This looms large in the early history of the Blantyre Mission since the Mission provided the voice of resistance to the advance of Cecil Rhodes' British South Africa Company, which aimed to include Malawi within its sphere of influence. Scott was alert to the racist ideology that guided Rhodes' operations and determined that this should not come to hold sway in Malawi. For Andrew Ross this provided inspiration when the question of racism had to be confronted again in the context of the State of Emergency in Malawi in 1959-60.

As John McCracken commented on the work of Andrew Ross: "Many academic historians see publication primarily as a means of enhancing their careers. Ross, by contrast, looked to the past to uncover examples of individual Scots whose struggles against racism and injustice could inspire those committed to similar campaigns in the present."[1] He saw Clement Scott and the Blantyre Mission as falling into this category. In an age when racism and xenophobia are resurgent in many different parts of the world, such inspiration is sorely needed. The lessons that can be learned from this book therefore have wide application and will repay study in many different contexts.

To end on a personal note, I owe a great debt to Andrew Ross. He was my doctoral supervisor at the University of Edinburgh in the 1980s, mentor and adviser when I was teaching at the University of Malawi in the 1990s, and fellow activist in rejuvenating Scotland-Malawi relations in the early 2000s. His death in 2008 deprived international scholarship of a distinctive voice and Malawi of an indefatigable champion. It is much to be welcomed that his contribution will continue to be made through this seminal book. It is an excellent choice to be the first in the projected series of Luviri Reprints that will keep important books in print for the benefit of the Malawian public and the global scholarly community.

Kenneth R. Ross

Argyll, Scotland

May 2018

---

1 John McCracken, "Andrew Ross and the Radical Strand in Scotland's Missionary Tradition", in Kenneth R. Ross ed., Roots and Fruits: Retrieving Scotland's Missionary Story, Oxford: Regnum, 2014, 86.

Abbreviations

ALC	The African Lakes Company, after 1895, the African Lakes Corporation
BCA	British Central Africa
BSA	British South Africa
BSACo	British South Africa Company
CCAP	Church of Central Africa Presbyterian
CMS	Church Mission Society
EUL	Edinburgh University Library
FMC	Foreign Mission Committee, the title of the General Assembly Committee with executive authority for the work of overseas missions in both the Church of Scotland and the Free Church of Scotland.
FO	Foreign *Office*
HMFR	*Home and Foreign Mission Record*
LMS	The London Missionary Society
LWBCA	*Life and Work in British Central Africa.* This was the monthly magazine published by the Blantyre Mission of the Church of Scotland and must not be confused with the entirely separate magazine of kindred name in Scotland. It was first published as *The Blantyre Mission Supplement* in February 1888, but soon in 1890 it took the above title. The words British Central Africa were replaced by Nyasaland, when the name of the Protectorate was changed by the British Government in 1907, and the periodical *became Life and Work in Nyasaland.*
Mal Arch	Malawi Archives
Sal Rhod Arch	Salisbury Rhodesia Archives - now the Zimbabwe National Archives
NLS	National Library of Scotland
UMCA	The Universities' Mission to Central Africa
ZIM	Zambezi Industrial Mission

Contents

Preface	11
Introduction	13
Chapter 1: The Scottish Base	19
Chapter 2: The Failure at Blantyre	49
Chapter 3: A New Beginning under David Clement Scott, 1881 - 1891	80
Chapter 4: The Need for a Protectorate	111
Chapter 5: Mission and Boma, 1889 - 1914	138
Chapter 6: The Growth of the Church: D.C. Scott as Leader	190
Chapter 7: Growth of the Church: Hetherwick as Leader	224
Chapter 8: The War and the Beginning of a New Day	242
Table of Sources	262

Preface

In March 1959 the Government of Nyasaland instituted a widespread series of arrests in order to break the power of the Nyasaland African National Congress which was threatening the authority of the Protectorate Government and the Government of the Federation of Rhodesia and Nyasaland. Many men and women were released from imprisonment in a matter of days, but at Kanjedza Camp in the town of Limbe, a thousand men and three women were held as the hard core leadership of Congress. During this time Dr. Hastings Kamuzu Banda together with Dunduzu and Yatuta Chisiza, Orton Chirwa, Masauko Chipembere, Augustine Bwanausi, David Rubadiri, Willie Chokani and other important national leaders were also briefly imprisoned in what was then Southern Rhodesia

The late Reverend Jonathan Sangaya and I were the Prebyterian ministers who went to minister to the detainees at Kanjedza Camp from September 1959. it was most exciting for me to find that approximately seven hundred of these men and two of the women were members of the Church of Central Africa Presbyterian (CCAP), mainly from the Livingstonia and Blantyre Synods. Indeed, the was a sufficient number of Church elders in the camp to enable it to be treated in practice as a congregation of the Blantyre Synod. During the time of detainment, a number of men were baptised and many others were restored to full membership in the church as a result of the ministry of the elders in the camp.

The sizable presence of Presbyterians and the faithfulness they exhibited while in prison prompted me to try to discover the source of the dynamism of the church which produced so many national leaders in what was then the British Protectorate of Nyasaland. While I was still ministering to these men and women and pondering this problem, I received a visit from Professor G.A. Shepperson, whom I had known when I was an undergraduate in Edinburgh. During that visit, he encouraged me to look into the early history of the Blantyre Mission leading up to the establishment of the CCAP, where it was hoped there might be found at least a partial answer to this problem. In 1962 the University of Edinburgh accepted this topic as a suitable one for a Ph.D. degree.

I must acknowledge my great debt to Professor Shepperson's stimulating influence on me throughout the whole period of my working on the dissertation that is the foundation of this book, an influence and friendship which has continued to this day. The Very Reverend Professor J.H.S. Burleigh, formerly Professor of Ecclesiastical History in the University, and his successor the Reverend Professor A.C. Cheyne also helped and encouraged me in those early years.

To many more African friends than I can mention, I owe a deep debt of gratitude for their affection, their teaching me to speak that very beautiful language, which I still prefer to call Nyanja, and teaching me to appreciate the traditional culture of the Nyanja, Ngoni and Yao peoples of Malawi. From among them some names must be mentioned because of their profound influence on my understanding of Malawi and the Church in Malawi. These are the late Reverend J.D. Sangaya, the late Reverend W.P. Pembeleka, as well as my dear old friend Simon Faiti Phiri. Three leading Blantyre Synod elders to whom I owe a great deal and whom I remember with warm affection are Mr Lewis Bandawe, Mr Lester Chopi, and Mr J.F. Sangala, the first President of the Nyasaland African National Congress. I must also mention two Ngoni elders, whose homes were always open to me as if they had been my own, the late Nkhosi Mandala Ngwangwa and Mr Edwin Chinkondenji.

The late Professor Eric Stokes of Cambridge University, Dr Robert Rotberg of M.I.T. and, in particular, Dr John McCracken of Stirling University all helped me on a number of occasions by their willingness to share ideas and knowledge about the Zambezian past and the European impact upon it.

Although the basic research for this book was done many years ago, I have not felt the need to make massive revisions to what I wrote then. The social and political changes in recent years have shown that the CCAP is still playing an important role in the life of the modern nation to whose early growth and shape it contributed significantly.

Andrew C. Ross

Edinburgh, February 1996

Introduction

It would be impossible to fully understand the modern nation of Malawi without reference to the Blantyre Mission of the Church of Scotland. First, this Mission played a decisive role in the establishment of the British Protectorate in 1889-91 which laid down Malawi's national borders. The same Mission, together with its northern sister, Livingstonia Mission, proved to be the seedbed of the nationalist movement which finally succeeded in achieving independence for Malawi in 1964.[2] More recently, when Malawi emerged from the repressive one-party era and the Second Republic was inaugurated in 1994, the Blantyre Synod made a strategic contribution to the political transition.[3] To trace the emergence and political development of Malawi up to the present day is an exercise which requires frequent reference to the Blantyre Mission. Malawian society, likewise, has been profoundly influenced by the missionary enterprise begun by a handful of Scots in the mid-1870s. Their vision of "Christianity and commerce" has to a remarkable extent been fulfilled as a great modem city has grown up around the Mission. Blantyre today is a thriving commercial community and the main urban centre between Harare and Dar-es-Salaam. The Mission has also been a major force in education and today there are cabinet ministers, diplomats and many other civic leaders who owe their education to Blantyre Mission. Biographies and autobiographies of Malawians who were trained and prepared for life by the Mission bear eloquent testimony to the impact which it had on African development.[4] Above all, however, this missionary endeavour has contributed substantially to a

---

[2] See KN. Mufuka, *Missions and Politics in Malawi*, (Kingston, Ontario: The Limestone Press, 1977), pp. 146-95.

[3] See KS. Nzunda & KR. Ross (eds.), *Church, Law and Political Transition in Malawi 1992-94*, (Gweru, Zimbabwe: Mambo Press, 1995), pp. 31-42; and KR. Ross, "The Renewal of the State by the Church: the Case of the Public Affairs Committee in Malawi", *Religion in Malawi*, no. 5 (1995), pp. 29-37.

[4] See e.g., LM. Bandawe, *Memoirs of a Malawian*, (Blantyre: CLAIM, 1971); S.S. Ncozana, *Sangaya*, (Blantyre: CLAIM, 1996); E.T. Ngwira, "The Life and "I lmes of Rev Harry Kambwiri Matecheta, 1870-1962", History Seminar Paper, Chancellor College, University of Malawi, 1973; D.D. Phiri, *James Frederick Sangala*, (Lilongwe: Longman, 1974).

religious transformation throughout what is now the Southern Region of Malawi. The early mission stations at Blantyre, Domasi, Zomba, Mulanje and Nthumbi have expanded into a network of congregations which fairly effectively covers the territory from Nsanje in the south to Ntcheu in the north, and from Mwanza in the west to Mangochi in the east. Today the Blantyre Synod of the Church of Central Africa Presbyterian comprises 13 Presbyteries, 300 congregations and 955,000 church members.[5] In these communities there has occurred the creative integration of Christian faith and African life of which the early missionaries dreamed, so that today an indigenous Christianity is a vibrant force shaping Malawian life and culture.

In order to account for these remarkable developments, it is necessary to attempt a thorough analysis of the origins of the Blantyre Mission and its early beginnings. This must begin with consideration of the Livingstone legend. Taking its name from the birthplace of the great explorer, there can be no doubt that the Mission was inspired by the vision and commitment of David Livingstone. Yet examination of the initial launching, organization and funding of the Mission will show that it worked from a very fragile home base. This partly accounts for the near-failure of the first five years when the missionaries' clumsy attempts to establish a civil jurisdiction almost resulted in a fate similar to that of the Anglican Mission (UMCA) which had been established at nearby Magomero in 1861 but which lasted less than a year.[6] The crisis of 1880-81 was surmounted, however, and during the 1880s the Mission began to take root under the leadership of David Clement Scott. It also built up sufficient support in Scotland to be able to put pressure on the British Government to declare a Protectorate after threats in the late 1880s that the Shire Highlands might become Portuguese territory. This set the scene for a new political tension in the 1890s as the colonialist approach of the British administration provoked opposition from Scott and his fellow missionaries with their "Africa for the Africans" vision. Fierce

---

[5] Letter from Rev. M.E. Kansilanga, General Secretary, CCAP Synod of Blantyre, 23 February 1996.

[6] See O. Chadwick, *Mackenziet Grave*, (London: Hodder & Stoughton, 1959); L White, *Magomero: Portrait of an African Village*, (Cambridge: Cambridge University Press, 1987).

debates raged on such issues as land, labour, taxation and the manner in which British rule was imposed. Meanwhile the Mission was engaging with the local communities at a deeper level. The missionaries mastered the Nyanja and Yao languages and began to take the biblical message into the vernacular world of the people of Malawi. In the villages there occurred the African appropriation of the Christian faith which would prove to be of momentous importance for the future. While the structures of colonial government erected by Sir Harry Johnston and his successors would one day have to be dismantled, the reception of the Christian faith among the people of Malawi would prove to be a much more profound and durable transformation. This book aims to give as full an account as possible of the early years of the Blantyre Mission so that its impact on Malawian life up to the present day might be more fully appreciated.

Before considering in detail the Scottish base from which the Mission originated, it is necessary to sketch very briefly some historical background to the Shire Highlands area, in what is now southern Malawi, where it came to establish its centre.[7] The original inhabitants were Nyanja/Mang'anja, branches of the once famous Maravi people. When David Livingstone first visited the area in 1859 he found a peaceful and fairly homogeneous society which, together with the favourable climate and topography, convinced him that he had found a place suitable for European settlement and for development as a base to combat the slave trade and preach the Christian message. The fact that a very different socio-political situation had developed by the time the Blantyre missionaries arrived in 1876 is primarily owing to two exceedingly disruptive forces which entered the scene. From the 1850s groups of Yao began to migrate into the Shire Highlands area from the direction of northern Mozambique.[8] Soon they would become the dominant ethnic group around the southern shores of Lake Malawi and across much of the Shire Highlands. It was partly an inability to come to terms with Yao-

---

[7] For a contemporary account see J. Buchanan, *The Shire Highlands as a Colony and Mission,* (Edinburgh: Blackwood, 1885).

[8] See KM. Phiri, 'Yao Intrusion into Southern Malawi, Nyanja Resistance, and Colonial Conquest, 1830-1900", *Transafrican Journal of History,* vol. 13 (1984), pp. 157-76.

Mang'anja conflict which led to the collapse of the short-lived Anglican Mission at Magomero in 1862. Soon, however, both Nyanja and Yao came under the threat of another group of immigrants. Amongst the groups of migrant Ngoni propelled northwards from Natal by the exploits of Shaka was one led by Maseko which in 1868 settled in the Ntcheu area just to the north of the Shire Highlands.[9] The military strength and formidable social organization of the Ngoni immediately made them a dominant force and most of the autochtonous peoples in the vicinity came under their rule. The Blantyre Mission, from the time of its establishment in the late 1870s, acted as a barrier to the construction of Ngoni hegemony in the Shire Highlands. A further development which owed something to Livingstone was the establishment of a Makololo state in the Shire Valley.[10] The Makololo were a people of Sotho stock who had moved northwards into Zambezia. Livingstone had recruited servants and porters from among them and, when his Zambezi expedition ended, some of these men decided to stay in Malawi. They quickly established their dominance over the indigenous Mang'anja and organized a little state in the Shire Valley under the Paramount Chief Ramakukan. Finally, in creating a haven of peace in what had been a turbulent environment, the Blantyre missionaries were responsible for drawing in the Lomwe people from their original homeland in Mozambique.[11] This meant that by the time the Mission became fully established in the 1890s, it was catering for an ethnically diverse African population amongst whom the Christian Gospel became a common denominator.

To begin the story, however, we must return to the situation in the 1870s when the combined impact of the "invasions" of Yao, Ngoni and Makololo had radically altered and thrown into flux the Shire Highlands society which Livingstone had known. It was into this fast-changing social

---

[9] See I. Linden, "The Maseko Ngoni at Domwe, 1870-1900", in B. Pachai ed., *Early History of Malawi*, (London: Longman, 1972), pp. 237-51.

[10] See N. Northrup, "The Migrations of the Yao and Kololo into Southern Malawi: Aspects of Migrations in 19th Century Africa', *International Journal of African Historical Studies*, vol. 19, no. 1 (1986), pp. 59-75.

[11] See R.B. Baader, *Silent Majority: A History of the Lomwe*, (Pretoria: Africa Institute, 1985).

and political environment that a further disturbance was introduced in 1875 when Lt E.D. Young led a party of Scots missionaries from the Free Church of Scotland to found a mission intended to fulfil Livingstone's intention of transforming African society through the impact of "commerce and Christianity."[12] Livingstone held that the barriers preventing the new life that the Gospel brings from coming to fruition in Africa were not primarily the sinfulness of individual Africans, but the actual structures of African society. Fundamentally the fact that Zambezia and the Lacustrine area of Africa were dominated by the slave trade meant that no new life for the people of the area could grow. A new pattern of trade and social relations had to be created. He believed that a legitimate European commercial presence could, when backed by the educational as well as evangelistic influence of Christian missions, set Africa free to find a new future. It was with this "Livingstonian" understanding of mission that the Free Church pioneers came to Malawi. Accompanying their first party was Henry Henderson, whose task it was to find a suitable site for the establishment of a second mission, that of the established Church of Scotland, the "Auld Kirk". This effort was organized by people imbued with a similar vision to that of the Free Church organizers, and it was hoped that the two would work together in one task. This final strand in the complicated weave of Malawi society in the 1870s was a decisive one. Its presence prevented the stabilizing of Malawi society around Ngoni or Yao power and began a new era of even more profound change and disturbance.

---

[12] See KJ. McCracken, *Politics and Christianity in Malawi 1875-1940: the Impact of Living-stonia Mission in the Northam Province*, (Cambridge: Cambridge University Press, 1977); 2nd ed. in preparation under ths Kachere Series, to be published by CLAIM, Blantyre, 1996.

Chapter 1: The Scottish Base

One of the main themes of this work is a study of the ideas of the Scottish missionaries who served the Blantyre Mission, the beliefs and ideas that are implied in their actual policy as well as those which they expressed when reflecting on their task. However, just as these must not be seen apart from African society, neither can they be properly understood without some reference to the Scotland and the Church of Scotland from which these men and women came.

The attitude of the Church of Scotland and the other Scottish Presbyterian churches to the task of mission needs more thorough investigation than it has yet received. It merits fresh study not only in its own right but as part of a much needed fresh look at the history of Scotland in the 19th century, but this is a design much too large for a single chapter in a work devoted to another subject.

What can be studied in the small compass available is the specific issue of how the Church of Scotland supported, in terms of personnel and money, the Blantyre Mission which was, at that time its only mission in Africa.

In almost every book which deals with Christian missions in the 19th century, there is reference to the enthusiasm in Scotland for a mission to Central Africa triggered off by the drama of David Livingstone's lonely death and the return of his body to Britain.[1] In popular books on the mission of the church, in the sermons preached on missionary themes, in Church magazines and newspapers, we find the full flower of this idea. The period from Livingstone's death until the First World War is viewed as the golden era of Scottish missionary activity. This period is often used as a ruler with which to measure, to its discredit, the missionary enthusiasm of the Church of Scotland in more recent periods.

Let us look then at the Church of Scotland and its Blantyre Mission during those forty years. The period is held to be one which began with a wave of enthusiasm in Scotland followed by years during which concern was maintained at a high level. The accuracy of this assumed view must be judged by the availability of suitable candidates for service, by the level

---

[1] See, e.g., C.P. Groves, *The Planting of Christianity in Africa*, (London: Lutterworth, 1948-1955), vol. 2, p.301.

of financial support and by the width of the constituency from which this support came.

The era can be conveniently divided into three parts: first, 1874, when Dr Macrae of Hawick first suggested the setting up of the mission, until 1881 when it had to be reconstituted under David Clement Scott; then from 1881 until 1898 when Dr Scott left Blantyre for good; and the third period which ends with the opening of the First World War during which time the Mission was led by Alexander Hetherwick.

The First Period

When the records of the period are examined the picture that emerges is not at all what might be expected from the description of the period in the traditional church history of Scotland. In 1874 after Livingstone's funeral "a thousand pulpits" are said to have taken up the missionary call he left with Scotland. As well as this urgent pressure, that year also saw the Moody and Sankey mission to Scotland. This mission was almost universally hailed as having been a success in deepening the Christian life of Scotland in all the main Protestant denominations, the Church of Scotland and Episcopal Church as well as the Free Church and the United Presbyterians. Dr J.R. Fleming wrote:

> When the General Assemblies met in May their members found themselves face to face with something almost unique in the religious experience of the land. One Free Church minister, Dr Julius Wood, went so far as to describe it as 'an outpouring of the Holy Spirit more extensive and remarkable than any that has taken place since Apostolic times.' In more sober language Professor Charteris, in the Church of Scotland Record, April 1874, bore testimony to the depth and reality of the movement.[2]

After attending Livingstone's funeral in Westminster Abbey, Dr James Stewart, who had visited Zambezia during Livingstone's Zambezi Expedition of 1858-63, now began to plan for the sending of a Free Church of Scotland Mission there. At the time of his original visit he had warned the Free Church of the inadvisability of a mission to the area, and indeed,

---

[2] J.R. Fleming, *The Church of Scotland, 1843-1874*, (Edinburgh: T. & T. Clark, 1933), pp. 236-237.

had come to dislike Dr Livingstone and disapprove of his methods. In 1873 he now changed his mind.

However, the first person to begin to gather funds and set in train detailed planning of a mission to Zambezia appears to have been, not Dr Stewart, but Dr John Macrae of Hawick, appointed by the Church of Scotland to chair an African Mission Committee. He approached Lt E.D. Young of the Royal Navy, who had been two years on the Zambezi with Livingstone, to lead a mission to the area. Almost immediately a similar request was made to Young from the Free Church side. Young replied to both suggesting a joint Scottish national mission but this idea did not appeal to either church.[3] Since Macrae had, as yet, no staff appointed nor even received any firm offers of service, Young turned to the Free Church whose scheme was more firmly underway. However, it should be noted that the main backing for the Free Church scheme came from a committee of Glasgow businessmen rather than from the Assembly of the Free Church. At the same time Dr Macrae was writing in every edition of the Missionary Herald and using all other means at his disposal to attract recruits for the new mission that had been formally approved by the General Assembly of the Church of Scotland of 1874. Yet in the months following that Assembly, which we have been told had come face to face with a great spiritual revival, during these same months when 'a thousand pulpits' had taken up Livingstone's call, Macrae almost despaired of getting the mission started at all. In November we find him writing in the Record:

> Will no successors from Scotland be found to tread the path of her Christian Warrior? No Volunteers of Scotland to go forth to endure hardness as becomes the soldiers of Christ ... and shall the Church of Scotland be the only communion which has not planted her disciples on African soil?[4]

In the January edition of the same magazine, Macrae reports that a final year theology student had volunteered, the sole candidate for service up till then. He went on to appeal for volunteers from among the younger clergy as leaders for the proposed expedition. In March 1875, he was

---

[3] D. MacDonald, *Africana,* (Edinburgh: Blackwood, 1893), vol. 2, p. 19.

[4] *Church of Scotland Home and Foreign Mission Record,* vol. 9, November, 1874.

driven to defending the setting up of an African mission at all, the needs of India and Scotland itself were suggested as being task enough. The spiritual revival would seem to have had a rather limited vision.

It was only that same month that the first serious candidate presented himself to Macrae's committee. This was Henry Henderson. He had lived for a number of years on the Queensland "frontier" and knew a great deal about pioneering in the "bush". Henderson volunteered to be a pioneer and pathfinder for the Church of Scotland Mission. He was accepted and hurried arrangements were made for him to travel out to the Lake Malawi region in company with Lt Young and the Free Church party. Henderson's task was to find a site for the new mission and then to await the arrival of the Church of Scotland party, when he would lead them in laying out and organizing their station. He set off, little worried, it appeared, by the fact that no such party had yet been recruited.

In the next chapter, the plan for the mission by Macrae's committee will be discussed. We will see how the missionaries sent out were put in a most difficult position, legally and morally, as well as geographically. For the moment, however, the point is that when Henderson sailed for Africa in 1875 there were as yet no other recruits even being considered, far less selected and ready to follow him.

The situation, then, of the Church of Scotland Foreign Mission Committee was desperate and any kind of careful process of selection of volunteers appears to have been dropped. Even when a very motley group had been got together, no ordained minister volunteered to go with the party. The party of volunteers who were assembled to go out to set up the first mission station was headed by a physician Dr T. Thornton Macklin. The others were John Buchanan, George Fenwick, Jonathan Duncan, William Milne and John Walker. There is always a great diversity of talent, temperament and character in any party of missionaries one cares to study, but this was a truly extraordinary group. They ranged from Dr Macklin and John Buchanan, dedicated Christian men with a passionate zeal to end the slave trade, even if it meant using force, to George Fenwick, an adventurer who would not have been out of place among the mercenaries from Scotland who played such a role in the Swedish and German armies of the 17th century.

Duff MacDonald, who went out in 1878 to be the pastor at Blantyre, in his important book, *Africana* (written in 1881), was very loyal to these men though they made his job exceedingly difficult. However, two passages reveal what some of these men were really like:

> We arrived at Blantyre at a very critical period of the mission's history.... Many of the artisans did not wish to continue in the service of the Mission, believing that they would find it better to become traders and chiefs among the natives ... some were large landed proprietors in their own right.[5]

Again in a period of depression over the attitude of the home authorities towards him and the mission, he recorded an even more devastating story in his journal:

> June 2nd. - Shortly after my return from Zomba, there occurred a melancholy incident which illustrates the difficulties that may flow from sending to a Mission men who do not even profess Christianity.... A misunderstanding arose between an artisan and a native headman, and the matter was being settled by the Lay Superintendent, when the artisan so far lost his temper, as to strike the poor headman a violent blow, which covered his face with blood ... in such cases little can be done. The artisan if dismissed, has it in his power to stay in the country and give a good deal of annoyance.... Indeed one often felt the need for a proper government in such a remote place. It was no uncommon thing for an artisan to threaten to shoot his fellow labourers, and to send them letters challenging them to deadly combat.[6]

The very strange "missionary" qualities of some of the Blantyre party was confirmed by David Clement Scott. Soon after his arrival at Blantyre in 1881 he wrote privately to his close friend, the Reverend James Robertson, about Fenwick and Walker.

> I fear heavy complications - Walker and Fenwick, in their intercourse with Chipatula and the Makololo chiefs, have lowered immensely their respect for the English. (This is hardly to be made public - Walker and Fenwick in the very house in which we are living for the present, used to drink with Chipatula when he came - the language

---

[5] MacDonald, *Africana*, vol. 2, p. 82.
[6] *Ibid*, pp. 258-9.

they used was fearful.) Walker afterwards went to Chipatula to try making use of him to make himself of some power, but Chipatula was trying to do the same with Walker. The chiefs liked Walker and Fenwick because they were war men and for other similar reasons.[7]

In the same letter Scott writes of having been at the valedictory service which sent that original party on its way to join Henry Henderson at Blantyre. He says:

> The men chosen for the mission were most unaccountably fit [sic] - without profession of Christian life or missionary spirit, and not even good workmen.[8]

Thus we have the witness of both MacDonald and D.C. Scott as to the character of the first missionary recruits. They did their work astonishingly well despite this in some ways. Jonathan Duncan began the cultivation of very successful gardens, and the others at least made a start to the training of Africans as artisans and the compilation of word lists of the Yao language. Under Dr Macklin's leadership a campaign against slave raiders in the areas of the chiefs with whom they had established good relations was initiated, and later, after MacDonald arrived with his wife, a school was begun.

However, apart from the MacDonalds, no new staff were forthcoming until the mission was dissolved and re-started in 1881. So for the first two years of its life, the Blantyre Mission of the Church of Scotland had no clergyman at all. At the Assembly of 1877 the Foreign Mission Committee was compelled to report that:

> It is with pain and regret that the Committee have to report that, notwithstanding many and sustained efforts, they have not succeeded in obtaining an ordained minister to the Mission.... It was scarcely dreamed of, that a year would pass, and yet, notwithstanding many calls, see the Mission without its spiritual leader. The want, indeed, is temporarily supplied by the charity of the

---

[7] D.C. Scott to James Robertson, December 1881. EUL Ms. 717/10.
[8] Ibid

> sister Mission but is it not a matter of humiliation that no one has come forth from the ordained ranks of the Church to go to Blantyre?[9]

It was in November 1877 that MacDonald was approached about going to Blantyre. He did not volunteer but unlike the many to whom an appeal had been made before, he did not refuse, and, after much thought, agreed to go. From then on, as we have seen, there were no volunteers nor did anyone else respond to approaches by the Foreign Mission Committee. We are therefore forced to ask, where was the response to the call to action presented by the loss of Scotland's missionary hero? Where was the practical effect of the revival to whose depth and effectiveness Professor Charteris had attested in the Assembly of 1874?

As we have already noted the Blantyre Mission was and is seen as a fruit of that revival and of the impact of Livingstone's death upon the Church of Scotland. Yet from the first calls that went out in 1874 it took four years to produce a response from one solitary minister out of a total 1,300 ordained men. The Kirk's pioneer party was made up of anyone who offered, two of whom, Walker and Fenwick, on the excellent authority of Duff MacDonald and D.C. Scott, were recognizably not men of Christian conviction let alone men on fire with concern for the spread of the Gospel in Africa. MacDonald at one point says:

> When our friends in Scotland had tried to dissuade us from going to Africa, they had pointed out how prudent the men were who got no further in mission work than to address drawing-room meetings.[10]

The enthusiasm of the years between Dr Macrae's first call for volunteers and the tragedy of the dismissal of MacDonald from Blantyre may have produced many of these prudent enthusiasts; it certainly did not produce candidates for service in Africa. What was the financial situation during those eight years? Was it that many people were moved by the appeals but could not go themselves and so contributed their wealth instead? The Reports of the Foreign Mission Committee to the General Assembly do not bear this out. Instead in the General Assembly of 1880 the Foreign Mission Committee had to point out the extreme seriousness of the

---

[9] *Reports of the General Assembly of the Church of Scotland 1877, Foreign Mission Committee Report* p. 134.

[10] *MacDonald, Africans,* vol. 2, p. 73.

situation. Its reserves had run out and it had no prospects unless things changed radically so that it could balance its income and expenditure. The figures that it presented were:

Year	Collections	Legacies	Total	Expenditures
1875	£9,720	£2,444	£12,416	£8,679
1876	10,306	4,490	14,796	13,881
1877	9,158	1,155	10,313	11,541
1878	8,793	4,892	13,685	13,367
1897	8,460	2,554	11,014	16,061

An impassioned appeal was made in the Report to all ministers and office-bearers to stimulate giving by their personal example. The next year things were even worse. An apparently higher total was achieved but only because of an extraordinarily large legacy; the actual giving by the congregations was down again, continuing the downward trend we see above. The figures were: Collections £7,697, legacies £7,512, a total of £15,209. This rate of decline in the regular giving to overseas mission of the Church led the FMC to declare:

> The state of the funds is of the gravest importance. In the last Report the steady growth of outlay was emphasized, with the need of a growing income. Founded on this, an urgent appeal was made in the pew-notice for the annual Collection in December. With rare exceptions, congregations have scarcely been moved to greater liberality as a consequence ... Retrenchment can be carried out only by abandoning stations and discharging agents. There is but one alternative - the immediate doubling of the ordinary income ... doubtless there are congregations and individuals who already do their utmost, but without controversy this cannot be said of the Church at large.[11]

With an income from giving which had fallen by 24% in five years, this was an understatement indeed. A warning to the General Assembly of

---

[11] *Assembly Reports, 1881.* FMC Report, pp. 51-2.

the possible need to close mission stations and to discharge missionaries because of the lack of financial support, when taken together with the desperate lengths the Committee had been driven to in order to get staff for Blantyre, makes nonsense of any claim that the Church of Scotland was awake to Livingstone's call for a mission to Central Africa, or for any other call to missionary action. Of the Moody and Sankey mission in Scotland, Dr Fleming reported:

> From Edinburgh the flame spread to Dundee, Glasgow and the West, Aberdeen, etc., and it may be said that by the end of the summer of 1874 the whole country was set on fire. James Stalker and other men of promise fresh from College entered with enthusiasm into the work of evangelism ... The central motive behind everything was the winning of human lives for the service of Christ. There never had been a revival more insistent on the connection between saving faith and redemptive effort for the world's good, and the fruits were manifest in the dedication of all that was best in young Scotland to this end.[12]

This blaze, this concern and dedication did not extend to the Foreign Missionary activity of the Church of Scotland, though this church was just as much caught up by the revival as were the Free Church and the United Presbyterian Church.

The Second Period

In December 1881 David Clement Scott arrived in Blantyre and the second period of the history of Blantyre Mission began. As we shall see in later chapters this was a period of success, the foundations of both the Church and of a new Malawi were laid during this time. It was of this period that Stephen Neill writes:

> Nyasaland was divided between the UMCA and the Scots, the two great Presbyterian Churches of Scotland coming in with a wonderful array of enterprises - evangelistic, educational, industrial and

---

[12] Fleming, *The Church of Scotland, 1843-1874*, p. 236.

agricultural, certainly among the best organised mission projects in the world.[13]

This judgement of the work done in the field is echoed by many contemporary observers, including hostile ones like Sir Harry Johnston. When D.C. Scott took leave of Blantyre for the last time in 1898, he left behind a rapidly growing primary school system, an apprenticeship programme, a growing literature in Yao and Nyanja, *an* efficient printing house, and, most important, a mushrooming African church. Does this mean that in Scotland the dreadful situation that existed during the first period of the mission's existence had been transformed into one of enthusiasm and concern for mission? Certainly more candidates came forward and at least some more money was produced than heretofore; but these changes were not big enough to be evidence of a growth in general concern for mission in the Auld Kirk.

During this period the Foreign Mission Committee had a full-time Convenor who had no other responsibilities but the work of this committee. He was Dr John McMurtrie, an extremely hard-working and committed man. All through the years we are considering, McMurtrie was torn by two opposing forces. One was the desire for a balanced budget of a General Assembly which rarely could get from the whole church the money to meet existing commitments. The other was the constant call from the missionaries in the field for more money and personnel to take advantage of the many new opportunities that were opening up, and to meet the desperate need for hospitals and schools which they saw around them. These needs the missionaries in Blantyre in this period often met by overspending their budget and further increasing Dr McMurtrie's difficulties with the General Assembly.

As we shall see candidates for service certainly came to be in better supply as the period went on, however, very often there was no money in the ordinary budget for their salaries. More rarely there was money but no candidate and still too often there were neither candidate nor money to carry out a task that D.C. Scott felt needed to be carried out.

---

[13] S. Neill, *A History of Christian Missions,* (Harmondsworth: Penguin, 1964), pp. 387-8.

When D.C. Scott went to Blantyre in 1881, he joined Henry Henderson and the gardener, Jonathan Duncan, both retained from the original mission party. By the time of the setting up of the British Protectorate in 1891, he had gathered around him a very able group of people, of whom the most outstanding were Dr Bowie, Reverend W.A. Scott, Reverend Henry Scott, Reverend Robert Cleland, Reverend Alexander Hetherwick, John McIlwain; Miss Janet Beck and Miss Margaret Christie. From then until 1914 many others came to serve, but none were of this calibre save Dr Neil Macvicar, who succeeded Dr Bowie, and the Reverend Robert Napier.

When we consider carefully the pre-1891 staff, the outstanding feature of them as a group is their close personal relationships to D.C. Scott. W.A. Scott was his brother; Bowie and Henderson were his brothers-in-law; Robert Cleland became a missionary as a result of meeting Scott; McIlwain was a carpenter already working in the Shire Highlands who was drawn into the service of the mission by Scott. Hetherwick alone was not related to him by family or sentiment, though he became a close friend and eventually his right hand man.

At first the Church in Scotland produced little or no support for Scott, and he was as understaffed as MacDonald had been, though the staff was of a high standard unlike those serving with MacDonald. Until late in 1887 Scott had only the aid of Hetherwick and five laymen, Dr Peden, Henry Henderson, Duncan, McIlwain and Hamilton, a teacher who went out in 1885, to run the two stations of Blantyre and Domasi. From 1887 till 1891 there was an increase in the number of recruits, most of whom, as we have noted, were in some sense Scott's own. As a result the year 1892 opened with the Mission staffed in a manner that Scott felt at last to be nearly adequate. The staff consisted of five ordained men, two of whom were also physicians, another physician and eight other lay missionaries who were teachers, craftsmen and agriculturalists. There were also four lady missionaries to take care of the girl boarders and for evangelistic work among women. From then until 1914 the staff was maintained at roughly this level but no positive response was made in Scotland to appeals for an increase in staff to meet the opportunities for advance in the Shire Valley, in Lomweland or Ngoniland. Even maintaining this level was difficult; for though there was a steady flow of candidates, the flow was never a flood, indeed, the officials of the FMC were easily upset if Blantyre missionaries on furlough insisted on a strict scrutiny of the candidates. Typically Dr McMurtrie complained to David Scott:

> We have been sorely tried by the difficulty of getting missionaries. You know the Doctor rejected two, and Mr Hetherwick is as hard to please as the Doctor; of course he is only thinking of what is best for the mission.[14]

The year 1888 and those that followed immediately saw the first real movement of men and women to serve in Africa. It was also the period when Blantyre became well known in many Scottish homes because of the powerful campaigns launched to provoke some sort of action on the part of the British Government to prevent a Portuguese or Arab take-over of Malawi. This agitation, which led to the declaration of a British Protectorate over what is now Malawi, was more effective than anything heretofore in bringing the cause of the mission to the attention of a wide circle of people. Indeed the campaigners mounted so many meetings and provoked such a mass of correspondence in the press that it must have been difficult for any educated Scots family to escape knowing about it. This was only a transient phenomenon but it played its part in producing recruits and financial support for Blantyre.

It was at this time that the Church of Scotland began the setting up of organizations at Presbytery and parish levels to work for the stimulation and maintaining of interest in the overseas work of the Church. The Assembly of 1886 began this process with the following resolution:

> The General Assembly believes that there is room for calling forth and sustaining increased interest in missions by improved organisation, and such other means as the observance of Mission Sundays, and visits from the Convenor and other deputies. They authorize the Committee to communicate with the Presbyteries, ministers and Kirk Sessions, with a view to the formation of organizing Mission commit-

---

[14] McMurtrie to D.C. Scott, 8 October 1897. Letter Book of Convenor of Church of Scotland, FMC, M.3.

tees or other similar agencies, which may benefit this and all the schemes of the Church.[15]

These associations came to be formed just at the time of the Protectorate agitation. Their principal aim was the raising of funds; but they also played their part in presenting the challenge to service abroad. However, it should be noted that only 460 out of the 1300 parishes of Scotland responded in any way at all to the letters of the FMC about the implementation of this decision of the General Assembly.

A further development took place as a result of the General Assembly of 1896, at which a new organization was begun called the Mission Advance Movement. It also was to be, like that of 1886, a network of organizations at Presbytery and parish level, they were to absorb the old mission committees set up as a result of the old scheme of 1886 where those existed. Again the prime aim was the raising of funds and the stimulation of candidates for service in mission abroad. Again the response was generally disappointing. Only one third of all parishes had taken up the scheme by the time of the Assembly of 1898. Therefore, in the twelve years since the original deliverance of the General Assembly of 1886, there had been no increase in the size of the sector of the Church showing any effective interest in the work of the Foreign Mission Committee. On the other hand, with the creation of parish level organizations, there was a definite increase in support over the days before 1886, when the only institution at parish level authorized by the General Assembly for the work of the FMC was the retiring collection once a year on Mission Sunday.

It is difficult to find any other general factors accounting for the increase in the number of candidates after 1888. It may be that more came forward as a result of the working out through the schools and universities of Scotland of the impact of the Moody and Sankey revival, more especially the influence on young people of Henry Drummond the "find" of the 1874-5 campaign of Moody and Sankey. However, to confirm this suggestion would be a major work of research in itself, and in any case there is no explicit reference supporting such a connection in any of the extant letters, reports, diaries, journal articles of any who

---

[15] *Assembly Reports,* 1886, FMC Report, Introduction, p. 51.

went to work for the Blantyre Mission. Indeed the only reference to Drummond in the available material is the scathing dismissal of Drummond's book, *Tropical Africa* as nonsense by D.C. Scott.[16]

This improvement in the staffing situation can only be called good when com-pared with the apparently hopeless situation of the years 1874 to 1888. The improvement was always just enough to maintain the staffing situation of 1892 for work that was centred on four stations, Blantyre, Zomba, Domasi and Mulanje. Again and again one or other of these stations was threatened with closure because of shortness of staff; but somehow such a disaster was always avoided. At no time did the staffing situation allow for the planning of a new station in any of the three newly opened up areas which Scott had set heart on from the mid-eighties; Ngoniland, Lomweland or Kawinga's chiefdom.

This precarious situation cannot be taken as proof of any great mission-ary concern in the Kirk; however, it must be added that it cannot be taken as proof of indifference either. When has there been a flood of volunteers for arduous missionary service within any communion? One perhaps has to go back to the stream of young men leaving the College at Geneva to spread Calvinist Christianity over Europe or the initial Jesuit missionary outreach when there were far more Jesuits willing to go forth from Europe than the Spanish and Portuguese colonial authorities would allow. Indeed it must be conceded that fewer deaths from tropical disease and only a very few more candidates would have allowed a massive expansion along the lines that D.C. Scott envisioned. Yet those changes while of enormous importance to Christianity in Malawi and Mozambique, would not have been significant as a sign of missionary enthusiasm in Scotland.

The situation within the Church of Scotland is more clearly seen when the fund-raising efforts of the Foreign Mission Committee are considered. Until the Assembly of 1886, the normal method of raising funds for the work of the FMC had been contributions from the parishes, from individuals and from legacies. The parish contributions were made by the kirk sessions from the offerings of the people, plus the proceeds of a special collection taken at the door of the Church on one Sunday of the

---

[16] D.C. Scott to James Robertson, 19 October 1888, EUL Ms. 717/10.

year. This money, as was the later source of funds provided by collections made by the Sunday Schools, was within the disposal of the kirk sessions and is what is listed in the first column of statistics at the end of the chapter. In that table legacies have a separate column. The centre column of figures, listed from 1881 onwards, is money received from local missionary societies and associations, at first privately organized but from 1886 the recommended missionary aid organization of the Kirk.

We have already seen how in Duff MacDonald's time the parish contributions fell by 24% in five years. From then on they rose until by 1891 the average was about £11,000 per year. Thereafter there appears to have been a large increase in support. However these figures are misleading because, from 1890 until 1899, they include money raised by special efforts made by informal groups and wealthy individuals as special contributions to clear the accumulated debts of the FMC. The present writer could find no financial records of the period that distinguished the routine parish contributions from these special debt clearing exercises which were organized on a different basis. Thus for these nine years it is impossible to gauge accurately the levels of parish contributions. The suspicion that they did not rise much is encouraged by the fact that when the Assembly of 1900 suspended the special debt-clearing efforts the figure in column one of the table falls again to around £11,000 per year. The centre column of figures representing the gifts of what came to be called the Missionary Advance Movement was the key new source of income which became especially important after the turn of the century.

The FMC officials of the day recognized the financial situation as a bad one and it was a source of constant difficulty and tension between them and the missionaries in the field. Dr McMurtrie, the Convenor, and his helpers had the depressing and frustrating task of raising the money from a Church that was, for the most part, indifferent to the Committee's concerns. They felt guilty about having to tell the missionaries in field to restrain their enthusiasm, to hold back developments about which they were excited, and at times, McMurtrie had the unpleasant task of reprimanding the missionaries for what appeared to be reckless overspending in the eyes of some of the very budget conscious men who served on the FMC and in the General Assembly. This often led to irritation, to say the least, among the staff in the field, who, in turn, became even less ready to be sympathetic to McMurtrie's com-plaints about the terrible burden he shouldered at home.

Again and again over the years, McMurtrie told D.C. Scott that the financial stringency was only temporary. If only the debt were cleared, the books balanced, then no one could be accused, no matter how unjust these accusations were, of being extravagant and recklessly over-spending. Only then, McMurtrie asserted, would the prosperous business people in the Kirk begin to contribute freely. He admitted that everything upon which they had spent money in Malawi had been essential, but, even if it meant cutting essential expenditure, he pleaded that this must be done if it was needed to create a credit balance in the accounts. Only then could the confidence of hard headed businessmen be gained; only then would there be available the necessary funds for the long awaited expansion after this *recueillir pour mieux sauter*.[17] 1887, the year that a real improvement in staffing took place, the financial situation was so bad that Dr McMurtrie had to turn down Hetherwick's plea for a teacher to be appointed to Domasi even when Hetherwick offered part of his salary to help pay the cost McMurtrie wrote:

> I need not tell you we dare not add any expense to the ordinary expenditure. We are very far from having fulfilled the Assembly's instruction to lessen expenditure by £2,000 (over all our missions).[18]

So, just when staff were becoming more readily available, the money available was even less than usual. The important and significant increase in the staff of the Blantyre Mission was paid for by sources outside the normal FMC channels. Janet Beck was supported by her two sisters who stayed at home in Scotland; the salaries of Dr Bowie and the Reverend Robert Cleland were guaranteed by private subscriptions. These were organized by Dr Archibald Scott of St. George's Church, Edinburgh, collected by members of his own congregation. A volunteer was found to answer Hetherwick's call for a teacher and he was able to be sent out

---

[17] McMurtrie to D.C. Scott, 2 February 1893, Convenor's Letterbook, M.1.
[18] McMurtrie to A. Hetherwick, 27 October 1887, Convenor's Letterbook, M.1.

because St. George's Session persuaded two other congregations to join them in guaranteeing his stipend.[19]

That same year, 1887, was one of crisis for the whole work of the FMC of the Church of Scotland. In the previous year a Special Committee of Assembly had been set up to consult with the FMC over what was considered the desperate financial situation. There was a debt of about £8,000, while the annual income had never reached higher than £16,000.

The recommendations of the Special Committee are summarized below. It is most significant for understanding the attitude of the Kirk in general to mission that the way out of the crisis was considered to be not a matter of planning a massive new effort to raise funds, but, with one pious generalization in paragraph 2, the essential task of the committee was seen as one of organizing effective retrenchment. Hetherwick asked plaintively when would the Kirk see mission as part of its essential life and not a side-show? The Special Committee clearly saw themselves dealing with a side-show. Their main recommendations can be summarized thus:

1. More funds were needed or there must be a severe cut in expenditure.
2. The Committee hoped that more might be found.
3. Until such times as more money was forthcoming the FMC must review all its work with a view to saving money.
4. The Committee felt that straightway each missionary responsible for expenditure should cut it by 10%.
5. Were paragraphs detailing specific cuts in the staffing of certain Indian establishments.
6. The FMC had suggested a doctor was necessary to make their China mission viable. The Committee's suggestion was that here was an opportunity for a major saving, no money for a doctor so simply shut down the mission.
7. The expenditure of the East African Mission needed to be checked sharply.[20]

---

[19] *Assembly Reports,* 1887, FMC Report, East Africa Section, p. 61.

[20] *Assembly Reports,* 1887, Report of the Special Committee on Mission Finance, pp. 185-8.

The emphasis then of the Special Committee's Report was not how to awaken the Kirk to her responsibilities, or even how do we raise our income to meet our obligations, but how do we curtail our obligations?

The staff increases in Blantyre did not involve an increase in the salary bill but they did increase not decrease overall costs for the mission. This reprehensible activity by the Blantyre Mission had been noted by the Special Committee, and well it might note them, for D.C. Scott, strongly supported by Hetherwick, although in no way spending recklessly, never cut down on any task he felt essential and so, in a period of decreasing funds and expanding work, he always overspent. So the Special Committee singled him out to have his accounts carefully checked.

The Special Committee made no effort at all to consider how to increase income though this was clearly the solution to the problem for a church that was barely giving at all of its wealth to the work of the FMC. The FMC was well aware of this and brought to the Assembly's notice these statistics which so clearly revealed the profound indifference to Foreign Mission of the Church of Scotland as a whole.

> Only 11 congregations gave last year, including what was raised by Sunday Schools, £100 or upwards for Foreign Missions (6 in Edinburgh, 2 in Glasgow, 2 in Aberdeen and 1 in Melrose.) Only 16 congregations gave £50 to £100 (5 in Edinburgh, 3 in Glasgow, and one in each of the following, Bothwell, Hamilton, Peebles, Galashiels, New Kirkpatrick, Aberdeen, Stirling and Dundee). Fifty-five congregations gave between £25 and £50. Of the remaining congregations (over 1000) hundreds gave only nominal contributions and 135 congregations worshipping in endowed parish churches gave nothing at all.[21]

The Foreign Mission Committee laid bare this dire situation but the General Assembly's response was not one of contrition and a promise to try harder but a command to the FMC to retrench vigorously.

Thus the incredible situation was created that new candidates for service in Blantyre had to be supported by privately raised funds and that Dr McMurtrie had to be apologetic when reporting their appointment, always reassuring the Assembly that they would not be an extra charge

---

[21] *Assembly Reports*, 1887, FMC Report, Introduction, p.65.

on the normal funds of the FMC. When in 1888 the Reverend Dr Willie Scott volunteered to join his brother in Blantyre this simply meant embarrassment for McMurtrie. Dr Archie Scott of St. George's and a group of friends came to the rescue and a very basic salary was guaranteed for a time. Thus Willie was enabled to go out and McMurtrie was able to report to the next Assembly that:

> Dr Scott was not deterred by the inability of the Committee to offer him the stipend of £300 and had gone on a salary of £150 for the first two years - that salary having been guaranteed without touching on the ordinary funds of the Mission.[22]

With the addition of the two lady teachers financed by the independent Ladies Committee for Foreign Missions, the staff of the East African Mission was beginning to reach the level D.C. Scott needed to press ahead with the developments he had been planning for so long. Here was the beginning of the organization which Bishop Neil praises as being the best in the world.[23] However, it was so only because of the personality and drive of D.C. Scott and the support of Dr A. Scott and his congregation of St. George's Edinburgh and not because of the Kirk in general.

As the eighties went on there was something of a lessening in tension over finance because of a slight increase in giving. However this did not keep up with the growing needs of the work in the field nor with the increase in candidates for service which occurred when Zambezia was so much in the newspaper headlines. Thus in 1892-93, the financial situation of the FMC was again a matter of concern for the General Assembly as it had been in 1886-87. Indeed the position was so serious that the Assembly of 1892 passed a solemn resolution calling on all missionaries,

> and especially those in Africa, where the increase in expenditure has been the greatest, to effect immediately, and for some years to come, a large saving, by reducing the number of persons employed by the Mission, or supported by the Mission; by withdrawing from

---

[22] *Ibid,* East Africa Section, p. 117.
[23] Neill, *A History of Christian Missions,* p. 387.

> undertakings not absolutely required; and generally by practicing the most rigid economy.[24]

The expenditure in Africa had been increasing because the Mission had, at last, an adequate staff due to the efforts of Dr Archibald Scott and his people. Though they alone took care of the additional salaries, an increase in the spending in the Shire Highlands was inevitable, since the new staff had to be housed, and they began new work which also led to the raising of costs. Thus just when D.C. Scott was beginning to see his work develop along the right lines; just when he had a staff that allowed him to go ahead with development instead of maintaining not much more than a holding operation, the Assembly insisted retrenchment was necessary. The very success of his work in attracting candidates for service in Scotland, in building new schools and new areas of evangelistic activity in Malawi, meant that his mission was singled out for what was in effect a rebuke from the General Assembly. On top of all this, the financial position of the FMC drove Dr McMurtrie to write a letter to every missionary individually, the most important paragraphs of which were as follows:

> The Committee was willing to fight this debt, and the friends that have stood by them will stand by them again, and new friends will join; but only on one condition - namely, that no money be spent that had not been given to us to spend. It must be felt by all that a new system of finance has begun, and that no more debt will, accrue ... The best friends of the Mission have little heart to help us, while they think that they are only prolonging an unsound system or delaying catastrophe ... We have, therefore, to ask that, for the sake of the future of the Mission, and even for its existence, you will, at any cost to the present work, prosecute retrenchment vigorously just now ... Endeavour to get local contributions, and to apply them in relief of expenditure that would otherwise fall on the Committee's funds ... Remember that our whole Mission in India, Africa and China is on its trial this year. We have to regain the confidence of friends whose sympathies are alienated by expenditure in excess of income year after year. Do not suppose for a moment that any of us think that the members of the Church of Scotland are giving enough for Foreign

---

[24] *Assembly Reports,* 1892, FMC Report, Finance Section, p. 72.

Missions. But the right way must be taken if we are to educate them to a higher ideal.[25]

The full text of this letter was presented to the General Assembly of 1894 when McMurtrie used it to attempt to awaken the Church to make a real effort to clear the FMC debt and to set the Committee's financial position in order. The Assembly agreed to take up the matter and efforts were made to respond to McMurtrie's call. By 1898 when D.C. Scott left Blantyre for good, the debt was cleared and the finances of the Foreign Mission Committee were on an even keel. It is very significant to contrast the response this call to clear the debt met with in the Shire Highlands with the response in Scotland.

In the Blantyre Mission every missionary gave one month's salary to the Treasurer in Edinburgh to help. Even more impressive was the response of the very poorly paid African teachers and artisans, forty-two of whom, almost all the African staff, also gave one month's salary. Dr McMurtrie wrote:

> I wish you very particularly to thank the 42 young people, including Nacho, who have so nobly given a month's salary for the Foreign Mission debt and to say how proud I am of their own letter to the Committee of date 26 October 1894, with all their signatures.[26]

He goes on to say that he and certain other officials in Edinburgh are going to make the very same gesture. In addition to all this, the small African congregation in Blantyre gave the proceeds of their annual sale of work, £42.7.1d. to help with the same task. This sum must be seen in the context of the difference between the standard of living in the Shire Highlands and Scotland, and the statistics of church giving in Scotland, where less than one hundred of the Kirk's thirteen hundred congregations ordinarily gave a sum larger than that of the Blantyre congregation to the work of the Foreign Mission Committee. In making this comparison it should be noted finally that the FMC had to report to the General Assembly of the Kirk in 1896 that 600 congregations, worshipping in endowed parish churches, had made no response

---

[25] *Assembly Reports,* 1894, FMC Report, Introduction, p. 60.
[26] McMurtrie to D.C. Scott, 3 January 1895, Convenor's Letter Book, M.2.

whatever to the Assembly's call for an effort to help put the finances of the FMC onto an even footing.[27]

It was in that same year, 1896, that a new development took place in the organization of support within the Church of Scotland for overseas mission. This was the Mission Advance Movement. This was the formalizing and bringing together of a number of private efforts that were already in existence along with the scheme started by Dr A. Scott, whereby certain prosperous families subscribed an annual amount, a substitute, as it were, for one of their number taking service overseas under the Committee.

The Advance Movement sub-committee endeavoured to help the creation of new Missionary Auxiliary Committees in the parishes, and to develop an organization at Presbytery level also. To this end missionaries on furlough and members of the subcommittee went out on intensive campaigns of visits to presbyteries and to address public meetings on the issue all over Scotland. They hoped to shape the attitudes of future generations by stimulating the organizing of junior groups in the parishes. They also tried to persuade parishes to organize quarterly collections in aid of mission to replace the system of the once a year retiring collection. A further development was the organizing of Mission Study Circles which were supplied with specially prepared leaflets and booklets.[28]

The Third Period

It was reported to the General Assembly of 1898 by the Advance sub-committee that one third of the parishes of Scotland had taken up the Advance Movement. This was an advance clearly in the Kirk's concern for mission on the situation in 1887 when it was reported that only 100 of the 1300 congregations gave anything more than a token sum to the work of the Foreign Mission Committee. However, it could hardly be thought of as satisfactory, because it also meant that two thirds of the parishes of the Kirk had not taken up the movement despite the really massive effort by the sub-committee It also meant that these two thirds

---

[27] *Assembly Reports*, 1896, FMC Report, Mission Advance Section, p. 57.
[28] *Assembly Reports*, 1896, 1897, 1898, FMC Report, Missions Advance Section.

had managed to ignore nearly twenty years of appeals and exhortations by the General Assembly. These had begun in the early eighties when it became clear that the recent modest expansion of the work overseas was outstripping the financial contributions of the Church to the work, which, in fact, were decreasing at this time.

The interesting fact that the work of the FMC did not even gain the support of the majority of parish ministers is clear from the drastic recommendation of the Advance sub-committee in 1898. That year it asked the General Assembly to call on the people of the Kirk, over the heads of their ministers as it were, to fulfil what the FMC insisted was their duty, to set up local Advance Movement groups even when their ministers showed no interest in the matter.

It was the work of the Advance Movement that finally cleared the debt that had so burdened the Foreign Mission Committee. It was the continued influence of the movement which made the last of our three periods in the life of the Blantyre Mission, that under Alexander Hetherwick, one where the pressure to retrench was lifted from the shoulders of the head of mission. Yet at no time in the period was the position such that any of the larger schemes of development planned in Blantyre could be initiated. The setting up of a small station in Portuguese Lomweland in this period does not alter this judgement because it was African staffed and paid for entirely by local African funds.

Although no crisis recurred in this period like those of 1876 or 1893, the FMC was never in a financially comfortable position during the years 1898 to 1914. Indeed as soon as 1902 the old song of the possible need to curtail work in the field due to financial stringency was being sung again. In 1907 the FMC noted with gratification effective church growth in its fields of work but was embarrassed at the same time by the financial implications of success. In the preface to the annual report of the General Assembly the Committee says:

> By God's blessing the results of the labours of our missionaries during many years, now become very apparent ... a vast increase in baptisms ... the greatest increase is in BCA ... No wise man judges a mission solely by the number of its converts. But other evidences of a healthy mission are not wanting. There is the solid structure of the African Church, as reported by our Deputy, Mr. McCallum ... It is not

> too much to say that the success granted in the Mission Field is God's challenge to this Church, to cease from its present parsimonious support of the Foreign Mission and rise to the greatness of its duty ... On the other hand, the clear message of the Committee to the General Assembly and through the Assembly to the Church, must be that the Foreign Mission, as it now is, cannot be carried on with its present income.[29]

After a temporary increase in financial support, a fall again ensued and in 1912 the Assembly was again being exhorted to further action in this field by the FMC. This call had to be made in the same city which two years before had housed the World Missionary Conference, 1910. In its report to the General Assembly the Foreign Mission Committee said:

> No one can peruse these without feeling that the information contained in them reveals very pointedly two things:
>
> 1. The devoted and efficient manner in which the existing staff of missionaries striving to cope with the task allotted to them.
>
> 2. The extremely inadequate measure in which the Church of Scotland is fulfilling her missionary obligation towards the people in the territories she has undertaken to evangelise.[30]

Also at this Assembly it was noted that the staffing position which had been in a not too unhealthy state since about 1886, at least for Africa, had again deteriorated. The FMC had insisted in its report that there were possibilities for advance and new development, but had to go on:

> there is thereby sounded a loud call to the Church of Scotland for advance in her missionary work abroad. At the same time, the F.M.C. are fully conscious of the fact that until their ordinary income has reached the level of maintaining the existing work (which is as yet far from accomplished) their primary endeavour as a Committee be directed towards bringing this about.[31]

So it was clear that the FMC was still struggling to maintain the status quo rather than trying to build the resources for advance and new

---

[29] *Assembly Reports,* 1907, FMC Report, Introduction, p. 67.
[30] *Assembly Reports,* 1912, FMC Report Introduction, p.83.
[31] *Ibid*

developments. As we saw the difficulties over staffing the existing work had also returned. Now in 1912 there was a crisis over the supply of new recruits similar in its seriousness to the crisis over financial resources in 1893. The FMC Report informed the Assembly that the Field Councils had made it clear that fifteen new recruits were necessary simply to cope with the existing work,[32] yet they had also to report that

> Only two new missionaries have been appointed since the last General Assembly, Dr T.C. Borthwick to China, Mr G. Dennis to Kikuyu. Other vacancies have occurred, for which, unfortunately, no suitable candidates have been forthcoming, and at the date of the Report they still remain unfilled.[33]

Faced with this unspecified number of vacancies plus the demand for the creation of fifteen new posts, the FMC took the drastic step of asking the authority of the General Assembly to recruit candidates from any Presbyterian Church in the world. So at the penultimate Assembly before the First World War which ended this era, we have the extraordinary situation of the FMC having to tell the Kirk that it was unable to supply the necessary number of candidates for its missionary work, and that its financial contributions were still not adequate for the maintenance of the existing work abroad. The total amount of money contributed to the funds of the FMC had increased, as we have seen mainly due to the work of Mission Advance groups throughout the country, but the level had by 1912 remained static for about a decade. A real breakthrough in evangelism and church growth had taken place in Africa and to a lesser extent in some parts of India, so that the work had developed beyond this static income.

In summing up, a picture very different from that traditionally painted of the missionary concern of the Church of Scotland in late Victorian and Edwardian times presents itself. Throughout the period from 1874 until 1914 the Foreign Mission Committee is never far from serious difficulties over finance, staffing or both. The taking over of the Kikuyu Mission in Kenya by the Kirk does not alter this picture significantly since it was already generously endowed.

---

[32] *Ibid*

[33] *Ibid*

In all of Dr McMurtrie's Letter-books, in all the Reports of the FMC to the General Assembly the questions were never, "Where do we go now? What new area contingent of our existing work can we occupy? What fresh need of the growing Christian communities of Africa or Asia can we help to fill?" On the contrary, the theme was always, "How can the work be restrained from developing beyond the present availability of money and personnel?" and tragically the question too often was "How can the work be curtailed to make financial savings?"

There is one more illusion current among Scottish church people which has little basis in the reality of the Victorian and Edwardian eras. During the last decade when much discussion has taken place about the nature of the Church, the nature of mission and of their mutual relationship, it has been the pride of the Church of Scotland spokesmen to point out that the essential unity of church and mission has been incarnated in the work of the Church of Scotland. The missionary outreach of the United Free and Parish Church traditions included in the present day Church of Scotland was carried out in each case by the institutional Church and not by voluntary societies.

Certainly, on the surface, that is the case and it is a clear contrast with what happened in England, Germany and Scandinavia, where no major denomination initiated overseas missionary work. In England the effective Anglican and Free Church work was initiated and carried out by Missionary Societies made up voluntarily by those interested in the task. Some societies were interdenominational, like the London Missionary Society.[34] Others were denominational in their basis such as the Church Missionary Society. The situation was similar in the Netherlands, Germany and the Scandinavian countries.

However, despite the great emphasis on this great difference in contemporary discussion was there any difference in reality? Was the situation in Scotland any different from the rest of European Protestantism? The fact that the General Assembly of the Church of Scotland had made overseas mission part of its task, setting up a

---

[34] This Society's work in Africa called forth a stream of very able Scots, among them Dr John Philip, Mary and Robert Moffat and David Livingstone.

standing committee of the Assembly for this purpose, does constitute a difference in principle.

In practice when the new challenge of Africa and the growth of work in India came before the Kirk in the late 1870s, the system can be seen to have failed. In 1880 the General Assembly was warned that the work would have to be reduced because of the imminent bankruptcy of the FMC. In response to this a variety of private groups of church members clubbing together began to make themselves felt. By 1882 their contributions were already making up a fifth of all funds available to the FMC.[35] In 1886 the existence of these groups was formally recognized and encouraged by the Assembly, which in 1896 merged them with certain other private groups into the Mission Advance Movement. As we have seen this was an organization with its own committees at parish and presbytery level. It collected its own funds and held its own meetings to increase concern for overseas mission. The only difference between it and the Church Missionary Society or the London Missionary Society was that their central committees were independent bodies while the central committee of Mission Advance was a sub-committee of a General Assembly Committee. However, up until that final level, there was almost no difference between the voluntary basis of all three organizations. Mission Advance was in practice a voluntary society also. Did the connection with the General Assembly help the Advance Movement? Despite twenty years of strong resolutions and vehement exhortations from the Assembly, the Advance Movement still only existed in one third of the parishes of the Kirk. Many Kirk Sessions were not only indifferent but hostile. This comes out in the startling appeal of the Assembly of 1898, which, as we noted, appealed to the people of the Kirk over the heads of their ministers and Sessions.

During the 1890s contributions from the Kirk sessions did increase but these were artificially inflated figures since included in them were the special contributions being raised by the Mission Advance Movement to clear the accumulated debt of the FMC. After 1900 the figures are recorded differently and it is clear that the money raised by the Mission

---

[35] See table outlining Givings to the FMC between 1875 and 1914 on page 36.

Advance Movement consistently surpasses the total receipts from Kirk sessions.

Thus it was only by the creation of the voluntary Advance Movement, a movement not essentially different from the home organizations of the LMS or the CMS, that the Foreign Mission Committee began to receive adequate and consistent sup-port.

However, even had the annual, later quarterly, collections made by the Kirk sessions produced an adequate support for the work of the FMC, this would not have been proof of a denomination taking on mission as an essential element of its life and work. At no time was there any suggestion that a simple proportion of all the Kirk's resources be assigned to overseas mission. Agreeing to take up special collections is an extra not an essential activity.

The existence of the Foreign Mission Committee as a standing committee of the General Assembly did at least remind members annually of the call of mission and perhaps it thus reached people who might not have been touched if mission had been solely a matter for a separate voluntary society, but in terms of making mission a central feature of the Church's life, it made no difference.

The first of our periods was one of declining financial support for overseas mission and an almost total inability to find suitable candidates for the work. Afterwards, during the period of Dr David Clement Scott's headship of the Blantyre Mission, there was slow improvement in the supply of both money and personnel. This- was the result of action by special groups like that which Dr Archibald Scott of St. George's managed to organize, a group that was supplying in 1890 the salaries of four out of the ten staff of the Blantyre Mission. The third period was that of the Advance Movement which formalized and channelled the work of these groups while attempting to increase their number and extend their influence. It must always be noted that while the Advance Movement was being set by the authority of the General Assembly, several presbyteries actually refused to receive a deputation sent by the FMC to explain the scheme, and no more than a third of the congregations of the Church ever took it up even in a token way.

The period of 1874 up to the First World War saw brilliant work done by Church of Scotland missionaries in many countries, but it was not a period when there was any widespread concern in the same church for the work these missionaries had been sent to do. A minority of its congregations contained groups of people, very often themselves small minorities, who cared and acted on this concern. The efforts of these groups were only channelled effectively when, in the Advance Movement, the Church of Scotland set up what was, in effect, a Missionary Society very little different from the Church Missionary Society or the London Missionary Society.

The situation for those who cared about overseas mission in the period is succinctly summed up in the words of a letter of Dr McMurtrie's where he says

> We work hard for improvement on two lines, (1) organisation in congregations, (2) special subscriptions from those who have means and convictions. Many - both ministers and people - offer a dull sand-bag resistance - which is discouraging to you and us. We must peg on and pray on.[36]

Givings to the Foreign Mission Committee 1875-1914

Year	Collections	Associations	Legacies	Total
1875	£9,972	2,444		12,416
1876	10,306	4,490		14,796
1877	9,158	1,155		10,313
1878	8,793	4,892		13,685
1879	8,460	2,544		11,014
1880	7,697	7,512		15,209
1881	9,223	2,599	1,801	13,623
1882	10,420	2,729	2,287	15,394
1883	9,701	1,588	2,733	14,023
1884	9,063	2,459	,907	12,430
1885	9,329	1,762	2,254	13,347
1886	11,012	6,219	1,340	18,573
1887	12,438	9,544	2,481	24,463

[36] Dr McMurtrie to H.E. Scott, 14 January 1902, Convenors Letter Book, M.6.

Year	Collections	Associations	Legacies	Total
1888	10,448	2,289	3,310	16,049
1889	13,309	4,935	4,177	22,421
1890	13,760	3,299	4,058	21,118
1891	12,718	3,262	6,889	22,871
1892	* 16,200	3,398	1,559	21,159
1893	* 13,614	4,075	5,427	23,117
1894	* 18,178	3,044	2,362	24,568
1895	* 14,676	4,585	2,309	21,573
1896	* 18,340	6,463	1,639	26,443
1897	* 19,585	10,298	4,094	29,252
1898	* 19,753	5,081	4,215	29,050
1899	* 19,767	5,124	2,778	27,669
1900	9,875	13,796	2,183	25,854
1901	9,733	13,391	1,735	24,859
1902	9,773	14,464	5,729	29,963
1903	11,168	12,617	2,348	27,133
1904	10,460	13,888	4,271	28,619
1905	10,237	13,969	3,774	27,970
1906	10,795	13,676	4,441	28,912
1907	10,196	13,402	6,044	29,642
1908	12,438	16,651	13,779	42,868
1909	10,983	14,357	12,442	37,782
1910	11,171	14,614	6,442	32,227
1911	10,887	16,548	9,603	37,028
1912	10,895	13,609	24,543	49,035
1913	11,189	15,485	3,123	29,797
1914	11,112	15,029	6,559	32,700

*   Special General Assembly debt-clearing assessments included in these figures.

It was originally intended that legacies should be set aside as capital, but the ordinary income was never enough so they had to be used for ordinary expenditure where their violent fluctuations caused the treasurer a major headache.

Chapter 2: The Failure at Blantyre

As we have seen, the funeral of David Livingstone on 17 April 1874, was the signal for the beginning of an interest among people in Scotland in sending a mission to Zambezia. It was Dr John Macrae of Hawick of the Church of Scotland who undertook to arouse that church to the task.

At the General Assembly of the Church of Scotland in May 1874, Dr Macrae presented an overture from his Presbytery, that of Jedburgh, calling for the establishment of a mission, among the natives of that part of Africa which has been hallowed by the last labours and death of Dr Livingstone.[1] The petition was accepted by the Assembly, which went on to instruct the Foreign Mission Committee to undertake the preparation for, and the carrying out of this mission. Dr A.J. Hanna in his book *The Beginnings of Nyasaland and North-Eastern Rhodesia,* makes a very strange comment about the work of the FMC with regard to the new mission, saying,

> The subject was first mooted on the 2nd June 1874, but the precise reason that brought it before the Committee has apparently been lost to history.[2]

The reason for it coming before the Committee is not lost, it was the simple one that the Committee was following the instructions given it by the Assembly held the month before. To carry out this remit, the FMC set up a special sub-committee with Dr Macrae as convener to supervise both the setting up and the carrying out of the mission. Dr Macrae already had experience of such a convenership, having been for some years convenor of the sub-committee of the FMC responsible for one of the Church's missions in India.

Macrae began his task in a most businesslike manner, consulting all the people who, as a result of experience of work in the area, might have good advice to give. He travelled to the south of England to interview Sir Bartle Frere, John Kirk and Horace Waller, amongst others. This

---

[1] A Hetherwick, *The Romance of Blantyre*, (London, James Clarke & Co., nd., 1931), p. 14.

[2] A.J. Hanna, *The Beginnings of Nyasaland and North-Eastern Rhodesia, 1859-1895* (Oxford: Clarendon Press, 1956), p.12.

admirable activity showed signs, however, of one of the most serious problems which existed from the beginning of the work of this sub-committee, which was that it was never united. Individuals, particularly Dr Macrae, appeared to do things on their own without the knowledge or understanding of the rest of the members of the sub-committee.[3]

It would have been more expensive, but perhaps a better plan if these and other distinguished informants had been brought to Edinburgh and addressed the whole sub-committee. Dr Macrae now approached Lt E.D. Young, asking him to lead the expedition. Young, who had been twice to the area of Lake Malawi, once with Livingstone and once to look for him, had also been approached by the Free Church of Scotland to lead their expedition to the same area. Duff MacDonald reports, though no documentary evidence is extant to confirm this, that Young suggested to both parties that a sort of Scottish National Mission be sent,[4] and that the authorities in both churches demurred. Dr Macrae's committee certainly did approach their opposite numbers in the Free Kirk about some sort of co-operation. In the Free Kirk Assembly of 1875, Dr Duff made a long speech reviewing the events leading up to the sending out of their mission to Lake Malawi. In the course of this he said:

> Further in January of this year Dr Macrae of Hawick, Convenor of the Special Committee appointed by the Established Church to prosecute a somewhat similar mission enterprise into Central Africa, addressed an official note to me, stating that some form of co-operation between the Foreign Mission Committees of both churches had been suggested. The letter was duly submitted to our committee, from whom it received an amount respectful attention proportionate to the importance of the matter to which it related ... But from the extreme vagueness and indefiniteness of the suggestion, and the absence of all details, the result of their most careful deliberation was that the best answer they could return to Dr Macrae's communication would be to let him know frankly, fully and in the

---

[3] MacDonald, *Africana,* vol. 2, pp. 80 and 259.
[4] *Ibid, vol.* 1, p. 19.

most friendly spirit, what the present position and views were respecting their projected mission to East Africa.[5]

Duff went on to report that he had met with Lord Polwarth, an elder serving on the Auld Kirk's committee, and that a statement which they drew up together was accepted by both the Foreign Mission Committees. The two key paragraphs were:

> As the slave-hunting region round Lake Nyassa is so large and populous as to afford abundant scope for many missions, it is expedient, under present circumstances, that each church should appoint its own body of management at home, send out its own staff of agents, and have its own stores and supplies as well as its distinct settlement and field of labour. The settlements, however, should not be so far from each other as to render easy intercourse at all difficult, it being most desirable that they should render each other all possible assistance.[6]

The statement went on to speak of a joint committee in Scotland to look after the joint property involved in sea and river transport in Africa. This joint committee ceased to have any function to perform after the setting up of the trading company of the Moir brothers, first known as the Livingstonia Trading Company and later as the African Lakes Company, when they extended their work to Lake Tanganyika.

As we saw in the previous chapter, Young agreed to go with the Free Church party because it was ready with men, equipment and funds, while Dr Macrae's was not. Also in the previous chapter we saw the great difficulty that faced Macrae, that there were simply no candidates coming forward to serve in the new venture. In the end Henry Henderson came forward to do the pioneer work just in time to go off with Young's Free Church party. He travelled with them as far as Lake Malawi, playing his full part in their arduous work which included the famous portage of their steamer, broken up into loads at Chikwawa and carried via Mbame and what was to become Blantyre to the headwaters of the Shire where it was re-assembled. Henderson was on board when the little vessel

---

[5] First pamphlet in Livingstonia, 1875-1900, bound collection of pamphlets in the National Library of Scotland.

[6] *Ibid*

sailed out of the Shire and onto the waters of the Lake on 11th of October 1875.

Henderson's task was to find a site for the mission of the Established Church that was both suitable in itself and conformed to the specifications of the agreement between the two churches that it should be close enough for each mission to be able to aid the other. In pursuit of this objective Henderson sailed with Young and Laws on the *Bala* when they circumnavigated the lake and made its full extent known for the first time. However he saw no suitable site on the journey and decided that it would be wiser to seek a site somewhere further back on their rather tenuous lines of communications. This certainly made sense in terms of propagating the faith since it took him into the densely populated Shire Highlands, the area that had been favoured by Livingstone himself as the best site for a mission.

The Livingstonia Mission lent Henderson an interpreter without whom Henderson would not have been a very effective agent. The interpreter was Tom Bokwito who had been freed from a slave party by Livingstone and Bishop Mackenzie. He had eventually gone to be educated at Lovedale Institution in the Cape Colony which was headed by Dr Stewart and was one of the three Lovedale 'graduates' who had volunteered to serve with the Livingstonia Mission.

According to both Hetherwick in his *Romance of Blantyre*[7] and the Reverend Harry Matecheta in *Blantyre Mission: Nkhani ya Ciyambi Cace*,[8] Henderson and Bokwito were still looking for a suitable spot when they reached the area of what is now the town of Blantyre/Limbe. From Cape Maclear they had come downstream on the Shire about as far south as where the Liwonde Barrage was built in 1965, and then struck off into the Highlands through the Machinga Pass. There they entered the territory of the Yao chief, Malemia, where they stayed for a while with one of his subchiefs, Kalimbuka whose village was where the first Malawi Parliament building stands in Zomba. The spot was well wooded and well watered; the people were friendly and both Malemia and Kalimbuka

---

[7] Hetherwick, *The Romance of Blantyre*, pp. 17-19.

[8] H.K Matecheta, *Blantyre Mission: Nkhani ya Ciyambi Cace,* (Blantyre: Hetherwick Press, 1951), p. 1.

appeared to want missionaries to come and settle under their patronage. This was almost certainly in the hope of gaining their help against Malemia's great enemy, Kawinga, the most powerful and aggressive of the Yao chiefs south of the Lake; one who was deeply involved in the Quelimane slave trade. Indeed the main route for slaves being taken to Quelimane skirted Malemia's land. It was for these very reasons that Henderson was not so keen on fixing Malemia's as the site for the new Mission. In addition he felt that there on the slopes of Zomba Mountain he was still too far from the furthest navigable point on the Shire.

So Henderson and Bokwito went on following a route which went roughly along the line of the later Zomba - Limbe road. They passed the old Magomero site of Bishop Mackenzie's mission, skirted Chiradzulu and then stayed for a while at Ngùludi Hill at the Yao village of Che Lopsa, where Bokwito knew some people. There a little boy named Kambwiri saw Henderson and heard the name of Jesus for the first time. This meant little or nothing to him then, though he grew up to be the Reverend Harry Kambwiri Matecheta, the Yao evangelist of the Ngoni.[9] Leaving Che Lopsa's the two pioneers had only reached the nearby village of Kapeni when Bokwito became seriously ill. This turned out to be a piece of good fortune for Henderson; he spent the three weeks of his comrade's illness in getting to know Chief Kapeni and the range of surrounding hills, Ndirande, Michiru and Soche. This was a spot that had been recommended by Livingstone to Mackenzie and Henderson soon came to see its advantages.

It was about this time that the Livingstonia people sent the *Bala* down the Shire to seek news of him. He went over to meet them at the river and insisted that

> he was in great spirits regarding the country he had explored. It was the most attractive he had seen, very fertile and as healthy as Scotland, and he had discovered an excellent site.[10]

---

[9] *Ibid;* the details of this story were confirmed in interviews with the Reverend H.K. Matecheta during 1960.

[10] W.P. Livingstone, *Laws of Livingstonia,* (London: Hodder and Stoughton, 1921), p. 90.

Without any reference to his source for the story, W.P. Livingstone says, at another point, in his life of Laws that the siting of Blantyre at Kapeni's was because the party of men sent out from Scotland under Macklin, were so exhausted by their journey that they could go no further, so there they stayed at Kapeni's, though Henderson had in fact chosen Magomero for the site of the mission.[11] This is quoted by Dr Hanna as the authoritative explanation of the siting of the Blantyre Mission.[12] Yet, W.P. Livingstone elsewhere in his book, quotes Henderson as saying he had discovered a site, a strange phrase to use of the ill-fated Magomero site of the old UMCA mission, a place which Bokwito knew well having stayed there as a boy.

Nowhere except in W.P. Livingstone and works which depend on him is there any reference to Henderson's having fixed on Magomero as the site for the new mission. We do know of Henderson and Bokwito's three long stays, first at Kalimbuka's, then at Nguludi and then the enforced three weeks at Kapeni's but nothing of even a visit to Magomero. We also have Hetherwick saying that after the Macklin party had been led by Henderson to Chikwawa, Henderson went up to Kapeni's ahead of them to confirm that the mission could settle there before returning to bring them up into the Highlands.[13] Harry Matecheta was also clear that he knew of no other plan than to settle at Kapeni's and insisted that Henderson and Kapeni had come to an agreement before Henderson went down the river to meet Macklin and the new arrivals. On a number of occasions afterwards, Henderson, in turning aside praise for having found such a marvellous site, often referred to it as being by chance. This would appear to be a reference to his having to stay at Kapeni's because of Bokwito's illness. Where W.P. Livingstone got his Magomero idea remains a mystery.

Taking up the thread of the narrative again, we find that Henderson, while at Kapeni's, heard that the pioneer party was coming out to start the work of the mission. He believed that his work would be over as soon as he had guided them to the spot he had chosen and had then seen

---

[11] *Ibid*, p. 106.

[12] Hanna, *The Beginnings of Nyasaland and North-Eastern Rhodesia*, p. 24.

[13] Hetherwick, *The Romance of Blantyre*, p. 21.

them settled in. He went down to Chikwawa to await them but after some weeks he got tired of waiting and set off for the Kongone mouth of the Zambezi to wait there. At Kongone he waited for a couple of weeks and then he received word that the Blantyre party, along with reinforcements for Livingstonia had landed at Ouelimane and would move up the Kwakwa river to portage across to the Zambezi at Mazaro where the two rivers came close together. At Mazaro, Henderson met up with the new men and led them to Chikwawa. He left them there with Chief Kasisi while he went up to Kapeni's via Mbame to confirm Kapeni's agreement to their siting the mission on his land. Kapeni assigned them an area where a village had stood till it had been destroyed by a Makololo raid.

With the help of some local men, Henderson put some of the houses into livable shape before going back to Kasisi's to collect the new men.[14] The chief provided a large number of porters for the mission party who, after a difficult climb, arrived at their site on Nyambadwe hill on October 23, 1876. They called the place Blantyre.

In the previous chapter we noted the very inappropriate character of many of this first group of missionaries. Fenwick and Walker in particular were simply adventurers; their attitude to life can be gauged by a remark of Dr Macklin's about someone else, "He is one of the Fenwick kind who believes himself equal to ten white men or one hundred natives."[15] Henderson has left no record of what he thought of the character of these men, but he was appalled by the fact that they were all in a state of collapse by the time they reached Blantyre.

Henderson was now faced with a problem which he confessed he was unqualified to solve.[16] How could he leave Dr Macklin and five sick artisans, none of whom had ever lived "in the bush" before, none of whom knew any local language, in their semi-repaired village houses in a society still badly troubled by slave raiding? MacDonald described their plight:

---

[14] *Ibid*

[15] Elmslie to Laws, 1 September 1885, NLS, Robert Laws Papers, vol. A.

[16] Livingstone, *Laws of Livingstonia*, p. 103.

> By the time they reached their destination some had suffered severely, and were unable to walk. In those days a large part of each man's time was spent in bed. In this condition they were cut off from all communication with their friends.[17]

Henderson, therefore, felt compelled to stay, although when Tom Bokwito returned to Livingstonia, he was of little help in communicating with the local people. More serious than this was that he soon despaired of their presence being of any use at all. He simply could not get the men out of their lethargy and depression. No work was done at all, not even to make decent living quarters let alone any evangelism or education.

In desperation, Henderson sent a letter to Dr Laws, who, as an agent of the United Presbyterian Church on loan to the Free Kirk mission, might have been free to come across and join them as a leader. The arrival of reinforcements for Livingstonia made this appear a possibility. Henderson had heard that Laws was on his way down river on some task and sent this letter to him at Chikwawa on December 1, 1876.

> Dear Doctor, - "Come over and help us." In other words, can you and will you come and take charge of this mission, at all events till next July or August; but I hope that you might be willing to stay here permanently, as the site is a good one in almost every way you look at it, and a good head is much required. I am not able, neither am I fitted to carry the work on. I should be perfectly willing to stay on as long as you wished, as it is no wish to bolt that makes me ask you to come, but the conviction that someone better qualified than myself is much required here at this outset ... All here have been and still are more or less down with fever and other complaints. The doctor a month confined to bed ... I much require to see you or someone like you. If Dr Black is disengaged perhaps he would consent to come if you can't. Let someone have pity on the Auld Kirk. Seriously, I do hope that someone with vigour and earnestness and practical knowledge will be head here soon, as it would be a sad matter to have a second failure on these highlands.... Hoping to see you soon....[18]

---

[17] MacDonald, *Africana, vol.* 1, p. 21.

[18] Livingstone, *Laws of Livingstonia,* p. 105.

Laws was dumbfounded as was Dr James Stewart who was with him having come up from Lovedale to help the Livingstonia Mission settle in. Laws was willing to go to Blantyre to help, but Dr Stewart was adamant that he could not be spared from Livingstonia. However, they both felt that Blantyre's plea could not be left go unheeded. So, after a discussion with Henderson, whether at Blantyre or Matope is not clear from any extant record, a decision was reached. This was that:

> The Free Church missionaries should take the work in turn and supply teachers and evangelists and artizans, this was decided and the financial terms arranged.[19]

In the event, the first man to take on this task at Blantyre, and a man of key importance to the mission's future, was not an official missionary of the Free Church at all. He was James Stewart, C.E., of the Public Works Department of the Government of India. He was a cousin of Dr Stewart's, the son of the pre-Disruption minister of Kirkmicheal.[20] Laws met him on the Shire only a few days after the Blantyre appeal had been received. Stewart was his way up river to offer his services to the Livingstonia Mission during his furlough from India. He agreed to do a stint of service at Blantyre as head of station.

Hetherwick[21] attested to the profound change in the situation at Blantyre which he brought about as did MacDonald.[22] He got the men shaken out of their lethargy and started them to work. He got a particularly good response from John Buchanan, who buckled to with his gardening as well as with language work to such an effect that he was later able to help MacDonald with Yao translations. It was only May or June 1877 that Stewart started his work but by December of the same year, when Laws visited Blantyre, he found the place transformed.[23] Hetherwick, in his book *The Romance of Blantyre,* summed up his achievement,

---

[19] *Ibid,* p. 107.
[20] This was perhaps seen by the Free Church men as a qualification for someone to go to head the Blantyre Mission.
[21] Hetherwick, *The Romance of Blantyre,* pp. 28-29.
[22] MacDonald, *Africana, vol.* 1, p. 21.
[23] Livingstone, *Laws of Livingstonia,* p. 131.

> He laid out the mission on the main lines of its present ground plan - an oblong - called the 'Square' - through which passed the main road from the Lower to the Upper River. On either side of the Square he built four bungalows in India fashion, which were used as dwelling houses, school, store and workshop. He laid out the mission garden, three terraces in a crescent, which remain to this day, and surveyed a channel over a mile long to bring into the mission water from a neighbouring stream.[24]

Perhaps his greatest feat was, with the co-operation of the staffs of both Blantyre and Livingstonia, the surveying and building of the road from Chikwawa to Matope. This road was essential to the transporting of goods from the Lower to the Upper River. Its Blantyre - Matope line was followed by the M2 Highway of the 1960s.

Thus we have the extraordinary situation of the Blantyre Mission, served by a staff still without a minister, some of whom we know not to have been committed Christians let alone missionaries, being brought to life and some sort of order by a man who was not a member of the Church of Scotland - nor was he a missionary in the strictly legal sense, though in the real sense of the word he certainly was.

This situation was typical of the totally inept organization of the work carried out by Macrae and his sub-committee. A man of vision and enthusiasm, he was clearly no organizer and his convenership of the committee was disastrous. Just how disorganized things were can be seen in a letter written to Macrae by McLagan, Treasurer of the FMC in February 1877. Only now, with Henderson already more than a year out in the field and the pioneer party in desperate need of leadership, was the FMC preparing an advertisement for the post of Mission Superintendent. Even more revealing of the lack of planning and the absence of effective communication between the various parts of the FMC organization were the questions McLagan still needed to ask. He wrote:

> What salary is to be given? What is to be the exact position with reference Macklin? What is to be the length of engagement? Would we now take a married man, allowing his wife to go with him, and if

---

[24] Hetherwick, *The Romance of Blantyre*, p. 29.

> so, would we pay his wife's passage? Would the terms for a clergyman or a layman be the same?[25]

In December 1877 Dr Laws took over from Stewart at Blantyre, he attempted to train Macklin, whom he found a likeable young man, to be able to shoulder the responsibility of leading the mission. He also continued to supply African teachers to keep the little school going; the only missionary work done till then apart from Macklin's medical care of those sick folk he could persuade to come to him. Laws left William Koyi and some other Livingstonia African staff to help at Blantyre when he went north again. Although some Livingstonia staff continued to pay visits to Blantyre, it was now to taste the cool air of the Shire Highlands and escape the lakeshore climate.

> Dr Laws was not at Blantyre to meet Duff MacDonald and his wife when they arrived there on July 12, 1878, but he went down soon afterwards. He was most impressed with the difference Mrs MacDonald had made to the place.[26]

After returning from the visit Laws wrote to Dr Macrae:

> In the providence of God, the two missions have been brought into very close relationship in the past, and I trust there will ever subsist between their various members that mutual goodwill and hearty co-operation which is of the utmost importance to them both in the peculiar circumstances of the land in which they are placed.[27]

Despite the temporary period of tension which was to exist between the missions over the Civil Authority issue, Laws hopes were fulfilled and the African church produced by the two missions felt itself to be one, almost from the beginning, largely due to the good relationship between the missionaries.

What was the mission to which the MacDonalds came, actually like? James Stewart had brought some kind of physical order to the site but we must read back into the 1870s H.H. Johnston's description of Blantyre in 1890 as an "English [sic] Arcadia". MacDonald loved Blantyre and the

---

[25] McLagan to Macrae, 15 February 1877, NLS, Ms, 7541.

[26] Livingstone, *Laws of Livingstonia*, p. 135.

[27] *Ibid*

African people; he was not a grumbler except, with justification when he was discussing the conduct of those in Scotland he chose to call the Mission Directors.[28]

It is interesting to have his straightforward description of what he found on his arrival:

> Blantyre, although highly praised at home, did not possess many attractions for the newcomer. In our first introduction to the manse we perceived that it contained two rooms. In the larger of these there was nothing but a huge table, which was noteworthy in many respects. It was the only one we had seen for a month, and with the exception of a board used by the artisans, it was the only table within a hundred miles. It had to serve too in surgical cases: when any poor native had to undergo an operation, it was on this the doctors had to place him. The smaller room we may describe as a bedroom, though when we were first ushered into it, it contained neither bedstead nor bed, and boasted only of one small chair of the rudest description. In our hut there were two doors, but neither of them had a lock and one had no fastening at all. When we learned that thieves and wild beasts were frequent visitors, we began to barricade doors with chairs, books and buckets.... There were three other inhabited houses built on the same plan as ours, but none of them was so well furnished! While there was one efficient door in the manse, and perhaps another in the doctor's house, the artisan's had no doors at all, but mattings of grass were propped up in doorways at night. Chairs were a great rarity; I do not think there were more than four in the whole station, old boxes doing duty instead.[29]

On arrival MacDonald immediately plunged into the work he felt he was sent out to do: learning the language, getting to know the people and working at developing the school. The school had been conducted by

---

[28] There were no officials of the Church of Scotland with the title of Mission Directors. MacDonald seems usually to have meant by this title the members of the responsible subcommittee of the FMC The official title of that group of men headed by Dr Macrae was "The Blantyre, East Africa, sub-committee of the FMC of the Church of Scotland." That they often acted as though they were the Directors of an independent mission may have been what MacDonald meant to imply by his use of this phrase.

[29] MacDonald, *Africana*, vol. 2, p. 74.

William Koyi.[30] MacDonald worked hard in the school and at learning the language and soon became a fluent speaker of Yao.[31] As a result he was able to wander into the nearby villages and make real contact with ordinary villagers. He was able to preach and teach in a way that none of the Blantyre staff had been able to do hitherto.

He was soon looking forward to starting another branch of the mission in the Shire Highlands and the earlier friendliness of Kalimbuka and his superior Malemia was pointed out to him. Accordingly MacDonald made two trips through to Zomba, the first one exploratory, the second in 1880, to see how John Buchanan was getting on at the new mission set up at Kalimbuka's. On this second trip he took Mrs MacDonald and was very pleased with what he found. Relations with Kalimbuka were warm and a small school was flourishing. Buchanan had been given land on behalf of the mission by Malemia, and on it he had begun planting coffee. The growing of coffee as a cash crop some in the mission hoped would help remove the need to participate in the slave trade. Buchanan could also speak Yao by this time and so within weeks of being established at Zomba he was preaching in Yao to sizeable congregations, a marked contrast to what had happened at Blantyre where months had passed before any attempt at the communication of the Gospel to local people had taken place. On the Sunday of this second visit, November 28, 1880, MacDonald took the service and found a congregation of about three hundred gathered to hear him.

Meanwhile MacDonald had also begun the translation of the New Testament into Yao as well as *Pilgrim's Progress*.

In so may ways MacDonald was an ideal missionary. He learned the language and tried to understand the ways of the local people. His description of African life in the Shire Highlands of that time is

---

[30] William Koyi and Shadrack Ngunana were the two most able of the group of South Africans of Nguni stock, trained at Lovedale, who went with the Free Church Mission to Malawi. Koyi was later the key man in Laws' building of good relations with the Ngoni of Mbelwa.

[31] The present writer has shown MacDonald's *Africana* to a number of Yao friends. They all commented on the accuracy of the Yao quoted, and on how well MacDonald had understood Yao idiom and Yao ways.

profoundly sympathetic in contrast to most other contemporary European descriptions of African life. Indeed his *Africana is* still useful to students of anthropology as well as history. However there were already serious problems bedeviling the Blantyre Mission which he was unable to solve. There were three main strands in this difficult situation: one was the quality of the original staff; the second was the intention and policy of the African Mission subcommittee in Scotland; and third was the political situation in the Shire Highlands.

In a situation of great difficulty, one presenting profoundly complex problems, men of genuine commitment to mission and of outstanding ability, such as Dr Stewart and Robert Laws, made serious errors; yet into this situation the Church of Scotland sent a party, the extraordinary nature of which we looked at in the previous chapter. Walker and Fenwick we have already characterized as a pair of "wild" men. Duncan is a shadowy figure about whom little can be found except that he was involved in the introduction of both tea and coffee to Malawi. Dr Macklin and John Buchanan were more clearly of the type needed in the situation, men who, though dispirited at first, did respond to James Stewart and then to MacDonald's inspiration. Like all the men aroused to go to Africa by Livingstone's direct call or the inspiration of his death, they saw one of the prime aims of missionary work in Africa as the ending of the slave trade. A paragraph of W.P. Livingstone throws a clear light on this strand in the motivation of these men:

> When Laws saw Young he was impressed by his 'limier and temperament: he was thorough going, earnest, determined and with a sense of humour which would be invaluable in Africa. His hatred of slavery amounted almost to an obsession, but this the Doctor thought was one of the best points in his favour.[32]

The same passion was a facet of Maddin's character, as can be seen in this letter from him preserved for us by Duff MacDonald. This was part of a report to the Africa sub-committee in March 1878.

> The Mission in its civil and social aspects is making reasonable and satisfactory progress. As an asylum for the poor and persecuted slave, Blantyre is becoming known and prized. We have now six

---

[32] Livingstone, *Laws of Livingstonia,* p. 41.

fellow creatures rescued from the lash of the slave-driver, and miseries worse than death. And this in turn prepares them for giving a ready reception to the free offers of the greater emancipation, salvation by grace through Christ our Lord. My present circumstances give a new emphasis to the old law of the city of refuge. Just think of the poor, fainting woman bearing her child, fleeing for her life, but sustained by the hope that she can reach the British flag, which already she sees fluttering in the evening breeze, her child shall live and herself be free.[33]

This passage from Dr Macklin is of great significance because it highlights two things, first, that the mission was seen as having some sort of "civic" status, and second, that deliberate interference with the slave trade and slavery was part of the policy of the Committee in Scotland which supervised the mission.

The slave trade was the "running sore" which both the Committee at home and the men in the field felt called to heal. This was a genuinely humanitarian motive but it could lead to enormous difficulties and to extreme complications for those who went with what they believed to be moral authority but with no political authority.

The Free Church of Scotland FMC felt that a British missionary presence, combined with the double effect of the new teaching of Christianity and the new economic activities they hoped to introduce in the form of "legitimate" commerce, would in the end kill the trade. However, they did realize that there might be vested interests strong enough to destroy this influence by force, and they sought to check this by getting Consular status for E.D. Young. The British Government refused this request. In the light of this the Free Church Committee was most precise in its instructions to the mission. These instructions[34] were particularly precise about the point that the mission should not interfere in the slave trade nor in the inter-tribal fighting except by persuasion. Indeed, patience, forbearance and persuasion are the keynotes in the pamphlet which was given to each member of the expedition. It has to be noted, however, that the feelings of the men about slavery were such that Young did

---

[33] MacDonald, *Mama,* vol. 2, p. 32.
[34] The instructions are bound into Livingstonia, 1875-1900.

board a dhow, fortunately empty of slaves and that Ross and Gunn, as well as others of the mission, did break up slave-gangs in the first days, though this was by bluff rather than violence.

The situation for the Blantyre Mission was completely different from this. The members of the home committee and the staff in the field, other than Walker and Fenwick, were also moved by this desire to heal the "running sore" of Africa. However, there was no one who was able to plan with the wise counsel that informed the "instructions" of the Livingstonia party. On the contrary, there seems to have been a determination to positively interfere with slave trading and with the indigenous institution of domestic slavery, which was not seen as the separate issue it was. There also seems to have been present in the thinking of Macrae and certain others of his sub-committee, the idea of Blantyre as a Christian colony. This was an idea very prevalent at that time. In 1875 both the Church Missionary Society and the Methodist Missionary Society had set up such colonies on what is now the Kenya coast at Frere Town and Ribe. These were communities of freed slaves under the civil authority of a group of missionaries headed by a superintendent. They acted as havens for runaways, and as a Christian and free presence in a slave area.[35] This intention for Blantyre was not specifically spelt out in any report to the General Assembly.

Because of the later similarities of the Blantyre and Livingstonia Missions, these troubles in the early period of the mission's history up until 1881 have been seen primarily as the result of the personalities involved and of the difficult situation. In fact a differing policy was at the root of the troubles. As MacDonald asserted, the maintenance of some sort of civil authority had been the policy of Macrae and his committee from the beginning.[36] Macrae's correspondence has not survived and because of this writers such as W.P. Livingstone and Hanna have suggested[37] that this idea was a matter of personal communication from Macrae to those

---

[35] R. Oliver, *The Missionary Factor in East Africa*, (London: Longmans, 1952), p. 56.

[36] MacDonald, vol. I, pp. 111 and 167.

[37] Hanna, *The Beginnings of Nyasaland and North-Eastern Rhodesia*, pp. 26-27; Livingstone, *Laws of Livingstonia*.

in the field. Although no formal discussion took place and the whole situation was one of bad administration, it is reasonable to assert that the members of the FMC must have been aware of what Macrae's intention was. In one particular article called, "An Appeal to the Ministers, Elders and Members of the Church of Scotland" which appeared in the Record, Macrae laid out his ideas unambiguously:

> The Committee are advised that the Mission should be of an industrial as well as an evangelic nature. In forming a Christian settlement, it would be necessary to teach the natives some of our industries, as gardening, ploughing and joinery work.

After a long passage about the horrors of the slave trade and the urgent need to check it, the article goes on:

> That this great sore of the world may be healed is certain. The commencement will be made as soon as mission is planted at Lake Nyassa. No Arab gang will come near an Englishman, if they can help it. With them the English name is synonymous with destroyer of slavery.... We are assured that a mission once established, they [the Africans] will settle around it, receive our instruction and our help, place themselves under our authority, and rise by order and Christian observance into the state of civilised communities.[38]

This article it is to be noted was signed by Lord Polwarth, Dr J.L. Herdman and Mr Alex Pringle, as well as by Dr Macrae. There is no need for the speculation put forward by W.P. Livingstone that the later instruction from Macrae to James Stewart for him to act as a magisterial head of Blantyre was a private communication out of line with policy. Here, in the appeal to the Church put out in the Church's official organ of missionary activity, was a clear indication of an intention to set up some kind of "authority" over an African population and also to create an instrument of interference with the slave trade. This idea of mission colonies received backing at that time from the great African mission figure, Dr J.L. Krapf, the hero of the early work of the CMS in what is now Kenya and Tanzania. In May 1875 he wrote a long letter to Macrae which the latter thought important enough to publish in full in the Record, though it was so long that it had to be done in two parts. Krapf advises that

---

[38] *HFMR*, February 1875, p. 271.

liberated slave groups should be the basis of the work, though he advises the Scots to get these freedmen from the colonies of liberated slaves on Mahe or the Seychelles. He continues:

> What a glorious event would it be, if the people residing around Lake Nyassa, and between the Lake and the coast should be christianised and civilised through their own people, under the instruction and superintendence of Christian Europeans![39]

He later goes on to refer to the work in the very dangerous image of being greater than the Crusades of the Middle Ages. In the few letters in Church of Scotland files that have survived from that period of the Blantyre Mission there is also confirmation that these ideas of Macrae's were quite public and well known. In July 1877 McLagan wrote to Macrae:

> I *have* lately seen a man Simons direct from Nyassa. He reports most favourably on Blantyre which is lofty, 3,000 feet, I think he said, above the sea - with abundant water and fertile soil. By his description the place is more suitable for a colony than Livingstonia which is at low level.[40]

Again, in his letter to Macrae about the necessary details for the advertisement of the post of Superintendent,[41] McLagan made it clear that the post was for a layman or minister. This would again reinforce the conclusion that a colony similar to Frere Town was intended and that this intention was known by the officials of the full Foreign Mission Committee.

Confusion and lack of any kind of decisive personality in the whole affair certainly made matters worse. As we saw from McLagan's letter about the post of Superintendent[42], he was not clear about that officer's relationship to Macklin. This never seemed to have been cleared up. To confound confusion further, Duff MacDonald was commissioned and sent out as Superintendent, but he refused from the beginning to act as a

---

[39] *HFMR*, August 1875, p. 4
[40] McLagan to Macrae, 24 July 1877, NLS, Ms. 75
[41] McLagan to Macrae, 15 February 1877, NLS, Ms. 7541.
[42] McLagan to Macrae, February 1877, NLS, Ms. 7541.

"civil governor"[43] or magistrate.[44] He was determined to be a missionary in the simplest sense of the term and that he was. But this left Blantyre after his arrival a Christian colony without a proper head. Stewart had acted firmly as such a head and the first floggings took place under him and were reported to the home authorities.[45] Macklin acted as head, with distant supervision from Dr Laws until the arrival of MacDonald.

From then the position was not very clear. MacDonald refused the role of governor; who then assumed it? As far as can be gathered from the evidence to the Com-mission of Enquiry and from MacDonald's own book, *Africana,* it was a committee of the laymen headed by Macklin. A series of letters from McLagan to MacDonald about rations and other matters, show that he was not at all certain as to whether he should not be writing to Macklin rather than MacDonald.[46] Late in 1879 Henderson arrived again in Blantyre. He had been instructed to act as "Christian Magistrate" and now he also refused this role, according to MacDonald.[47] There seem to have been no serious incidents after this date, the Commission of Enquiry declared the trouble to have ceased in September 1879.[48] But MacDonald insisted that even after Henderson's refusal to act as a governor, the home authorities still had "colonial" ideas. In the part of Volume Two of *Africana* which deals with January to June 1880, he says:

> The Mission Directors had been for a long time debating whether the Mission could really exercise civil or criminal jurisdiction at all. At first they had claimed such jurisdiction, but grave doubts arose on the execution for murder (page 109), and we did not yet know which way they were likely to decide. They had taken about a year to consider the subject, and no decision had yet reached us. The matter had an important bearing on the question of fugitive slaves.... In official letters received at the time we were urged to adopt a spirited

---

[43] MacDonald, *Africana,* vol. 2, p. 252.

[44] *Ibid,* vol. 2, pp. 111 and 167.

[45] *Ibid,* pp. 31-35.

[46] McLagan to MacDonald, 19, 23 September 23 October; 18 December 1878, NLS, Ms. 7543.

[47] MacDonald, *Africana,* vol. 2, p. 167.

[48] Para. 1 of Minutes of FMC meeting, 16 February, 1881.

Foreign Policy towards certain troublesome chiefs. The Directors indicated a plan of punishing some of these offenders, but as the layman that they had sent out to act as a Christian Magistrate declined to take such a delicate task, I was puzzled to know who was to be responsible for carrying out the scheme, and on April 5th, I wrote to the Directors with reference to this plan: "But take into account that we are only poor dominies and tradesmen." The dominies have the Saturday holiday at their disposal, but no other day without injustice to school-work.[49]

In June 1880 there arrived with the new doctor, Henry Dean, the letter of the Africa sub-committee to say that Britons by law could not exercise magisterial functions in a situation such as that at Blantyre.[50] MacDonald felt that they had been a bit slow in finding that out. The third difficulty facing MacDonald was the political situation in what is now the southern half of the Central Region, together with the Southern Region of Malawi. The Makololo state of Ramakukan in the Shire Valley was antagonistic to the Yao chieftaincies in the Shire Highlands.

These chieftaincies themselves had not settled into any permanent set of relationships, but were involved in raiding and skirmishing with each other and with the few remaining independent groups of Nyanja and Amanganja. This situation was continually being made worse by the activity of those chiefs like Kawinga, Matapwiri and Chikumbu, who had become slave traders. Other chiefs also involved themselves in the trade when the visit of coastmen made a market readily available.

However, a large shadow hung over all the Yao people. This was formed by the threat of the devastating raids of the Maseko Ngoni of Nkosi Chikuse. The Blantyre Mission was seen by the Yao people living near it as some sort of security or insurance against the Ngoni, and the warm welcome to the new extension of the mission at Zomba probably stemmed from the same source. The fact that there was no major Ngoni raid after 1875 seemed to confirm this in the minds of the Yao people, all the more when a threatened raid in 1877 never came.

---

[49] MacDonald, *Africana*, vol. Z p. 167.
[50] Ibid, p. 209

This situation meant two things for the mission. First it meant that there was no paramount such as the Kabaka in Buganda, Moshweshwe among the Sotho or Sebituane among the Makololo for the mission to deal with in matters of law and order. This in turn led to the second problem that there was a great deal of lawlessness, with a vast amount of kidnapping and stealing going on. This was a very serious problem for the small group of missionaries and their "foreign Africans" at the end of a very long line of communication which was extremely vulnerable. In the situation the depredations of even a petty thief took on serious proportions. Dr Stewart wrote to Laws that, "This thieving must be brought to an end or it will end us."[51]

Faced with this situation and having had much of his goods stolen, the other Stewart, an Indian civil servant after all, was determined to act firmly. People like Fenwick and Walker, willing to kill each other over trifles were likely to welcome tough action. In February 1878 after a very exciting chase in the bush, which let Macklin enthuse, to his credit, about British pluck in the African[52], Mapas Ntithili, one of the Livingstonia teachers lent to Blantyre, caught one of the thieves that had been plaguing Blantyre. To the joy of the Yao he was shown to be Nyanja from the river. After a trial he was given nine dozen lashes in two instalments. Macklin's report to Scotland, it must be emphasized, a report received long before the publication of Chirnside's pamphlet[53], went on:

> We kept him in all about a month, and then the people being all assembled, we made proclamation that if after two days the prisoner should be found on the Yao territory, or on this side of the Kabula river, the people were at liberty to kill him. Of course this proclamation was made by the Yao headman. After this proclamation

---

[51] Livingstone, *Laws of Livingstonia,* p. 134.

[52] MacDonald, *Africana,* vol. 2, p. 33. Macklin wrote "We are British and fond of British pluck, but in what is this young man's blood and spirit inferior to our own? and surely there is good hope for a race that can furnish such men."

[53] A. Chirnside, *The Blantyre Missionaries: Discreditable Disclosures,* (London: Ridgeway, 1880).

was made, the prisoner was escorted out of the Yao country by armed men.[54]

This letter shows a colony with its prison and its alliances with neighbouring chiefs.

When MacDonald refused to act as magistrate, it is not clear from any record how the gap was filled. This was MacDonald's real mistake, he took the first step in making a change by refusing to act as magistrate, but did not go on to organize the relationship of the mission to its client villages, and to the local Yao chiefs on any new basis. Men like Fenwick, violent in all their relations, continued to beat offenders caught red-handed in theft, so they maintained a de facto magistracy. This situation was made much worse, as Dr Hanna has pointed out, by the arrival of the Africa Lakes Company.[55]

They were short staffed and made the Blantyre Mission one of their staging posts, where the missionaries were responsible for checking goods going in and out. This involved them even further in the problem of crime and punishment. MacDonald, though trying to steer clear of being personally involved, did not try to extricate the mission as an institution and try out some new practical arrangement, based on his good relations with the Yao chiefs and his respect for African ways. He did complain to Edinburgh, however, that the fact that having refused to be what he called "the Civil Governor of the Colony", MacDonald was not at all clear even as to his authority over the lay members of the mission. The FMC sent him no clear remit about this. As we have seen from McLagan's letter, the FMC did not seem to be clear in its own minds what to do now. At the time of a skirmish between mission carriers and men of Mitochi, a Yao headman near Chiradzulu, the Africa Mission sub-committee took, according to MacDonald, ,a step which, though it could be called a step towards colonial self-rule, still was consistent with its being a colonial power. They:

> advised that the natives living at Blantyre should select one of the laymen to carry out some sort of government. Mr Walker perhaps

---

[54] Macklin to FMC, March 1878, reproduced in full in MacDonald, *Africans*, vol. 2, pp. 31-37.

[55] Hanna, *The Beginnings of Nyasaland and North-Eastern Rhodesia,* p. 22.

would have been the successful candidate, and might have been willing to take the duty, but I learned from other home letters that he and other artisans were required to work under Mr Henderson, who had returned to Blantyre a few days before, and who was expected to 'act as a Christian Magistrate'. But Mr Henderson declined to take the responsibility of the office.[56]

So the situation was again one of confusion, lacking any clear authority in the mission. By this time the FMC had been told by the Blantyre sub-committee about the carrying out of capital punishment, and word was sent out to Blantyre that the FMC

> while deeply sympathising with the missionaries in the great difficulties of the position in which they found themselves, felt constrained in the meantime to disavow all responsibility in regard to the infliction of capital punishment in the case in question.[57]

They also said in the letter that they were going to consult with the Free Church as to how the mission could be carried on without the exercise of civil authority by the missionaries.

The result of these deliberations seems to have been a letter dated March 1880, arriving in Blantyre with the new doctor, Dr Dean, in June 1880. This letter pointed out that there were specific statutes of the UK Parliament forbidding British subjects from exercising the type of authority hitherto done at Blantyre. It also contained this paragraph:

> Your position must be understood as excluding the power and jurisdiction known as civil government. We have no right to give, and you have no right to receive from us, any jurisdiction whatever over the lives, persons or property of the natives who live round about you. We cannot make you civil magistrates over any portion of Africa, even though we possess property therein; and we desire you to understand that the only commission which you can hold from the Church of Scotland is that of the ambassadors of Christ sent to preach the gospel of His love and grace, and to train the native in precept and example the usages of the Christian life.[58]

---

[56] MacDonald, *Africana,* vol. 2, p. 167.
[57] *Ibid*
[58] *Ibid*

MacDonald's response was one of amazement. Had he not been complaining about this very issue throughout his time there? Yet the response from Edinburgh had been a consistent attempt to maintain Blantyre as a colony and a complete contradiction of this last letter. If the FMC decided now that they could not authorize magistrates,

> Well, why had they given commission to various individuals to act as magistrates? Why had they from the beginning of the mission down to the very last mail, urged the carrying out of civil jurisdiction? We could only hold up our hands in amazement.[59]

The worst cases of flogging were by this time over, and a system of handing serious troublemakers back to their masters or chiefs had been begun as an attempt to at least minimize civil jurisdiction. However, the matter could not rest there, because Andrew Chirnside, a traveller who had visited the mission in 1879 and had been horrified by the execution and several of the savage floggings, had published an account of them which caused a scandal in Scotland. The UK Government were also informed, but they seemed keen to wait and see if the Church of Scotland could clear the situation without their intervention. Dr Rankin of Muthill Parish and Mr Pringle, an Edinburgh lawyer, were sent out as the General Assembly's Commissioners to investigate the situation, which, it must again be noted, had in fact been fully reported to the appropriate authorities in Edinburgh. MacDonald was able to quote in *Africana* letters from Macklin, James Stewart and himself which show that severe floggings, including one associated with a man's death, the clash with Mitochi and the execution, had all been reported to Edinburgh. One of McLagan's letters appears to confirm MacDonald's assertion. In May 1880 he wrote to MacDonald asking for detailed answers to all Chirnside's complaints. He went on,

> Be particular as to dates, for in regard to the murder of the woman and the execution of the murderer he is evidently all wrong - placing the whole of these events subsequent to March 1879 - whereas the woman was shot in December 1878, and the execution took place in February, 1879.[60]

---

[59] *Ibid*, 209.
[60] McLagan to MacDonald, May 1880, NLS, Ms. 7545.

He was asking MacDonald for confirmation of what he already seemed to know. Rankin and Pringle went to Blantyre and returned and the result of their report was that MacDonald, Buchanan and Fenwick were dismissed. Macklin who was held to be very blameworthy for several of the floggings had already left the service of the committee, as had Walker.[61]

At the Commission of the General Assembly on March 2, 1881, their report had been heard and several resolutions adopted including this:

> III. That while regretting that the Church did not, through the Foreign Mission Committee, distinctly instruct their agents, when the Blantyre Mission was originally established, that they must not in any circumstances attempt to exercise civil jurisdiction there the Commission condemn in the strongest terms, and bitterly deplore, the conduct of which certain of these agents - assuming that jurisdiction - were on various occasions guilty of in the earlier days of the Blantyre Mission.[62]

They said 'in the earlier days' because it was accepted by them that flogging had ceased in mid-1879. The Report of the FMC on East Africa to the General Assembly concludes with this paragraph:

> After anxious deliberation, your Committee are prepared unanimously to recommend the continuance of the East Africa Mission, abandoning, however, as soon as practicable, the Industrial department, and aiming at Evangelistic and Educational work alone in the Blantyre District and among the Makololo. Of course it will be understood that the Mission is not to exercise civil or criminal jurisdiction of any kind, but will leave that to the native chiefs."[63]

These last words show just what a strange corner the FMC had been driven into. Chirnside's complaints about ill-treatment of Africans included one about the handing over of people to African chiefs for punishment. On Chirnside's last night in Blantyre, MacDonald had begun to implement, with Henderson's help, what he had always wanted to do, which was to hand back runaways and troublemakers to the chief claiming authority over them.

---

[61] *Assembly Reports*, 1881, FMC Report, East Africa Section, p. 78.

[62] *Ibid*, p. 79.

[63] *Ibid, p.* 80.

The bitter protests of the persons involved, who knew they were going into slavery or to their deaths, disturbed Chirnside's sleep and his conscience. However, this was the only possible alternative to the exercise of civil authority of the kind Chirnside rightly deplored, but which, it is clear, the missionaries sent to Blantyre had been instructed to exercise. W.P. Livingstone and Dr Hanna both think that the instruction was one from Macrae personally and had not the approval of the Africa Mission sub-committee or the Foreign Mission Committee. What the latter Committee was informed of as to policy in Blantyre cannot now be known; it is clear though that the policy at Blantyre was supported by the Africa Mission subcommittee and it was not simply a matter of one letter from Dr Macrae. In the Foreign Mission Committee's Special Report to the General Assembly of 1882[64], it is stated that Dr Macrae had all the correspondence between his sub-committee and Blantyre in his own personal possession. The sub-committee moved that he should return it. However, when all the Blantyre Mission material was sent to the National Library of Scotland, the correspondence for Blantyre for that period was not there, nor was it to be found in the Church headquarters, so it can only be assumed that Dr Macrae was allowed to keep it. MacDonald did have access to it in preparing his case for the Assembly, presumably in Blantyre and it is from this correspondence that he quotes extensively in *Africana,* volume two, which in turn is quoted in this chapter. These letters leave no doubt about the fact that the policy in Blantyre was not unknown in Edinburgh, even if there was no other evidence but the long letter from Dr Macklin sent in March 1878 to the Africa sub-committee which is referred to above. The fact of civil jurisdiction is clearly reported and its implementation, including severe flogging, is also reported. The contents of the few letters of McLagan which have come to light and been deposited in the National Library also confirm this. One can come to no other conclusion than that Duff MacDonald was made a scapegoat for the Africa Mission sub-committee, whose policy he had consistently opposed.

The question of civil jurisdiction was not critical for the Blantyre Mission alone; it was a pressing one wherever there was any kind of missionary entry to a country where there was not a strong paramount, as among

---

[64] *Assembly Reports,* 1882, FMC Special Report, pp. 51-53.

the Baganda, the Lozi or the Ndebele. It was an extremely acute problem for missions like those in the region of Lake Malawi who entered, under the impetus of an anti-slavery passion, a semi-anarchic situation in which there was a constant danger of slave raiding and kidnapping. While being quite clear that they were not to attack slavers to free slaves, the Blantyre missionaries believed it their duty to accept runaways. Laws and the others at Livingstonia felt this also as Dr Hanna has pointed out,[65] but they had quite specific instructions not to take in runaways, except in specifically restricted circumstances.

However, even then around Livingstonia at Cape Maclear, there grew up a community that looked to the mission head as to a chief. As a result they also exercised "civil jurisdiction", for some kind of law and order had to be maintained. That this was the case at Cape Maclear and that he thought it to have been no bad thing, is clear from the letter written by James Stewart to Laws in March 1881, where among other things he says:

> It is generally supposed that all exercise of jurisdiction is illegal, and I fear that nobody will say a word for it after the mess that MacDonald has made of it.... I cannot say what position they [Livingstonia Committee] will take up, but they are quite prepared, I think, to defend your action and mine on moral grounds, though not legally.... You must keep yourself from all magisterial powers in the future. Make the principal headmen into a council and throw all responsibility on them and give your advice to them only privately.[66]

It is acknowledged by his biographer that Laws once ordered a man to be flogged for the rape of a young girl, but after a few strokes he ordered it to be stopped.[67]

From about the end of 1880 Laws had done what MacDonald had been doing from the end of 1879, that is, returning runaways to their masters, and trying to get local headmen to deal with all cases which arose among the people who were permanently settled around the mission. This permanent community was a more complex problem, especially because

---

[65] Hanna, *The Beginnings of Nyasaland and North-Eastern Rhodesia*, p. 35.

[66] James Stewart to Laws, 2 March 2 1881, Laws Papers, vol. A.

[67] Livingstone, *Laws of Livingstonia*, p. 138.

a number of them were runaways, but of such long standing that they could not possibly be sent back.

This solution may seem obvious to us now but it was extremely difficult to carry out for men who had come to Africa on fire with the idea of halting the slave trade. Indeed, Dr Macklin had refused to return to Blantyre because of the decision at the end of 1879 to implement this policy of turning back runaways.[68]

Even for someone like MacDonald, who was almost unique among all the members of the staffs of either mission in feeling that the ending of the slave trade was not one of the prime aims of the mission, found it hard. He could write in a letter to the home authorities:

> All the missions to this region have run their heads against the question of slavery, and out of it have sprung a world of troubles. We might have done our duty as missionaries, and let slavery alone entirely. We do not find that the great Church of the Middle Ages ran against the question, and it had as many opportunities as we have now. To say the least of it, our taking the matter up hitherto, has been premature; we have not Such knowledge of the language and the feelings of the natives as to justify us dashing at once into a difficult question like this.[69]

Yet even he, who could look on the issue so objectively, was in fact upset when handing back some of those who came. Some who came were rascals, but many were not, and he recalls a number of these cases in *Africana*, some of which he calls "unspeakably sad" as when he had to hand back a widow and her five children to Chief Mtambo, knowing they were almost certainly going to their death. At that time he wrote to the Directors that he was having to put "a remorseless logic in the place of mercy."[70] The problem of civil jurisdiction was brought to a head by the capital punishment carried out by the Blantyre Mission and reported to the appropriate committee in Scotland, which woke up to where its instructions had lead the mission. The issue became a public one because of the stir raised by Chirnside's polemic, which touched on the complex

---

[68] MacDonald, *Africana*, vol. 1, p. 204.
[69] *Ibid*, p. 168.
[70] Ibid, p. 202.

heart of the matter when it complained both of the cruel exercise of civil authority by the mission and about the mission's handing back of people to a chief to exercise his authority. It might be suggested that it was the brutality of the flogging that was really the issue, a brutality which one could only expect from some of the men involved, as has already been suggested. However, that was not the real issue. At Cape Maclear no brutality took place, yet the Free Church felt the real issue keenly, which was, how was law and order to be maintained among the communities of people who gathered round a mission station? The statute law of the UK was quite clear that no "colony" could be set up as the Blantyre Mission party had been instructed to create, yet the alternative to missionary authority was the handing of malefactors back to chiefs who would kill or enslave them. This was the very thing that most of these men felt they had been sent out to stop.

In the case of Blantyre, the case was further complicated because acting on what they believed were their instructions, and in keeping with the spirit of the humanitarian circles in Britain, the staff made Blantyre a refuge for runaway slaves. These were not always fleeing from being sold to the coast, but were fleeing traditional African domestic slavery. This increased greatly the numbers and therefore the difficulties of maintaining law and order, and it also made for bad relations with local chiefs and headmen.

When the policy of being a refuge for all was stopped because of these troubles, the whole cutting edge of the mission as a Christian colony was blunted in the eyes of a man like Dr Macklin, as we have seen. Surely many others like Lt Young must have felt the same; where was the work of healing the "running sore of the world" going? Yet this new policy was that which enabled David Scott when he arrived to create good relations with the chiefs around Blantyre, and it enabled Laws to steer a difficult but effective course between the Tonga and Mbelwa's Ngoni when the Livingstonia Mission moved to Bandawe. It must be recognized that it was a new policy, and perhaps it was a key factor in the long-range success of these two missions, a success which did not attend the efforts of the Church Missionary Society at Frere Town, nor the Wesleyans at Ribe, both of whom remained caught in the web of being a missionary colony of freed slaves, acting as a refuge for free slaves, and so effectively cut off from the surrounding population.

The Free Kirk and the Auld Kirk Missions learned from the "Blantyre Scandals". MacDonald had begun the new policies already in 1880 as the Commission of Enquiry acknowledged,[71] but had to carry the blame for the original policy going awry. He left to his successors very good notes on the Yao language, as well as some good translations, good relations with many people, Mpama, Malemia, Kalimbuka and Kapeni, to name a few. He also left a flourishing school and a group of African men, Bismarck, Kagaso Rondau, Nacho and others who, like the children of the school, had a great affection for him, and who were of immense help to David Clement Scott later.

The General Assembly of 1882 at least partly redeemed this story of very unfair dealing with MacDonald. During the actual sittings of the Assembly a special committee was set up to review the whole situation, and especially the evidence which MacDonald had submitted to the FMC appealing against his sentence. This evidence had been taken from the correspondence of the Blantyre Mission with the authorities in Edinburgh, on which evidence he also drew for the second volume of *Africana*. His appeal was reported to the General Assembly. A Special Committee of Assembly was appointed to hear it, reported back before the Assembly ended, and although it said it could not reverse the findings of the Foreign Mission Committee, it in fact went on to modify them considerably.[72] Their findings were passed by the Assembly, the third and parts of the fourth and fifth points of their resolutions are important in that they went very far indeed to vindicate MacDonald.

3. The Committee gladly record their opinion that in much of the conduct thus condemned and deplored, Mr MacDonald was in no degree implicated, and, in particular, he was not guilty of cruelty ...

---

[71] All the discussions reported as taking place in the Commission of Assembly and full Assembly of 1881, acknowledged that what they considered to be a reprehensible policy ended in September 1879.

[72] *Assembly Reports,* 1882, Special Report to Assembly on Duff MacDonald's Petition, pp. 147-149.

4. The Committee are further of the opinion that in estimating any amount of indiscretion with which Mr MacDonald is fairly chargeable, every possible allowance must be made for the extremely difficult circumstances in which he was placed by his comparative youth and want of knowledge of affairs, the indefinite and perplexing instructions given by those by whom he was commissioned ...

5. The Committee express their conviction that nothing which has occurred can detract from the testimony of the Commission to the good work, earnestly and successfully done by Mr. Duff MacDonald in the general supervision of the religious work of the mission, and that no reason exists why his high character and proved zeal should not be made available in any field of Christian usefulness to which he may be called.[73]

"Indefinite and perplexing instructions" is the phrase which indicates that the Assembly Commission accepted to some real degree that the home authorities were at fault. This is also borne out by the fact that the Blantyre sub-committee of the FMC was discharged by the Assembly of 1881 and a new one appointed by the Assembly of 1882. Regrettably no inquiry was held into the sub-committee's work, nor was MacDonald's case against the committee ever printed in any report or document of the Church.

However, 1882 was the beginning of a new era in the history of Blantyre, with the Mission headed by David Clement Scott, and the sub-committee in Edinburgh by Dr Archibald Scott of St. George's.

---

[73] *Ibid,* p. 148.

Chapter 3: A New Beginning under David Clement Scott, 1881 - 1891

> People will not believe how much the African is capable of until they have tried. Our aim is always to teach responsibility, and at the proper time to lay it on those who have to bear it. In many ways the time has now come. It is a fatal mistake to keep the African in leading strings. We cannot too soon teach him to realise he has a part to play in the education and life of Christ's Church and Kingdom. The more he realises this, the greater his progress will be.[1]

The above quotation from one of David Clement Scott's many articles in *Life and Work in British Central Africa,* can be taken as the keynote of his work in Malawi. All of this work was based on two firm convictions, first, that Africans were human beings, essentially no different from Europeans, and second, that they were ready for responsibility, both in the Church and in the new society being created in Africa by the coming of European power.

D.C. Scott saw the task of the missionary in Africa as being both a bearer of the Gospel and of modern culture. This was how he interpreted Livingstone's dictum about the need for "Christianity and Commerce" in Africa. The culture brought by the missionaries was not, he believed, simply European culture but a modern culture, world-wide in its significance. He insisted that Africans were its inheritors as much as Europeans. He fully realized that when missionaries dwelt in a place and

attempted to propagate the Christian faith, they could not help imparting something of their culture other than the religious, even if they tried not to, as some did. Scott held that since Africans were co-inheritors of modem culture it should be imparted consciously in the educational process, hoping that, as with the Gospel it would ground itself in African forms.

D.C. Scott took over the leadership of the Blantyre Mission at a time which was very unpropitious for the working out of his ideas. Although these ideas were a good deal more sophisticated than those of most of

---

[1] *Life and Work in British Central Africa,* June 1895.

the supporters of "industrial missions", they were very closely related to them, striving after the same end of a total renewal of African society. The "Blantyre Scandals" had sown grave doubts in the minds of many about this concept of mission which, under MacDonald, had seemed to lead to miserable failure. No one was more clear about this than the two commissioners sent by the General Assembly to Blantyre to investigate the troubles there. They both made reports recommending a very definite and specifically different form for the future of the work in the Shire Highlands.

The Reverend Dr Thomas Rankine,[2] the Senior Commissioner, was most insistent that the work was to be clearly and simply evangelistic in its nature. A change of the geographical distribution of the work was also recommended by him. The mission was to be centred in the Shire Valley rather than in the Shire Highlands. Rankine specifically recommended two sites in the valley, one a hill, Namkango, near Katunga's village and another near the village of Chipatula. These stations, with the existing two at Zomba and Blantyre, were to be the basis of the new developments.

Another remarkable feature of Dr Rankine's plans shows an understanding of the missionary task very different from that of "industrial mission". He laid down that the staff necessary for the work as he envisaged it, with its greatly expanded area of operation, was that of one ordained man and one doctor at Blantyre with a single lay evangelist at each of the other stations. This scheme clearly implied that there was no need for any kind of sophisticated instruction of African people nor much concern for their medical care; it also implied that Dr Rankine had not thought very clearly about the very important matters of health and furloughs for European staff.

The other commissioner, the Edinburgh lawyer, Thomas Pringle, also favoured a development of the mission's work in the Shire Valley among the Makololo. His report[3] dwelt at length on the advantages that would accrue from such a move. Pringle's report was much more explicit than Rankine's in its refusal to accept the missionary as having any "civilising"

---

[2] *Assembly Reports,* 1881, FMC Report, Appendix A, pp. 86-90.
[3] *Ibid,* pp. 90-97.

role to play. His view was that successful evangelization could take place apart from any great cultural change among African people. His view was so narrow that even care of the sick was not seen as an essential part of obedience to the Gospel, but as a subordinate adjunct to the work of evangelization. He says:

> The specific object of the Mission should, I decidedly believe, be only to evangelise and to educate and to heal the sick. I here mention the medical department, not to put it on a par with the other two, but because the amount of time and means which it would be legitimate to spend upon the healing is more than I would have deemed legitimate to spend upon any other work than evangelising and educating.[4]

He goes on to explain his understanding of education in the mission field.

> When I advocate educating along with evangelising this is mainly for the purpose of evangelising ... It is with a view of training Scripture-readers from among the natives.[5]

The next two pages of his report are devoted to showing that "Arts and Industry" are not needed in Malawi because the standard of living was fair, and, in any case, this whole realm of activity had little or nothing to do with the work of the Mission, except where necessary to attract people to it. Since people were already attracted to the Mission in the Shire Highlands, that was sufficient as far as Pringle was concerned. Further, Pringle asserted that artisans were simply not a suitable class from which to recruit missionaries.[6] This was an extraordinary assertion for a Scot to make, despite the misbehaviour of Fenwick and some others of the original Blantyre staff.

These two reports were accepted by the General Assembly, though no attempt seems to have been made to reconcile their far from identical practical recommendations. Their tenor was, however, the same and this presumably was what was endorsed by the Assembly in accepting them. That is, the Assembly decided to reject the concept of the missionary

---

[4] *Ibid*, p. 92.

[5] *Ibid*, p. 93.

[6] *Ibid*, p. 97.

task as seen by Livingstone, a member of that very class which Pringle thought of as unsuitable material for the work of missions. Livingstone had appealed to Christianity and Commerce to transform the old society of East and Central Africa which was being profoundly altered by the pressure of the slave trade. Pringle insisted that Malawi society best be left alone except for evangelization.

Quite apart from asserting that the lay elements of "industrial mission", modern education, technical training and the development of trading - all that Livingstone meant by "Commerce" - was out, as far as the Church of Scotland was concerned, the Commissioner's report completely failed to grasp the problem of religion and culture. How can a person's view of God and their relation to Him be changed without changing their view of society and its customs, and indeed beginning a process of change in the society itself?

This feeling that it was simply the business of the missions to change only the religious side of man and society was widespread in Church circles at the time. It was expressed most clearly by Bishop Steere in an article quoted by Mr H.A.C. Cairns in his book *Prelude to Imperialism*.[7] Cairns also quotes in this context some remarks of Duff MacDonald about a simple village person being capable of being a good Christian.[8] They can be seen, Cairns asserts, as representing an attitude which respected African culture as over against the very prevalent missionary attitude of aversion to things African. Cairns goes on to say about this attitude:

> Kerr, Jephson and Bruce-Knight, tended to express comparatively favourable attitudes to African culture. Yet, as Jephson indicated, this could be coupled with the assumption that Africans were incapable of becoming Europeanised, and with a distaste which existed even at this early date, for the Africans who "aped" the European in such matters as clothing.
>
> An apparent respect for African culture may veil a disrespect for African capacity, or a distaste for the breaking down of cultural distinctions. The Scottish Missions with their emphasis on civilisation

---

[7] H.A.C. Cairns, *Prelude to Imperialism: British Reaction to Central African Society 1840-1890*, (London: Routledge & Kegan Paul, 1965), p.219.

[8] MacDonald, *Africana*, vol. 2, p. 248

displayed less respect for tribalism, but their approach was possibly indicative of a greater optimism as to the capacity of the African to assimilate a range of western values and traits which would eventually place him on a level of equality with Europeans in more than spiritual matters. This, however, is dangerous ground for which explicit evidence is sparse.[9]

Quite apart from what Scottish missionaries thought or did, it is significant that modern African nationalists have been most suspicious of those who would insist on the preservation of the integrity of African culture, with some justification since the whole structure of "apartheid" was built on such an insistence.

In Malawi itself, the first overt political rebel against European rule, John Chilembwe, was a man who was certainly not opposed to the social, technical and other non-religious changes brought in by missions.[10]

A look at the extant writings of D.C. Scott would have given Cairns the explicit evidence of which he was short. Joseph Bismarck, a man who worked with Scott, having begun his mission career with MacDonald, used to tell a story which illustrated very clearly that Scott certainly believed that an African gained equality in more than spiritual affairs by becoming a member of the Christian Church. Bismarck used to tell how one day he was standing outside the carpenter's office on Blantyre Mission, waiting to speak to John McIlwain, head of that department. He was standing, hat in hand, when D.C. Scott approached. Scott came up to him and said, "No, no Bismarck, when McDwain comes up you simply raise your hat, that's all, you and he are brothers. You both keep your hats off while speaking to me, because I am your Father, but you two, no, you are brothers."[11]

In his articles in *Life and Work in British Central Africa*, Scott was quite explicit in giving his reasons for wanting an "industrial", a civilizing mission. He did not despise African culture, as undoubtedly some of his

---

[9] Cairns, *Prelude to Imperialism,* p. 221.

[10] G. Shepperson and T. Price, *Independent African: John Chilembwe and the Nyasaland Rising,* Edinburgh: The University Press, 1959).

[11] Interview with Mr Lewis Bandawe, M.B.E., Bismarck's son-in-law and confidant, October, 1963.

colleagues and successors did, but felt that a fertilization was necessary for its development. At one point Scott specifically answered an article in an unnamed British journal which opposed civilizing missions as did Pringle and Rankine. He said:[12]

> When one comes, however, here in Africa into practical touch with the everyday life of the native, and has to live in their midst, one cannot help imparting the civilisation one has received to those whose co-inheritance it is and who certainly desire it ... unless then he (the missionary) cut himself off from all that is human and declare himself an ascetic, or unless he fall below the appreciation of culture he must perforce take interest in and develop the people round him to the best of his ability.
>
> He does not produce a non-native product, he only brings a civilisation before the native spirit not merely to develop a native Christianity but to become a conscious member of the Catholic Church of Christ.
>
> At Blantyre we have striven accordingly to the impress with which the Mission started and in answer to Livingstone's appeal and prayer, to supply an ideal of Christian industry; to tangibly aid the colony; to give the native the place in the development of this land to which he is called to prove he is fit for it; and to see him through.

David Scott was not a man of the mid-twentieth century who could benefit from fifty years of anthropological study; from time to time he misunderstood aspects of African culture as we shall see, but he had a firm grasp of certain essentials upon which all his work was based. The essentials for him were that Africans were part of the same humanity as Scotsmen or Portuguese, that they could contribute to the Christian Church as well as receive from it, that the civilizing and Christianizing task of the mission must result in a civilization and Church that was African as well as being Christian.

Were his *Cyclopaedic Dictionary of the Mang'anja Language* the only thing of his left to us, it would be enough to convince of his fundamental respect and affection for African culture, despite his being a "civiliser".

---

[12] *LWBCA* May 1894.

Cairns has shown that many missionaries of the mid-19th century lacked any real sympathy or understanding of the people of Africa; that some, on contact with Africans, came to dislike them intensely, and, unfortunately, stayed on to "convert" the objects of their dislike.[13] Scott was to have trouble with members of staff who typified these assertions of Cairns. The liberal paternalist form of the denial of the human equality of Africans also brought out his anger. When Henry Drummond, the hero of the Churches in the United Kingdom and of student Christian circles there, published his book about his visit to Malawi[14], Scott's wrath was aroused, as well as an honest realism not often noticed by contemporaries, dazzled by his eloquence. He said to a close friend in Scotland:

> I never read such nonsense as Drummond's book: it is a frightful libel on humanity, I would write but he praises the Mission so much one's mouth is shut, and one's time is so limited.[15]

In Scott's eyes, Drummond's kindliness towards Africans could not make up for the denial of their shared humanity, a denial implicit in Drummond's exposition of the moral authority and superiority of the European over the African.

To return to 1881, we find Scott, a man who was both a respecter of Africans and yet a firm believer in the civilizing role of missions, as head of Blantyre Mission. He was appointed by the authority of the General Assembly which had endorsed the reports of its two Commissioners who supported a very different view of the role of missions.

In a letter to his close friend James Robertson,[16] written only a month after he had arrived in Blantyre, Scott outlined what he believed were the problems that faced him. These were four.

First, the aftermath of bad relations created during MacDonald's time with a number of neighbouring chiefs, and the continued presence in the district of troublemakers like Fenwick, was a serious handicap to the new

---

[13] Cairns, *Prelude to Imperialism,* chapter 7.

[14] H. Drummond, *Tropical Africa,* (London: Hodder and Stoughton, 1888).

[15] Scott to James Robertson, 14 October 1881, EUL Ms. 717/10.

[16] Scott to Robertson, 20 December 1880, EUL Ms. 717/10.

beginning. Second, the antagonism of the Portuguese who controlled the mission's only lines of communication was a constant threat to the continued existence of the work. Third, the existence of three large villages of freed slaves on the land of the mission, was an immediate administrative problem. On grounds of humanity, they could not simply be dispersed. Scott's realism again appeared when he pointed out to Robertson that it would take considerable force to disperse them anyway. The fourth problem was the one which he thought most difficult and was not peculiar to Blantyre but was common to all missionaries in Africa at that time. This was the contrast between his situation and that of St. Paul. The latter was of a poor nation going to rich rulers, in contrast to himself, as Scott said, who was of a conquering nation going to the conquered.[17]

Scott was almost alone in the new situation. Only Jonathan Duncan, the gardener and Dr Henry Dean were left of the old staff, though Henry Henderson had now rejoined the work. However, in Blantyre he found some very important assistants waiting his arrival, whose ready help, wisdom and integrity left a lasting mark on Scott's attitudes. These were a small group of Africans who had been attracted to the mission in MacDonald's time and had stayed on. They included Joseph Bismarck, Rondau Kaferanjila and Donald Malota.

The mission station proper, as opposed to the mission villages, still consisted of the eight daub and wattle houses built round a square, with their roads and gardens as laid out by James Stewart. The stone house built by John Buchanan for MacDonald had fallen into an uninhabitable state and was abandoned. There was no church building. Scott thought that this was of some significance after a four-year missionary presence, and the building of a small thatched adobe church was the first task undertaken and completed under his new regime.

The four key problems which he had outlined to Robertson in his first letter after his arrival had to be dealt with. The fourth was one which would be always present in everything he did during his time in Africa

---

[17] It is not without significance that as early as this Scott sees Europe as conquering Africa.

and had no specific solution. The other three were specific and he dealt first with the nearest, that of the freed slave villages.

He had clear instructions from the General Assembly that he was not to exercise magisterial functions.[18] Since, as we have seen, he believed that it was both morally and physically impossible to disperse these villages, what was to be done about law and order within them, and what was to be done about relations between them and neighbouring villages? A solution to this difficulty involved the first of the problems he listed, because part of the cause of the strained relations with neighbouring Yao chiefs was the fact that some of the villagers were runaways and the villages continued to act as a haven for runaways. Law and order had to be maintained, good relations with neighbours had to be restored, yet the new head of mission could not break trust with the villagers.

Scott began by making it known in the surrounding area, that all who had any claim to any of the runaway slaves who were living in the mission villages, should come to see him. If they could substantiate that claim, then they would be paid compensation by Scott. This compensation would act as the legal redemption of the person involved, legal in traditional African law that is. The redeemed person would then work off his price in labour to the mission.[19] Thus Scott, who was just as passionately opposed to the slave trade to the coast be it Portuguese or Arab, as had been Young or Macklin, took the very important step of distinguishing between traditional African domestic slavery and the coast trade, and recognizing the validity of the former for the society in which the mission was living. This move was accepted and welcomed by all the local Yao chiefs except two. These were Mitochi of Chiradzulu, who had actually fought a skirmish with the mission's people in MacDonald's time, and the mission's former near neighbour, Chikumbu of Nsoni. From his arrival Scott had tried to maintain the close relations that MacDonald had built up with Chief Mpama and Chief Kapeni. With their help as go-betweens, it was arranged for him to go with Mrs Scott to visit Mitochi at Chiradzulu. This visit was highly successful and created a bond between the two men that was never broken. As we shall see in a later chapter,

---

[18] *Assembly Reports,* 1880, FMC Report, p. 78.
[19] Hetherwick, *The Romance of Blantyre,* p. 39.

one of Scott's earliest quarrels with Commissioner Harry Johnston, was over the latter's treatment of Mitochi in 1892. However, no negotiations got anywhere with Chikumbu, who was a very aggressive person closely associated with the coast trade, and whose presence so close to the mission was a constant menace to the peace. However, Chikumbu's very aggressiveness was his undoing and solved Scott's problem. As the Reverend Harry Matecheta records:

> *Chikumbu anali ndi anthu alcudziwa cifwamba, ndipo anthu ambili anasauka.* [Chikumbu had many people who were expert man-stealers and many people suffered].[20]

At length the Yao chiefs Mkanda and Kapeni got together and called on the aid of Kasisi, the Paramount of the Makololo, to help them remove this danger to their people's peace. Chikumbu was forced to leave the district and settled in an area which was later called the Fort Lister Gap, astride the trade route to Quelimane under the shadow of Mulanje Mountain. There he was still a nuisance, but not the immediate menace that he had been at Nsoni. His hostility again became a critical problem for the mission when its work expanded and entered the Mulanje area in the 1890s.

These newly established good relations with the Yao chiefs, were only maintained by Scott's ruthless insistence on refusing to accept runaways. This was often a very painful rule to carry out in practice, as we have already seen MacDonald point out. The problem of relations between the mission villages and their neighbours, was, by this step, greatly reduced, but there still remained the problem of law and order within those villages, the problem which had so desperately troubled MacDonald. The people in these villages undoubtedly looked to the mission as the source of authority and Scott felt that this was a responsibility that could not be shirked. However, he did not attempt to set up any kind of European magistracy as had been so tragically attempted by his predecessors. He tried to organize the mission community in as African a way as possible. Each village had its headman, who with his elders heard each case of complain according to the

---

[20] Matecheta, *Blantyre Mission: Nkhani ya Ciyambo Cace*, (Blantyre: Hetherwick Press, 1951), p.2.

traditional form of the *miandu*.[21] If no decision could be reached or there was an appeal, then the matter came to Scott, as did any inter-village dispute. He then gathered all the headmen and elders together and presided over the *mlandu* himself. His role was that of any important chief in such a situation, to hear all sides of the argument, to listen to the opinions of the headmen and elders, to articulate the consensus of the meeting when all had had their say, and to back up the headmen with his authority so that the decision reached was carried out.

There was thus created a very different atmosphere from that of the 1870s, when the word colony, used by Macrae in his appeals, was not an inappropriate designation for the mission. Alexander Hetherwick, in a short article he wrote years later describing his first few days in Blantyre in 1884, gives us a picture of the new situation and Scott's role in it. The problem confronting the missionaries was again murder as at the moment of crisis for the old MacDonald regime, but there was no attempt at following European practice or law as was done then. Hetherwick wrote:

> then came lunch. In the middle of it we were interrupted by a native rushing up to the door with the shout of 'War, war at the Chipeta village'[22] ... A man or men of Kuntaja, a small headman of a Yao village within a few hundred yards of the mission ... had joined in the beer-drinking and quarrelled with one of the Chipeta and stabbed him. It was war with a vengeance, and the whole of the Chipeta clan were said to be gathering to make an attack on the village of Kuntaja. They were out on the war-path armed with spear and shield ... Clement Scott and the Doctor set out for the scene of the trouble. The newcomer followed interested in the novel experience ... the Chipeta looked warlike advancing in the Zulu battle formation of the crescent, brandishing spear and shield and calling out *nkhondo! nkhondo!* Kuntaja did not seem very much perturbed ... Scott gathered the Chipeta together on an anthill ... and there harangued

---

21 Mlandu (plural milandu) is a meeting for discussion held by a headman with his elders along with the parties involved in some dispute, to resolve the dispute. It can be a matter that would be called civil as well as what would be called criminal in Britain. The word can also mean case or dispute, but primarily refers to the meeting called to resolve it.

[22] One of the three principal villages on mission land.

> them in what was to me an unknown tongue but it seemed to make some impression ... at any rate the warriors agreed to come and face Kuntaja on the morrow and have their say at the Manse. The *Mlandu* occupied two days. I forget the terms of the agreement but no doubt it contained payment by Kuntaja of certain goods as compensation to the Chipeta.[23]

This way of using the institution of the *mlandu* was very slow and time consuming. It demanded patience and sympathy. It meant that Scott became a chief among chiefs and had to go to many *mlandu* with his neighbours such as Kapeni and Mpama. Exhausting and time consuming it was, but what better form of language instruction, what better introduction to African ways and philosophy could anyone have had? However, the officials in Scotland were very unhappy about the whole matter, partly because it was something that verged on the forbidden "civil jurisdiction", but more because it seemed to them to be terribly time wasting. Dr McMurtrie wrote complaining that Scott spent too much time and energy in *mlandu.* McMurtrie went on to suggest that getting rid of all people from mission land except the committed church men, seemed the only way out. This was exactly what Scott could not do.[24] But what better use of his time could D.C. Scott have found? Where else could he have gained such knowledge of the language and way of life of the people to whom he wished to preach the Gospel? To be effective the Gospel must be preached in terms relevant to the situation of the hearers, relevant to where they are, where they see themselves to be. The world view of the Malawian people is similar to that of the other Bantu peoples, a view which has been given its first clear exposition in Father Temples' *Bantu Philosophy.*[25] Clement Scott did no such systematic study of Bantu thought, but through the many, many *milandu* in which he took part, he became deeply appreciative of the Bantu thought-world, the results of which are most clearly seen in his *Dictionary.* In any case, the problem of law and order simply had to be solved, and the way chosen by Scott was as close as was possible to

---

[23] *Central Africa News and Views,* vol. 2, no. 1, July 1896. *Nkhondo* means war.

[24] McMurtrie to D.C. Scott, 27 October 1887, Convenor's Letter Book, M.1.

[25] P. Temples, *Bantu Philosophy* (Paris: Presence Atricatne, 1959).

traditional ways; it minimized the foreigness of the mission though it could not remove it.

Face to face with the next problem, that of the form of the mission's proclamation of the Gospel, Scott encountered a difficulty which he did not mention in his letter to James Robertson. This was that he was emotionally and intellectually on the side of the "industrial mission", but the Assembly which had sent him out had accepted the reports of Rankin and Pringle which clearly recommended a change to a narrowly evangelistic form of mission. There is no record at present available that shows Clement Scott paying any heed at all to these recommendations. This total disregard for the reports of the Commissioners and Scott's profound difference with them over the nature of the task in the Shire Highlands, possibly accounts for the bitter antagonism towards Scott shown by Dr Rankin, for as long as Scott was head of Blantyre Mission. Rankin was an able man who was concerned for the future of the people in the area. He was very sympathetic to John Buchanan and got the Assembly to recognize formally the school on his estate at Zomba as a missionary school.[26] There were times when he seemed to be simply cantankerous, as during his attacks on the mission in the columns of *The Scotsman* and in the General Assemblies of 1896-7.[27] However, it would seem to be fairer to see his behaviour as stemming from the total disregard of his work, advice and concern as a Commissioner, by Scott and the latter's continuing the work of the mission along lines which Rankin disliked and felt to be unsound.

D.C. Scott seemed completely oblivious to any doubts about industrial mission in the minds of the Assembly and set about getting the work of the mission going again along "industrial" lines. He inherited from MacDonald a school which was a boarding establishment for both boys and girls. It was not simply a school to produce readers of Scripture in the vernacular, of the type Pringle recommended, but had attempted a more general education including the use of English. It had been reasonably successful in this with some very surprising results, as one of the early employees of the African Lakes Company recorded. Frederick T.

---

[26] *Assembly Reports,* 1885, FMC Report, Appendix 5, p. 110.
[27] *The Scotsman,* 25 March 1897.

Morrison, one of the many pious young Glasgow men who joined the service of the ALC in fulfilment of a missionary vocation, kept an interesting diary which gives a detailed picture of life in Blantyre in the 1880s. He recorded an extraordinary manifestation of the effectiveness of the work of MacDonald's school.

During the crisis in the relations between the white community and the Makololo after Fenwick's murder of Chipatula and the killing of Fenwick by the chiefs enraged people, he tells us that the Makololo sent their terms for re-opening the Shire to navigation by letter, not by word of mouth.[28] The new knowledge was put to an even more enterprising use in that another letter was written, this time in English, by a former Blantyre pupil, purporting to come from Mandala. It was sent to a man called Gowk,[29] captain of the ALC steamer waiting for permission to come upstream. It said that the troubles were over and ordered him up river; he complied with the false instructions and his boat fell into the hands of the Makololo.[30] MacDonald's short-lived school undoubtedly added a new dimension to Makololo diplomacy and espionage.

Despite this interesting proof of the initiative of MacDonald's "old boys", and their ability to adapt their school lessons to the realities of African life, Scott was not happy about the way the school had been organised up till then. In MacDonald's day most of the boys had been Makololo. They, being part of a ruling aristocracy, had brought with them their personal slaves, and the boarding establishment had been a sort of young men's village, though inhibited and controlled to some extent by MacDonald. That control certainly never extended to any attempt to develop a new pattern of living. How tenuous the authority was, is

---

[28] Journal of F.J. Morrison, EUL Ms. Room. 7 March, 1884: 'Visit from Mr. Moir, he had with him a letter he had received from Ramk., it was written in Mang'anja to this effect: We want nothing but war. Give us Fenwick's wife, an his goods. You Mr. Moir come down here and I win rejoice with you. If you do not do these things we understand you want war.'

[29] Gowk in Scots means a fool or gullible person - singularly appropriate in the circumstances.

[30] Morrison's Journal, 24 May 24 1884.

recorded by MacDonald himself, who refers to the death of a boy after a quarrel had led to fighting.[31]

Scott decided to start the school again on a new basis. Boys who wished to attend the school had to be boarders except for a few children belonging to mission families. The boarders had to come without personal slaves. In the school a definite pattern of work, manual work, recreation and rest, was laid down by Scott. It was in this establishment that Scott got to know the young men whom he believed he was called to train so that they might create a new Church in a new Africa. Hetherwick records how on his first day in Blantyre he accompanied Scott on his daily visit to the boarders after evening prayers. An exhausting time mediating between Chipeta wishing to revenge themselves on Kuntaja's people, could not stop Scott having his chat with his "laddies".[32] This was all part of his wishing to really know folk and for them to know him, in order that the Gospel might be spread.[33] The first Christians and the first African staff of the mission came primarily from this school. However, they supplemented a very important nucleus, the group of men who had served MacDonald and waited on to serve his successor.

The most outstanding of these men was Joseph Bismarck, who originally came from the Mozambique coast. He had received there the name Bismarck from some Frenchmen at the time of the Franco-Prussian War of 1870-71. Bismarck had been very close to MacDonald and went with him to the coast on his journey back to Scotland. He became a key man in Scott's re-starting of the work. Bismarck and his colleagues were the

---

[31] MacDonald, *Aftfcana,* vol. 2, p. 181.

[32] *Central Africa News and Views,* vol. 2, no. 1. July 1896.

[33] Just how effective Scott was in establishing close relations with the mission boarders was brought home to the writer while visiting the home of Mr John Likagwa in Ndirande village in June 1960. The grandmother of the house, a very old lady, had been baptised by Scott, and had been married by him to one of his 'laddies". She reminisced a good deal about her youth on the mission, never referring to Scott as *bwana* (master) or *mbusa* (pastor), but always as *Wokondedwa wathu dotolo* Scott (our beloved Dr Scott - beloved is the usual but rather stilted translation for *wokondedwa* which is the normal word for close and deep affection).

first teachers and supervisors of labour on the mission, interpreters and preachers in the nearby villages. To their number were added the men who finished what schooling was available, from their ranks came the first brick-makers, brick-layers, carpenters and printers.

The real development of this technical training in things other than agriculture which continued from the old regime under Jonathan Duncan, came when John McDwain joined the staff in 1884. McDwain was another of these young evangelical Scots in the service of the ALC, who after working four years for them was persuaded by D.C. Scott to join the Blantyre staff. He immediately began the training of young men as builders and carpenters.

It was the next year that Scott himself began work as an industrial missionary when the printing press, which he felt to be essential to the development of both evangelism and education, was sent out. With the aid of the accompanying instruction manual, he and a young lad named Chisuse (later baptised Mungo)[34] assembled it and began to teach themselves to use it. By the end of 1887 there was a group of young "apprentice printers" working the press and cutting and stitching together books and pamphlets in English, Nyanja and Yao. Scott used this new tool to create Zambezia's first newspaper. In January 1888 he began the production of a monthly news magazine, *Life and Work,* which in 1892 became *Life and Work in British Central Africa.* There was not simply mission news in this magazine; political news and comments were regular features along with occasional anthropological or botanical studies, indeed anything of interest that someone wished to contribute. It was in the columns of this magazine that Scott explained his aims for the new church, his hopes for the future; it was through this magazine that he campaigned to improve the attitudes of the European population towards Africans, to get British Protection in the area and so forestall the Portuguese; he also used the journal as a stick with which to beat the

---

[34] A man of the chiefly clan of the Amangoche Yao. Head of a family that produced in the 1950% and 1960s, many leaders in Malawi life, including Dr Augustine Bwanausi, a minister in the first Malawi Cabinet, and Mrs Dina Khonje, Malawi's first BBC trained radio announcer.

very British administration he had campaigned to obtain, when he thought it was doing wrong.

Through the school, the printing press, through industrial training, Scott met and influenced people. There was one more field where the mission attracted people to it and so opened an avenue for influence and evangelization. This was through the large need the mission had for labour of a more or less casual nature. Labourers to help the skilled men with building, porters to carry from Mandala to the mission the goods which the ALC had brought up river, men to work in the fields of maize and beans which were grown to help feed this new community. During the period of 1888 to 1891 when the Blantyre church was being built around 2,000 people a year were being employed on that task.[35] Some of these men became more or less permanently attached to the mission, but the vast majority came only for a time, attracted by the chance to get cloth, the form of wealth and of exchange of the time. Matecheta reports that men were paid eight yards of cloth a month and women six yards. He also goes on to point out that at that time a goat sold for about six yards of cloth and a ram for nine yards.[36] This is perhaps a better way to estimate the value of the wages than any transfer into cash values of then or now. These folk were brought into contact with the Christian gospel by attending morning and evening services of worship. Very few at that time became Christians, but on going back to their villages, which covered a large area of the Southern Region of Malawi and the Ntcheu district of the Central Region, they helped prepare the way for the spread of Christian teaching when more formal missionaries arrived. They also spread news of the mission and its doings which attracted more enterprising young men to go there to learn what they could in the school.

Daily life on the station was not very different in most details from what can be read in most of the popular mission magazines of the period about life on any African station. Bugles awoke the people of the mission, who breakfasted and went to morning prayers, which were followed by assemblies for work or school. A mid-day meal was followed by the daily

---

[35] *LVVBCA* June 1891.
[36] Matecheta, *Nkhani ya Ciyambo Cace,* p. 22.

service at 1.30 p.m., then there was more school or work. There was then a period of rest, followed by prayers for those who could understand English - this was at first intended for the missionaries, but the number of Africans attending rapidly grew - then followed the evening meal. We have already made mention of Scott's evening chats with the boarders, which in their informality and friendliness were not as typical of missions in general as the daily timetable was.

Another of Scott's ideas was very far from typical of the Victorian mission station, this was moonlight dancing. On the nights when the moon was full and there was no cloud, Scott had the boarders gather on the *bwalo*[37] to dance and play games and sing as they would have done at home in the villages on such a night. He presided and saw that no unseemly songs were sung or dances danced. This must be contrasted with the fact that African dancing, often dancing of any kind, was frowned on by most missionaries working in Central Africa at the time. Blantyre's nearest neighbour, the Zambezi Industrial Mission founded in 1892, banned dancing and then went on to ban drumming also as evil.

Another feature of the Scott routine at Blantyre was the weekly tea-party at the Manse. Every Saturday afternoon, if there was no *mlandu to call* Scott away to some village, senior boys or senior girls were invited to the Manse for tea. These were meant to be relaxed friendly occasions which Scott hoped to use in a twofold way. First he taught the young folk how to behave easily in European company, secondly, he got a chance to have them talk and to learn from them not only customs and traditions of African life, but also their ideas and feelings about what was going on around them. Later in the 1890s this became a meeting of the senior African staff and their wives, Scott's "deacons", whom he hoped would be leaders of a new African Church.[38]

The actual Blantyre Mission station under Scott was soon a thriving and well-organised community, but it would have to expand if it were to

---

[37] *Bwalo* is any large open space in front of a house or in the centre of a village where people meet and talk. A chief would always hold his *mlandu* on such a *bwalo*, so the word also comes to mean court.

[38] These paragraphs are based on conversations with the Reverend Harry Matecheta and Mr Lewis Bandawe.

evangelize the Shire Highlands. It could expand in two ways, firstly by using new staff to start stations along similar lines to that of Blantyre in new areas. The second way was by the creation first of schools and then worshipping communities in the villages in the area around the station. The methods were not exclusive, but more properly complementary, though with a limited supply of staff and money, choices had sometimes to be made between them. A third form that the expansion of Christian activity took, was that little worshipping groups gathered around other Europeans in the area, not formally attached to the mission but sympathetic to it.

In practice this kind of help came from the employees of the African Lakes Corporation and the Buchanan family; John Buchanan and his brothers who came out to join him at Zomba after John left the service of the mission in 1881. The majority of the white men who came into the Southern Region of Malawi in the 1880s were not particularly committed to Christianity and did little or nothing to help propagate it. It was difficult enough for Blantyre Mission to attract a few of them who lived in the vicinity even to attend worship on a Sunday morning. A number of the African Lakes men were different. They, like McIlwain and Morrison, went with the ALC as a form of response to a missionary calling. Wherever they worked they tried to teach the Christian faith, and they regularly held services of prayer. Extracts from Frederick Morrison's Journal give an indication of the pattern of their life.

On first seeing Africa when his ship called at Algiers he wrote:

> When I sighted Africa I lifted up my eyes to God asking I might be used in that land in a special manner.[39]

At Quelimane where the Moirs were staying at he ALC post he records that Moir conducted an English service in the morning and one in Nyanja in the evening. A typical entry in Morrison's Journal is that of March 1, 1885:

> Held evening service with the staff. After giving a short address myself I asked James Mvula to finish, his address was just grand and the real gospel ring about it, no uncertain sound. John Kurakura also

---

[39] Morrison's Journal, 23 April 1882.

> engaged in prayer. I trust it was a meeting for an eternity rejoicing ...
> I have no selfish motive in this company other than to save their souls.

Others of the ALC staff were not of this stamp but a great many were. Their senior African helpers were often people like James Mvula, a product of the mission school, and together they gathered little congregations about the ALC posts.

Scott hoped both to expand the influence of the mission through schools and congregations in the neighbouring villages and by setting up new stations. He had real difficulty in doing either. The constant problem that the FMC had in raising money and staff in Scotland meant that the creation of new stations was not easy. The setting up of schools and congregations outside the actual mission station was also a difficult process, both because such institutions did not fit readily into traditional society and because society was in a state of turmoil and thus inimical to this kind of growth. Everyone in the Shire Highlands was afraid of the Ngoni coming to raid, but Yao chiefs were also at odds with each other due to man-stealing. A ready market for slaves was provided both by the Portuguese and by visiting Swahili coast-men. The existence of this market and the presence of the traders in slaves prodded some Yao chiefs into a constant aggressive search for slaves. It also upset the military balance of the area, at times appearing to threaten the small white community consisting of the mission, the ALC and the few hunters and traders who were beginning to come into the country. The situation is typified by an extract from Morrison's diary in March of 1883, on going ashore at Mponda's, where he saw Mponda sitting around with many well-armed Arabs, the presence of which he suggested "bespeaks no good, as the most of them who find their way up here are confirmed slavers"; Morrison continues that Mponda displayed "a goodly number of Enfield rifles, and as he showed them he boasted that now he had as many guns as the white man."[40] Mponda went on to point out the guns were vital to defend himself from the Ngoni.

Despite this constant and widespread fear, there was not a raid from the Maseko Ngoni of Ntcheu and Dedza, though in 1883 there was a raid as

---

[40] Morrison's Journal, 2 March 1883

far south as Zomba by the Makwangwala Ngoni from the far north-east side of the Lake. The first menace to the peace of the communities of the Shire Highlands, and to the security of the mission came from a surprising quarter, the Makololo.

The Makololo were held to be the special friends of the British, yet it was they who in February 1884 threatened to make it impossible for the ALC to continue operations and thus make the position of the missions untenable. The cause of this was the man who so often featured as the villain in the story of the first years of European presence in the Shire Highlands, George Fenwick.

After his dismissal from the mission he had existed as a hunter and part-time employee of the ALC. His behaviour made it impossible for the Moirs to go on employing him and he was dismissed.[41] He then tried to set up as an independent trader using his good relations with the Makololo and other chiefs to help him with trade in ivory. On one occasion returning from Quelimane he stopped at the court of Chipatula, one of the most important of the Makololo chiefs; they were boon companions and often drank together. Fenwick seems to have involved Chipatula in some of his enterprises because they now quarrelled about whether Chipatula was cheating Fenwick or not. The exact circumstances are not clear, but he seems to have taken some of Chipatula's ivory to sell for him and there was a quarrel about the price. Fenwick who was always ready to threaten violence, really acted this time and killed Chipatula. He almost escaped in the confusion, but the people of the village managed to catch and kill Fenwick in turn, a justifiable reaction. However, when the people of the village got word to Ramakukan, the Paramount, he and his elders were, understandably, not clear about the relationship of Fenwick and the ALC and so held the company responsible and demanded compensation. The Makololo effectively cut off the white community of the Shire Highlands from the coast. The newly appointed British Consul, Captain Foot, and John Moir eventually settled the matter peacefully, though not until July 1884. This caused great hardship

---

[41] Morrison's Journal, 24 December 1883, where Morrison records being present when Fenwick actually aimed his rifle at Moir and threatened to shoot him.

because there were no trade goods, no supplies and no mail for the small community during that time.

Monteith and Morrison of the ALC were sent with two little expeditions by overland routes to get round the blockade caused by the Makololo; though they were able to bring back some mail and trade goods, they were unable to pioneer any effective alternative to the river route.

Peace with the Makololo in July did not end the troubles of the mission and the ALC, for there immediately followed a rising of Africans in the Zambezi valley against the Portuguese. This was even more effective in isolating the mission from outside contact. Only an overland expedition to the coast itself by John Buchanan relieved the situation. The rebellion was broken by a white force, none of whom were Portuguese, led by Frederick Moir.[42]

The two incidents only reinforced the belief in Scott's mind that the vulnerability of the mission to this kind of blow could only be ended by the coming of some kind of British authority which could also help to end slaving. The presence of Captain Foot as United Kingdom Consul, Shire Districts, was a beginning and perhaps little more was needed. Despite this period of tension, Scott still tried to expand the work and sent out Alexander Hetherwick with Henry Henderson to find a site for a new station. They went on a long journey via Mulanje Mountain to Lake Chirwa and across to the massif of Zomba and Malosa mountains. There Henderson was welcomed by his old acquaintance of nine years before, Malemia. Hetherwick and Henderson agreed this well watered, fertile and populous spot on the approaches to the top of the high pass that separates the two mountains, was a good spot and made an agreement with Malemia. Hetherwick then hurried back to Blantyre to prepare to go to set up his new station on the banks of the Domasi stream.

He was not able to go immediately because Scott himself now wanted to carry out a long projected journey, to the chief of the Maseko Ngoni, in the hope of gaining his friendship and bringing peace. He set off with Mrs Scott, a symbol of his peaceful intentions, and Dr Peden. They travelled for two weeks and finally reached the court of the Paramount, Chikuse

---

[42] Morrison's Journal, 11 August 1884.

Kaphatikiza, grandfather of the paramount of the writer's acquaintance, Nkosi Gomani II. Hetherwick in *The Romance of Blantyre,* says that they only met Chikuse's mother, the *Nkosikazi,* a very important person none the less, while Matecheta insisted that they saw Chikuse himself.[43] Both were agreed and this is confirmed in oral tradition, that a real bond was created between the Ngoni and Scott as representing the mission. Scott hurried back because he saw that an *impi*[44] was being prepared to raid across the Shire. On Scott's return, Hetherwick immediately set out for Domasi, while Scott set about warning his Yao neighbours, many of whom would not listen. Those that did listen fled with as much as they could carry to the tops of the nearby high hills such as Soche, Ndirande, Malavi and Michiru, others fled into Makololo country and some came on to mission land, presumably hoping that since Scott had just visited the Ngoni, his land would not suffer in the raid. Matecheta points out though, that many deliberately avoided the mission because they interpreted the friendship differently and thought that the Europeans would hand them over to the Ngoni.[45]

On his way to Domasi, Hetherwick crossed the track of the *impi* and leaving his porters hiding in the bush, he hurried on to Buchanan's place in Zomba. Here his porters turned up the next day having been sent there by the Ngoni *induna*[46] who wanted Scott's boys to be safe. These porters had learned while with the Ngoni that the raid was to go on to Blantyre, though intending to leave the mission intact. Scott was warned of this, and continued his attempts to get people to come on to the mission. After the *impi* had been in the area of Blantyre for several days and showed no signs of leaving, Scott and Henderson went out to the camp and after a long discussion persuaded them to go back. They had probably been hanging around because of the Yao still on top of Malavi, who had repulsed their attacks. Hetherwick asserted that they stormed Malavi,[47] but Matecheta said, and Yao oral tradition confirms, that they

---

[43] Matecheta, *Nkhani ya Ciyambo Cace,* p. 2, and in an interview with the present writer.

[44] War party.

[45] Matecheta, *Nkhani ya Ciyambo Cace,* p. 3.

[46] Royal advisor.

[47] Hetherwick, *The Romance of Blantyre,* p. 52.

did not, though they did storm some of the other hills where Yao had taken refuge, like nearby Nguludi. This raid of June 1884 was the last great raid of the Maseko Ngoni into the Shire Highlands. It had some important effects on the situation of the mission. First, it gave Scott some sense of security, since it was clear that the most powerful military influence in the area was friendly towards him. Second, this friendship greatly increased the prestige of the mission in the eyes of the neighbouring Nyanja and Yao people. Third, both his visit to Ntcheu and the raid fired Scott with a vision of the Ngoni as warriors for Christ.

The excitement over, Hetherwick began the building of his station at Domasi. He built a large, two-roomed, wattle-and-daub shed with wide verandas. One room was his living accommodation, the other along with the veranda, was the school. Hetherwick had barely got his work going when he had to return to Blantyre; this was in February 1885. Scott's throat was badly strained and infected, and as his furlough was almost due, the new mission doctor, Dr Millen, who had replaced Dr Peden, ordered him home.

For the next two years Scott was at home, while Hetherwick continued his work in Blantyre, with Joseph Bismarck maintaining the little school at Domasi and Rondau Kaferanjila and some of the others of the African staff relieving him from time to time. With no additional staff, in Scott's absence Hetherwick carried on as best he could, following as much as possible in Scott's footsteps. The routine that had been established carried on with little incident. It was a time of no major external alarm, when the pattern of life and work created by Scott had time to operate in a peaceful atmosphere. Under his direction the small missionary staff of Jonathan Duncan, John McIlwain, and James Hamilton and Miss Walker, who were both teachers, aided by Mrs Fenwick[48] and the trained African staff led by Joseph Bismarck, established firmly a pattern of worship,

---

[48] Mrs Fenwick came back to live on the mission at the time of her husband's death. She became an assistant to Mrs Scott. She appears to have recovered at this time her Christian faith, after having lost it, as far as one can judge from Morrison's description of her son Jose's funeral. On October 4, 1883, he recorded: "Poor Mrs Fenwick was very calm and resigned like, I trust it might be a means of blessing to her and her husband, at present they give no countenance to the services by way of attending them."

teaching, technical instruction and labour on the mission station at Blantyre. Outside that area little went on except for regular services at the Mandala compound and the maintaining of the little schools at Domasi and on the Buchanan estate at Zomba. That did not matter at that time because at Blantyre itself the school and apprentice programmes were producing a number of young men as well as a few young women who would become the real means of expansion in the future.

This opportunity for expansion came with the return of Clement Scott in June 1887 along with reinforcements for the mission, his brother-in-law, Dr John Bowie, the Reverend Robert Cleland and a teacher, Miss Janet Beck. Also back with him came Nacho Ntimawanzako, whom Scott had taken to Scotland at his own expense to widen his education and also to help him with the preparation of his *Dictionary*. These two years in Scotland had seen the *Dictionary* approach completion and a leap forward in Nacho's education. Scott believed in sending Malawi youths outside for further education. A scheme for such training to be carried on regularly was begun by MacDonald. He sent Kagaso Sazuze, Joseph Bismarck, Rondau Kaferanjila, Evangel Sawelayera and Chinkolimbo to Lovedale. The worth of this was confirmed by the sterling service they gave Scott when he came to reform the mission. Dr Rankin, who had been most impressed by some of the men he had met as Commissioner in 1881, arranged for two of them to come to Scotland; these were Henry Cowan Kapito and Donald Malota.[49] They returned to Blantyre in 1884.

It is not clear from the records whether Rankin did this spontaneously or because of the General Assembly's decision to stop the training of Africans outside their own land. In 1882 the Foreign Mission Committee had stated in its report, endorsed by the Assembly that:

> No small expense has been incurred by the sending of boys to and from Lovedale, and the Committee cannot in some cases get information as to the parties who ordered or authorized this procedure. They have found it necessary to prohibit it in the future;

---

[49] They were baptised while in Scotland at Muthill, Kapito in April 1882 and Malota in April 1884.

as it is evident that if Blantyre cannot train its own youths, it fails in the very purpose for which the Mission has been instituted.[50]

This decision is an astonishing one, and must surely be related primarily to the usual desire of the FMC to spend as little as possible. The remark about Blantyre failing as an institution if young men had to be sent to Lovedale, was very unreasonable when it is remembered that the old staff had been dismissed only a year before and the new staff of only three missionaries had re-started the work under Scott, only six months before the FMC report was prepared.

Be that as it may, by the middle of 1887, Scott had at last a reasonable staff of missionaries and trained Africans, one station of considerable size which was running well as a base, many long and well-tried friendly contacts with chiefs and people throughout the whole area, and so was ready to begin the extension of the work of the mission of which he had dreamed for a long time.

Hetherwick went through to Domasi and took up again the work which had been carried on primarily by Bismarck. Robert Cleland was sent to start work on the slopes of Chiradzulu Mountain near to Mitochi's. Chiradzulu lies about mid-way between Blantyre and Zomba, and is also conveniently placed for an approach to the Mulanje Mountain area across the Phalombe Plain. Cleland began to make journeys across the plain to Mulanje and initiated negotiations with that old enemy of the mission, Chief Chikumbu.

Earlier in 1887 Scott had gone with Duncan to clear up once and for all the old quarrel over runaways, but Chikumbu had not even spoken to them though they had stayed two days at the village. A way for Cleland was finally opened when in May 1888 Chikumbu invited Scott to come back and see him. Scott went there with Dr Bowie and this time was able to clear up the trouble, Chikumbu accepting the offered cloth as compensation for the runaways who had been harboured nearly ten years before on the mission. However, Cleland could not go immediately to Mulanje as Hetherwick was now due for leave, and so in November 1888 he went to Domasi to take over the little station there.

---

[50] *Assembly Reports,* 1882, FMC Report, p. 84.

It was only in May 1890 that Cleland was able finally to go to settle in the Mulanje area and begin the building of a station, the site of which he had got Chikumbu to agree to during the visits in 1889. However, Chikumbu was still a very difficult customer to get on with, and continued to assume that his Nyanja neighbours, the people of Chief Chipoka, were his natural prey, their belongings, their harvest, their sons and daughters should be his for the taking. Cleland did, however, establish a very close relationship with the old man. The impact of this was very short-lived, however, because in December 1890 Cleland had an attack of blackwater fever from which he died. Of him, Chikumbu said: "He is a brave man, he has a heart like Chikumbu."[51] Despite this tragedy, by January 1891, a real geo-graphical expansion of the work had taken place. Chiradzulu, Domasi and Mulanje were all now stations with some degree of stability. At Chiradzulu there was a school and regular worship; at Mulanje a school was started; at Domasi there was a school, and two other village schools, one at Katangulu and one at Mulunguzi, which was a continuation of the old school of MacDonald's days, continued independently by Buchanan, and was now a mission school again. There had also been an expansion of the work of the mission ecclesiastically, with a real movement of people into membership of the Church.

The form that this church was to take had still to be worked out, and its Christian life built up. This movement, which began in 1887, was the result of patient work over the previous six years. This was not a mass movement, in the technical sense of that term as used by writers on missiology, but a movement of individuals. These were, at first, mainly the young men who had gathered round Scott as teachers and helpers, and followed by some of the boys and girls (mostly in their late teens) at the school. Older people living in the mission villages also came forward. Hetherwick described the movement in these words:

> Many a quiet knock came to the manse study door at night, and in response to the invitation 'Come in', the door would be opened and a shy voice would plead, 'I want word'. And the words would be that a desire for more knowledge of higher things had come, and the speaker had many questions to ask. Not a few times the 'words' would be about a dream that had come once, twice, thrice, in the

---

[51] *LWBCA* December 1890.

night, and whose interpretation the visitor greatly desired ... Another would come with a text that he could not understand. Another wanted to join the *'class'* ... 'Why do you want to join the class?' Because of So and So' - a friend who had lately joined and whose action led to a desire to follow his steps. An old man or woman, grey-haired and wrinkled, would follow the minister after Sunday morning service and say 'I want God' ... and so the numbers of those gathering on a communion Sunday in the little wattle and daub church gradually increased till on occasion it could hold no more.[52]

In the 1960s these motives were still the ones put forward by people who wished to enter "class".

The pressure of dreams was important in this and other vital decisions, and Professor Bengt Sundkler has discussed its importance in the calling of men to the ministry and priesthood of the Churches.[53] A very important aspect of this growth was that no one was ever asked or told to join this "class". Naturally living and working on the mission, with its atmosphere of worship and prayer, was itself a pressure. This was intended, but it was an encouragement and not coercion; it would seem to merit being thought of as legitimate as opposed to various forms of "pressure", which could be called illegitimate. These have been listed for Zambezia by R.I. Rotberg, and certainly applied to some extent at least elsewhere in Africa and Asia. Rotberg's two main accusations of "coercion" are that the missionaries,

> reserved the educational experience to nominal Christians. More significantly they provided employment only for those who professed some seemingly sincere interest in the Christian message.[54]

At Blantyre, apart from attendance at the brief morning prayers and the noon service, nothing else was demanded of scholars or employees. A man could become an employee of the mission at any level from labourer (of whom some 2,000 were employed on the building of Blantyre Church) to teacher, without having to be baptised, or indeed,

---

[52] Hetherwick, *The Romance of Blantyre,* p. 73.

[53] B. Sundkler, *The Christian Ministry in Africa,* (London: SCM, 1960), Chapter 1.

[54] R.I. Rotberg, *The Rise of Nationalism in Central Africa,* (Cambridge: Harvard, 1959), p.9.

even become a member of the "class". Scott naturally hoped that they would become Christians, but he deliberately avoided creating the situation whereby the "class" became an entry into paid employment. The real physical benefits of living on mission land, of working for it, of trading with it, were not made the exclusive preserve of those who made some sort of profession.

Many of the Makololo, who were the majority of the boys in the school until the last two or three years of the decade, went home without making any kind of profession of faith. They were still thought of as his "boys" by Scott. The very existence, as much as the content, of the following obituary from the mission magazine is a witness to this.

> Kainga, Kasisi's son is dead. He was crossing the river in a very small canoe with his wife, when a crocodile caught the boat in the middle and sank it. Kainga was eaten by one crocodile, his wife by another. He was one of the old School boys.[55]

Much more important and significant are the examples of John Chipuliko and Mungo Chisuse. They did not become baptised Christians until November 1889, when they had already been responsible members of the staff for five years. Indeed, they were second only to Joseph Bismarck in authority. Chisuse was in charge of the printing press from the beginning of its work, and printed the very issue of the magazine which published the notice of his baptism.[56] Scott was quite explicit in his insistence on a policy of freedom.

> The service and hymns of the native church are written by us, but the free teaching and preaching is as freely received without forcing and without terrorism or tyranny as any congregation of free thinkers could desire.[57]

Though slowly, the number of Christians was growing and Scott had to plan how he was to deal with them.

In order to deal with the increasing numbers and to symbolize his dreams, Scott began the planning of a central church at Blantyre. He, a

---

[55] *LWBCA* April 1888.
[56] *LWBCA* December 1889.
[57] *LWBCA* October 1890.

philosopher and theologian, was to be the architect, John McDwain and his untried builders were to build it, with the help of labourers recruited from the many folk who wanted cloth. It was in May 1888 that the foundations for this building began to be dug.[58] In November of that year the foundation bricks were laid by Scott himself. The building is still one of the sights for tourists in Malawi. Its walls are adorned with many designs which come from the many differently shaped forms of brick used. The eighty-one different patterns of the moulds for these bricks were carved by D.C. Scott himself, along with his brother Willie.

The completion and dedication of St Micheal's and All Angels Church in May 1891 marked the end of this period of the life of Blantyre Mission. In its very design, Scott attempted to portray what he dreamed of creating, a catholic African Church. The building was of African bricks built into the catholic cruciform shape, topped by Byzantine domes and turrets. Sad to relate, the main stumbling block lying between Scott and the fulfilment of his dream lay in Scotland and the staff sent from there. However, there were growing difficulties in Malawi; the deaths of Robert Cleland,[59] John Bowie[60] and Henry Henderson[61] meant major changes in the composition of the missionary staff. Would the new men be able to work with Scott as those now gone had done?[62] The pressure of the advance of the Portuguese and Arabs on Malawi had now led to the declaration of a British Protectorate. What would this mean for Scott's vision? Could he work as well with a British Commissioner as he had done with Ramakukan, with Chikuse and the other chiefs? What was the Church's role to be in the life of the increasingly large European community in the Shire Highlands? Perhaps the biggest problem facing Scott in the new stage into which the mission was now entering, was that the little Christian community was still confined to people living on the mission lands or at Mandala. Although there were village schools near Blantyre

---

[58] *LWBCA* May 1888.

[59] 10 November 1890 at Blantyre.

[60] In the first few days of January 1891, when he and his sister, Mrs Henderson, and her child all died.

[61] At Quelimane on 12 February 1891, on his way back to Scotland.

[62] *Assembly Reports,* 1881, FMC Report, Appendix A, 86-90.

and Domasi,[63] there were no communities of village Christians. Unless the Church took root in the villages then Scott's vision could never come to pass.

---

[63] Blantyre had village schools at Mandala, Chilimoni and Ndirande, while Domasi had village schools at Mulunguzi and Katangulu's.

Chapter 4: The Need for a Protectorate

The growth and development of the work of the Blantyre Mission, which was surveyed in the last chapter, took place in an atmosphere of growing apprehension. During the 1880s sense of insecurity grew in the minds of the Scots in the Shire Highlands. This feeling had nothing to do with the recurring petty difficulties they encountered with the local Yao chiefs, nor with any fear that the Maseko Ngoni would again cross the Shire and sweep through the Highlands as they had in 1884; the leading men of the mission and the Company were fairly confident by about the middle of the decade that they had reached a reasonable modus vivendi with these forces. It was from outside that they saw the danger coming to threaten all that they hoped to achieve in the land. The threat came from both the Portuguese, and the Arabs.

The Portuguese had been a problem from the beginnings of British interest in Zambezia. From Livingstone's Zambezi expedition onwards, the control of the lines communication by the Portuguese was a, constant threat to any operation in the interior. The Portuguese claims to authority inland may have been a laughing matter but they did have power on the coast, where they were in a position to cut off essential supplies to anyone operating inland. This was simply a hard fact of life for the British interests in the Lake region. It was listed in 1881 by Clement Scott as one of the four key problems facing him as the new head of Blantyre Mission.[1] As the decade went on, the problem grew because the Portuguese entered upon a new period of colonial activity, their first on the East Coast of Africa in the 19th century. Scott could not deal with this problem as he had resolved, with great diplomatic skill, the problems created by Chikuse of the Ngoni or Yao chiefs like Mitochi. Diplomatic activity was needed to resolve the problem but on a level that was beyond the reach of the mission or the African Lakes Company.

The very presence of the missions and the Company in the Portuguese hinterland necessarily embroiled Britain in a tricky diplomatic situation, but their presence was a result of the original British Government interest in suppressing the slave trade in East Africa. Livingstone, for at

---

[1] D.C. Scott to James Robertson, December 1880, EUL Ms. 717/10.

least part of the time acting as British Consul, had exposed the terrible results of the impact of that trade on the area stretching from the Zambezi northwards past Lake Tanganyika. The Scottish Missions, the Universities' Mission and the African Lakes Company were all operating where they were, in a belated response to his appeal for help on behalf of the region.

The idea of working so far from the coast and from direct contact with Europe was criticized by Bishop Tozer when he withdrew the original UMCA party, and his criticism continued to have force. However, at first, the Portuguese had not figured as the key problem so much as the sheer distance and difficulty of communications.

This was because Portuguese power had been such a shadowy affair, even on the coast. The dispatches of the British Consuls at Mozambique, first Elton and then O'Neill, constantly reported African defiance of Portuguese authority right down to the coast itself. Indeed, as late as 1884, what little authority the Portuguese had along the Zambezi was saved from total extinction by a force led by Fred Moir, which was wholly non-Portuguese in its composition.[2] Some of the ALC men very soon regretted their action and felt it would have been better to let Machinjili destroy the Portuguese attempt to maintain a facade of occupation of the Zambezi valley.[3]

However, on the coast and along the Zambezi, there was a more formidable Portuguese presence, in the form of the holders of *"prazo"*. These men were as often as not a threat to the official Portuguese authority of the Governor General at Mozambique, but when his and their interests coincided, then Portuguese power did become a significant factor in Zambezia.

The growth of the British settlements in Malawi threatened the dream of a Portuguese empire in Africa from coast to coast which was beginning to excite some of the leading Portuguese officials both in Lisbon and Mozambique. The Scots with their anti-slave trade objectives, were also, to put it at its lowest, a nuisance to the *prazo* holders, about whose

---

[2] Morrison's Journal, 11 August 1884.

[3] Ibid, 4 September 1884.

complicity in the trade all reliable witnesses from Livingstone onwards agree.[4] Thus *prazeros* and officials came to unite in wishing to get rid of the British presence in Malawi. From about 1882 onwards there was a perceptible though gradual increase in petty difficulties put in the way of communications between the Lake area and the outside world. Along with this activity the Portuguese began to put forward claims to jurisdiction in the Shire Highlands and on the lakeshore.

The pioneer missionaries in Zambezia were all committed to ending the slave trade, and all looked on the Portuguese presence as a hindrance to this end.[5] For some, like Waller of the original UMCA party and Young, the leader of the Free Church pioneers, the ending of the slave trade was their primary concern, and they were willing to subordinate all else to that end. The creation of the African Lakes Company was part of this effort, as it was intended to be the channel of that legitimate commerce which Livingstone hoped would drive out the illigitimate slave trade.

Since, therefore, the missions and the ALC were following on the aims of Livingstone's Government-sponsored Zambezi Expedition, was the Government not obliged to help them? Dr McMurtrie took up this idea in a letter to the MP, Sir John Nelson Cuthbertson, in 1888, early in the campaign of the Scottish churches to persuade the Government to take a more positive line in the face of the threat of the Portuguese to the British presence in the area of the Lake. McMurtrie said in the letter[6] that the answers given in the House of Commons by the Under-Secretary for

---

[4] The *prazo* was an estate granted by the Portuguese crown, similar to the encomienda of Spanish America. The holder of the *prazo* was the supreme authority on his own land; he received bead tax, usually in ivory, from the African headmen of the villages on his land, though slaves were acceptable in lieu. James Duffy in *Portugal in Africa,* (Cambridge: Harvard University Press), p. 93, says of them, "acting together they were the strongest force in Mozambique, able to contain the Monomotapa and to bend the Portuguese captains to their will.

[5] See, e.g., F. D. Lugard, *The Rise of our East African Empire,* (Edinburgh: Blackwood, 1893), p. 25-29. and R. Foskett (ed.), *The Zambesi Journal and Letters of Dr igrk* (Edinburgh: Oliver & Boyd, 1966), p. 351-359.

[6] McMurtrie to Sir John Cuthbertson, MP, 29 Febrary. 1888, Convenor's Letter-Book, M. 1.

Foreign Affairs, Sir James Fergusson, indicated that the missionaries and traders in the area of Lake Malawi were going to be left to their own fate. Fergusson had insisted that the settlements had been made "without our concurrence", and McMurtrie countered that Fergusson was wrong since the whole Scottish effort arose out of Livingstone's Government-sponsored expedition of 1858. The Foreign Office had organised it with the intention of "engaging the inhabitants in industrial pursuits and was avowedly sent in the interest of the extinction of the slave trade."[7] Its withdrawal by the Government led to its purpose being taken up again by the churches, said McMurtrie. Dr McMurtrie was wrong in his insistence that the Government had dropped all attempts to end the slave trade at its source in the Lake area. What had been dropped was any large commitment, of the kind Livingstone had as his remit, to transform African society in the area.

Although even slower than the churches to follow Livingstone, the first British Consul in the area, the British Government did appoint in October 1883, Captain Foot, RN, to be Consul accredited to the African chiefs "in the districts adjacent to Lake Nyassa." Consul Foot was quite specifically not accredited to the Portuguese, who were simply informed of his appointment, so that they would know who he was when he passed through Quelimane. Foot was told quite clearly and specifically that his primary task was the suppression of the slave trade. There were remarks in the instruction made in the Livingstonian vein about the development of the civilization and the commerce of the country, though how one man without any staff was to do this was not at all made clear. What was made clear, however, was what he had to do about slaving.

The Consul was to gain the confidence of the chiefs and help them to trade through legitimate channels, which at that time could mean only the ALC, since there were no other legitimate channels.[8] Dr Hanna makes a good case for supposing that the pressure of the Free Church for some Government interest in Nyasaland helped to bring the Foreign Office to the point of making this appointment.[9] That Foot made an official call on

---

[7] Quoted in *Ibid*

[8] Lister to Foot, 1 October 1883, A. and P. 1884, p. 370.

[9] Hanna, *The Beginnings of Nyasaland and North-Eastern Rhodesia,* pp. 64-65.

the Secretary of the Foreign Mission Committee of the Free Church would seem to support his contention. However, the fact that Foot lived in a house on Blantyre Mission when he arrived in Nyasaland is no more significant than that there was no other place to live.

It could be asserted that the Consul and the missionaries were following where Livingstone, Consul and missionary had led, but the position was a very muddled and unsatisfactory one. Captain Foot died of fever in August 1884, having only reached Blantyre in January. His assistant, Goodrich, continued his task of reporting on the activities on the slavers and visiting the chiefs with a view to persuading them to give up participating in the trade. In October 1885 he was relieved by Foot's successor, Consul Hawes. During this official's tenure of office the position of the British community became precarious and the anomalous nature of the role of the consulate became exposed to view.

The arrival of Captain Foot led to no noticeable decrease in the activity of the slavers in the Lake area, indeed, some observers would insist that there was an increase.[10] However friendly and co-operative a Yao chief might be for most of the time (for example, Mponda), the presence of a Swahili caravan from the coast changed the whole situation. The chief again became a man-stealer in order to satisfy the traders and his own desire for their goods. Morrison of the ALC experienced this transformation at his third meeting with Mponda, up till then friendly in his manner to the Scots. He recalls that he went ashore,

> and saw Mponda, he had sitting round him about 40 of these low-caste Arabs, and all were armed with guns. The presence of these fellows bespeaks no good, as the most of them who find their way up here are confirmed slavers. Mponda showed the Capn. a goodly number of Enfield rifles and as he showed he boasted that he now had as many guns as the white man.[11]

Only a few Yao chiefs who were closely associated with the Blantyre Mission, like Kapeni and Kuntaja, stayed clear of this activity, while at the other extreme were chiefs like Kawinga, Matipwiri and Makanjila who

---

[10] O'Neill to Salisbury, 6 February 1888, no. 2 Africa, FO 84/1901.
[11] Morrison's Journal, 2 March 1883.

were in constant contact with the coast and had no intention at all of changing their ways.

When raiding for slaves did take place, there was nothing that the Consul could do, except protest orally, which the ALC men or missionaries had previously done and continued to do. Kawinga, however, would not even receive him. Why should anyone listen to the Consul anyway? When he did protest, he did so as a representative of a great nation, and though this was no simple protest by missionary or trader, the Consul never had any power to back up his official protest with their implied threats. He had no force with which to make good any stand he wished to take on any issue; indeed, he had the greatest difficulty in getting the Foreign Office to allow him enough money to maintain a small personal guard. He had no military force, neither had he any effective means of carrying out the other aspect of his mission, which was the development of trade.

This was brought home to Consul Hawes very forcibly on a journey he made in May 1886 from Blantyre to Old Livingstonia (Cape Maclear). He found the land between Blantyre and Zomba comparatively empty and also very fertile. At Zomba, the Buchanan brothers had shown already the feasibility of producing both tobacco and coffee. Hawes raised the possibility of following this example, at least with regard to coffee, in his conversations with some chiefs. The response was good, but he was asked where the necessary initial capital was to come from, and also how cash crops were to be got to markets in sufficient quantity without a road being built. Were the capital able to be found and if a road were constructed, this would be to take the first practical steps to implement the remit of the consulate that had been taken since its inception.[12]

The reply given by the Foreign Office to Hawes' enquiries shows up the emptiness of its high-sounding instructions:

> With regard to the two suggestions made by you in your first mentioned despatch that HMG should afford assistance to the chiefs of the country between Blantyre and Zomba for the purpose of encouraging the cultivation of coffee in the district in question and that they should also give some aid towards the completion of the road between the two points above mentioned, I am to state to you

---

[12] Hawes to Salisbury, 3 June 1886, no. 19, CA, FO 84/1829.

that HMG are unable to apply public funds to either of these objects.[13]

So it was clear that the British Consul, who was in the area to attempt to stop the slave trade and to encourage the development of civilization and commerce, had neither the military force nor the financial power to take any effective steps towards either end.

Things took an even worse turn in February 1887 when Hawes had to report that his escort of Swahili men had deserted him with their weapons and had gone to Mulanje to join with Matipwiri, one of the most aggressive of the Yao chiefs. Although he was able to recruit men locally - and he then rationalized that they were probably better in any case - the outcome was that the hitherto insoluble problem of Matipwiri's aggressiveness was made all the more dangerous with this reinforcement of the well-armed Swahili.[14] Hawes was driven to suggest that the Portuguese authorities might be asked to deal with this dangerous slaver.[15] This request is a measure of the despair that Hawes must then have been feeling, for he knew well that, implicit in the appointment of a Consul to the chiefs around the Lake, was the desire to keep the Portuguese out of the area, quite apart from the fact that the Portuguese were involved in the slave trade in any case and Matipwiri went to the Portuguese town of Quelimane for his supplies.

Salisbury replied to Hawes, stating that the purpose of the consulate was to report on the slave trade and assist the local whites in their attempts to spread civilization and legitimate trade.[16] This is distinctly different from the instruction to Foot, already noted above, which talked of checking the trade, not simply reporting upon its growth. Salisbury went on to say that Britain would not and could not use force in an area to which she had no access. It was impossible to ask for Portuguese help in an area beyond the recognized boundaries of Mozambique as this would arouse the antagonism of the missionaries and traders. T.V. Lister commenting on that July dispatch of Hawes wrote, This dispatch raises

---

[13] FO to Hawes, 22 September 1886, no. 16, Confidential, FO 84/1886.
[14] Hawes to Salisbury, February 1887, Nos. 5,6, CA, FO 84/1829.
[15] Hawes to Salisbury, 4 July 1887, no. 29, CA, FO 84/1829.
[16] FO to Hawes, 22 October 1887, no. 22, Confidential, FO, 84/1829.

doubts in my mind (not for the first time) as to the utility of the Lakes Consulate." Lister's handwriting makes the word "dispatch" look like "despair" and it would be an appropriate alternative reading in the circumstances.

Hawes was also troubled by an increase in thefts and general lawlessness in the Shire Highlands and on the river. This was partly because of tension between the Makololo and the ALC, of which the Fenwick incident was only one example, and also because of the increasing aggressiveness of some Yao chiefs like Matipwiri. Thefts of trade goods in transit became commonplace during 1886, and on August 28 of that year a British subject of Australian extraction named Hinkleman was killed by a Makololo headman, named, like the Paramount of the Maseko Ngoni, Chikuse. Hinkleman was a particularly disreputable character, but his death was a murder, for there had been no *mlandu,* nor had there been an attack by Hinkleman on the headman's people. Hawes, on receiving a report of the incident, immediately began negotiations with the Paramount Chief, Ramakukan, who pointed out that he did not approve of the action and that there was no danger of any general anti-white activity by the Makololo.[17] However, Hawes was unhappy that Ramakukan was not making any very clear move to punish Chikuse.

Like most contemporary Europeans, Hawes did not understand that it was not so simple for a paramount chief to punish an important headman. However, Chikuse wrote to Hawes asking for his friendship, which was probably a result of pressure from Ramakukan and also possibly a result of Chikuse's own initiative to try to placate the European and thus ease the pressure they were exerting on Ramakukan to punish him.[18] Hawes rejected Chikuse's advances and said that he could have accepted the killing of Hinkleman as due punishment for a criminal if Chikuse had returned all the trader's goods to the Consul for return to his principals.[19] This was a misunderstanding of the legal system of the

---

[17] Hawes to Iddesleigh, 7 September 1886, no. 27 CA, FO 84/1751.
[18] Hawes to Iddesleigh, 19 October 1886, no. 37 CA, FO 84/1751.
[19] *Ibid*

Malawi tribes[20] where the lack of a *mlandu* was what made the killing murder, and where an alien criminal's goods would have been the chiefs due anyway.

The Foreign Office reply to Hawes on this matter and the general increase of lawlessness was based on a minute penned on Hawes' dispatch of October 19, 1886. In this minute Sir Percy Anderson said:

> Unless the English settlers have sufficient influence to cause murder of whites and theft of their property to be punished, it will be impossible for HMG to resist the offers of the Portuguese Govt. to chastise the offenders even if their doing so should lead to their occupation of the country.[21]

The next month Hawes was able to report that Ramakukan had at last got enough support from the other headmen to go in and depose Chikuse, and to take his villages directly under his own control.[22] Hawes, in the same dispatch, raised the possibility of forming some kind of military force:

> I venture to ask your Lordship whether the establishing of a military police force for defensive purposes would be approved of by Her Majesty's Government. My advice is frequently sought in cases of difficulties, but on this point I feel uncertain as to whether legal questions might not be raised and have therefore hesitated to express an opinion.

Anderson minuted on this dispatch:

> Answer that the settlers in a barbarous country have the right to protect their property but that only the administering power can establish a military police force.

What seemed to be absent from these exchanges was any recollection of the troubles of the Blantyre Mission in the 1870s and the very strict insistence of the Foreign Office at that time on the impossibility of any

---

[20] The Makololo were not a Malawian tribe, but being a very small ruling minority, had been integrated into Malawian custom.

[21] Minuted by Sir Percy Anderson on Hawes to Iddesleigh, 19 October 1886, no. 37 CA, FO 84/1751

[22] Hawes to Iddesleigh, 19 November 1886. no. 43 CA, FO 84/1751.

kind of authority being exercised by Europeans in the Lake area. If what was done at Blantyre was illegal, what did Sir Percy mean by saying that settlers "had the right to protect their property"?

As Sir Percy's minute on the dispatch of October 19, 1886, referred to above, shows, the Portuguese at that time were showing a revived interest in Nyasaland. They talked of sending up forces to punish the "murderers" of Hinkleman.[23] This thoroughly alarmed Hawes who warned the British Government that the Makololo would resist any Portuguese move into what they considered their territory:

> I trust HMG will use their influence with the Portuguese Government to prevent any occupation of the Makololo country which could lead to deplorable results and engender bitter feelings towards the English by a tribe whose friendship we might depend on in case of necessity and who practically look on the country they hold as belonging to the Government of England.[24]

Ten days later on November 29, 1886, Hawes reported that he had seen Ramakukan (or Kasisi as he called him in that dispatch and in some others) and warned him that the Portuguese might come. He went on to ask him to receive them courteously, but to be alert and to resist any Portuguese force.[25]

This was a situation in which the British Consulate seemed to be not "of doubtful utility" as Lister put it, but positively immoral and a dangerous threat to the continued presence of British traders and missionaries in the area. As we noted above the Consul could do nothing that the traders or missionaries could not do themselves in terms of influencing chiefs to change their ways. Indeed, the Consul's official status created problems because about it hung the threat of power, yet a power that the Consul, in practice, did not have. Coast men could tell Matipwiri or Makanjila that a consul's presence was a sign of a possible British conquest, which confirmed the suspicion and antagonism of such chiefs, yet the Consul who aroused such feelings had no means of dealing with their results. The Consul could not even help chiefs willing to try to

---

[23] *Ibid*

[24] *Ibid*

[25] Hawes to Iddesleigh, 29 November 1866, no. 45 CA, FO 84/1751.

develop cash crops, the very simplest step forward for the territory. Yet in this situation the Consul was encouraging resistance to Portuguese invasion. Hawes gave encouragement but he knew very well, as we have just seen, that it was all he could offer. Hawes, personally an honourable man, was being driven by the barren state of the Foreign Office's policy into urging a friend to engage in a fight which might lose that friend his lands and the lives of many of his people, without even the hope of helping him with weapons and ammunition, let alone troops.

The men of the ALC and the Scottish Mission came into the area with their wives and children; they invested capital in the country; they undertook fairly long contracts and had that much commitment to Malawi and her future. They had achieved some kind of modus vivendi with the indigenous power structure. However, the "coast" influence always rendered this precarious and they had, from the beginning, wanted some kind of British protection from these threats which they could not deal with themselves. But the Lakes Consulate was worse than no help at all. It aroused both Arab and Portuguese suspicions without any compensatory gain. The fault was not with Foot or Goodrich or Hawes, but in the policy they had to carry through, a policy which, by the end of 1886, was simply to observe and report.

The hopelessness of the situation was patent by the end of 1886 but it could have been seen perhaps even on Foot's first appointment. He received very positive instructions, yet with them there came none of the financial or military resources which would have enabled him do anything that would improve the situation.

The Free Church of Scotland and other anti-slave trade people went on pressing for a More positive British presence on the Lake, even after Foot's appointment. These efforts centred round the African Lakes Company, whose managers in Africa, the Moir brothers, and the directors in Glasgow, were both Free Church and anti-slave trade. The Moirs during their travels in the Shire Highlands and the lakeshore area in 1885, began to collect signatures of chiefs on treaty forms which called for British Protection, a protection to be exercised through the Company.

With these treaties to back up their claims the Company hoped that a Charter might be granted to them to rule Malawi on behalf of the British

Government. The slave trade could then be effectively suppressed, the missions encouraged and legitimate commerce and trade developed. There was much to be said, however, against any such Charter being given to the ALC. From the beginning of its existence the Company never had enough capital for any large-scale development, their service on the Zambezi and Shire Rivers, the key to Nyasaland's contact with the outside world, was always very unsatisfactory, even when allowances are made for the difficulties of the route.[26] Their relations with the Makololo were not very good. At the time of the Fenwick incident the Makololo were quite clear that their quarrel was not with the British in general, but with the ALC, especially the Moir brothers.[27]

It was at this stage that the Church of Scotland took the initiative in the matter for the first time. As soon as the plan of the Moirs became known to them, they began to press the British Government not to grant a Charter to the Company. Hawes had himself already found that Ramakukan and Moir disagreed about the nature of the treaty that they had signed,[28] and now Hetherwick submitted to him a long memorandum protesting about the unsuitability of granting of the powers of a chartered company to the ALC.[29] He pointed out the "manifest incapacity of the Lakes Company as presently constituted for undertaking any such administration..." recalling that in Consul Foot's time it took all his time and energy to extricate them from their contretemps with the Makololo. Hetherwick also questioned the worth of the treaties, insisting that, apart from Mpama and Kapeni, no important Yao chief had signed anything at all; Malemia, Kawinga, Matipwiri, Mkanda and Mitochi were all absent quite apart from the Ngoni. He went on to insist that the Blantyre Mission would support any proper administration - but not one as envisaged by the ALC.

---

[26] Hawes to Roseberry, 11 February 1886, no. 6 CA, FO 84/1751; D.J. Rankin, *The Zambezi Basin and Nyasaland,* (Edinburgh: Blackwood, 1893), Chapter 1; W.H. Rankine, *Hero of a Dark Continent,* (Edinburgh: Blackwood, 1897), p. 87.

[27] Morrison's Journal, entries for March and April 1884.

[28] Hawes to Salisbury, 1 December 1885, no. 5 Africa, FO 84/1751.

[29] Enclosed in Hawes to Roseberry, 30 March 1886, no. 13 CA, FO 84/1720.

Hawes enclosed the memorandum in his dispatch to the Foreign Office and commented that, while he thought the mission was not very important, he agreed with its judgement about the incapacity of the Company. He went on to say that Kapeni, the mission's neighbour, who had signed a "treaty", had not got any idea of the cession of sovereignty involved. Hawes then went on in a sentence ominous for the future, and of importance for the discussion of the early policies of Sir Harry Johnston:

> The discussion that took place was long and animated, and I am of the opinion, for what was said, that any attempt to levy taxes for the administration of the country would lead to opposition on the part of the chiefs which might result in difficulties.[30]

Also of significance for the story of later relations between the British administration and the mission was Hawes' remark about the significance of the mission. Even if only for the relationship of Clement Scott and the Maseko Ngoni, which had saved many Yao from the Ngoni in the last great raid of 1884, this would appear to be an inaccurate assessment of the mission's importance. Indeed, less than a year later, Hawes was praising Scott's ability to get on with African people and saying how useful and helpful it was. This was in connection with the establishment of good relations between the British and Chikumbu, a powerful Yao chief at Mulanje and a close ally of the noted slaver Matipwiri.[31]

However, on Hawes' dispatch enclosing Hetherwick's memorandum of March 1886, T.V. Lister in his minute added malice to inaccuracy:

> Blantyre Mission deserves little favour from us. They were guilty of some horrible murders and tortures of natives which were hushed up. The Lakes Company is not yet a very flourishing affair but is much more likely to introduce good government and trade than any missionaries.[32]

---

[30] Ibid

[31] Hawes to Salisbury, 3 October 1887, no. 43 CA, FO 84/1829.

[32] Minute initialled T.V.L on Hawes to Roseberry, 30 October 1887, no. 13 CA, FO 84/1751. This totally ignored the Commission of 1880-1 and the fresh start with a new staff.

In Scotland the Foreign Committee of the Church of Scotland, advised by Clement Scott, who was on leave at the time, backed up the initiative Hetherwick had taken. They took part in a series of meetings with anti-slavery interests, the Free Church and the ALC which culminated in a conference at Glasgow that sent a petition to the British Government asking for a real measure of British authority in Nyasaland to protect the British there; not from African people but from the threat of Portuguese advance.[33] However, in those meetings the Church of Scotland was adamant that they could not accept the Moir treaties as valid nor could they accept a Protectorate exercised by the ALC. Dr McMurtrie wrote to the Secretary of the Company in Glasgow after the Glasgow conference, reporting the attitude of a meeting of the Foreign Mission Committee:

> With reference to treaties with native chiefs, the meeting felt strongly that this Committee could not agree to receive any benefits under the treaties of which they disapprove; and they requested me to ask whether your Company is willing to renounce all benefits stipulated to your Company in the series of treaties entered into by Ramakukan and other African chiefs, and to hold these treaties as non-existent.[34]

Lister's prejudices did not blind him to the validity of the case made out by the mission, that the Company should not be granted a Charter. Lord Roseberry replied to Hawes at the end of July, saying that the Government could not administer a Protectorate approachable only through the territory of a European power to which the Protectorate was distasteful. They could not delegate to the Company an authority they did not have, and in any case, the ALC was not much good and the treaties were to be taken as inoperative due to the protests of the missionaries.[35] Roseberry did not say that the treaties were illegal and thus left them as a possible option for the future. Hawes, therefore, reported only a little later that he was trying to persuade Hetherwick that the treaties might be worthy of some kind of recognition, even if only to stop the wrong kind of trader coming into the area; for example someone like Hinkleman who had just been reported as selling guns and

---

[33] McMurtrie to D.C. Scott, 22 September 1886, Convenor's Letter Book, M.1.
[34] McMurtrie to Secretary, ALC, 10 February 1886, Convenor's Letter Book, M.1.
[35] FO to Hawes, 24 July 1886, no. 11 Confidential, FO 84/1751.

spirits to the Makololo.³⁶ In this dispatch Hawes says that part of the mission's opposition was due to Hetherwick's jealousy of Moir.

There is no doubt that Hetherwick had a very unfortunate and at times malicious attitude to certain individuals, which sometimes marred the effectiveness of cases he argued,³⁷ but on this issue Hawes himself had consistently complained of the Company; and Hetherwick's prejudices against Moir were not factors in the thinking of the Foreign Mission Committee, which at that time was advised by Clement Scott who was then in Scotland. Hawes' attempts to persuade the missionaries of the validity of the Company's treaties were an extraordinary performance. Hawes himself had reported his doubts about their validity, and about the ALC's bad relations with the Makololo, the one really pro-British group in the country. It would seem that the only explanation of this behaviour is that Hawes saw only too clearly the fruitlessness of the Consulate and was casting around for anything to protect British interests.

1887 was the darkest year yet for the British in Malawi, especially those in the Shire Highlands. The Portuguese were claiming the Shire Highlands as theirs.³⁸ Throughout the year Matipwiri and his Swahili allies openly flouted what semblance of authority Hawes had,³⁹ and Kawinga raided for slaves right to the door of the Consular buildings that Hawes had caused to be erected at Zomba.⁴⁰ He reported that local headmen had asked him for assistance against the raids. What was he to do? he asked; especially what was he to do if some of his own employees were taken to help make up a caravan? All that Whitehall could say in reply was:

> It is difficult to give advice in such matters inasmuch as, during the time required for the interchange of communications new and different phases of the question may be entered upon. I am at the

---

[36] Hawes to Iddesleigh, 28 August 1886, no. 26 CA, FO 84/1751.

[37] Notably during 1893 in some of his letters to McMurtrie and in some of his contributions to *LWBCA*.

[38] Hawes to Iddesleigh, 20 November 1886, no. 44 CA, FO 84/1751.

[39] Hawes to Iddesleigh, 25 February, no. 6 CA, 25 Mar. no. 7 CA, 27 June, no. 27 CA, 6 July, no. 29 CA, all 1887, FO 84/1829.

[40] Hawes to Salisbury, 25 April 1887, no. 20 CA, FO 84/1829.

> same time to observe that His Lordship has every confidence in your tact and general management of the natives of your District and relies upon you to keep clear of any unnecessary complications in your dealing with them.[41]

Hawes then applied for leave, which may not have been unconnected with the extremely frustrating situation in which he found himself. He nominated as his acting Consul for the period when he or his successor would be out of the country, John Buchanan, whom he had used a good deal as an interpreter.[42] T.V. Lister minuted his approval of this appointment, despite the waspish tone of his previous minutes on Blantyre Mission and missionaries.

It was at this time, when British policy towards northern Zambezia appeared totally bankrupt, or perhaps more accurately, non-existent, that a critical situation arose which forced the Foreign Office to make up its mind about whether to make British authority effective or to end the charade by withdrawing altogether.

The crisis began with Hawes reporting in November 1887 that there was serious fighting at the north end of the Lake between coastmen, led by an Arab slaver called Mlozi, and the local Nkhonde people. He reported that the Arabs had shown no antagonism to the English; therefore, if caution and discretion were exercised by the Europeans at Karonga, their interests would not be in danger. He went on to warn, however, that:

> I am not satisfied with the attitude assumed by Mr Monteith and have told the A.L.C. to warn employees not to meddle in native quarrels, as interference of that kind might lead to hostilities between European and natives, will not in any way be supported by me, and have asked them to caution their subordinates to avoid using language in their discussions with the natives that might involve the responsibility of HM Consul.[43]

He continued that he was on his way to Karonga and that at Old Livingstonia he had encountered O'Neill, Consul at Mozambique. O'Neill had told him that he also was going up to Karonga, and was embarking

---

[41] FO to Hawes, 9 August 1887, no. 16 Confidential, FO 84/1829.
[42] Hawes to Salisbury, 15 August 1887, no. 36 CA, FO 84/1829.
[43] Hawes to Salisbury, 16 November 1887, no. 47 CA, FO 84/1829.

immediately on the ALC steamer the *Ilala*. He would do his best to prevent bloodshed. "I conclude that Mr O'Neill will not undertake to act in an official capacity", Hawes rather plaintively remarked.[44]

Hawes was really asking for the impossible when he wanted someone like Monteith to stand aloof from such a fight as the one that was then in progress at Karonga. The whole purpose of the ALCs coming to Zambezia was the suppression of the slave trade, and to help the missions build up a peaceable and prosperous African society.

How could Monteith be expected to play the role of disinterested spectator, the role that Hawes had been essaying for the previous year? Hawes misunderstood the ALC position completely when he said that their interests and that of the other Europeans, missionaries mostly, would not be in danger if they steered clear of this fight. The prime interest of the Company and the missions was the support of a peaceful and prosperous people like the Nkonde and in driving from Malawi the slaving coastmen like Mlozi. O'Neill, on the other hand, was a man who understood the attitude of Monteith very well. He also was an anti-slave trade crusader, always having interpreted his position as Consul at Mozambique in as active and anti-slave trade a fashion as had been possible. He had been on the Lake before and knew the ALC and both the Scottish missions well.[45] Even when on leave he had kept up a stream of letters to the Foreign Office, pressing the vital importance of a strong British presence on the lake and on the Shire for stopping the east coast slave trade.[46]

It was in August 1884 that the Lakes Company first put up a post at Karonga. It was planned as a base from which to pass goods along the Stevenson Road to the London Missionary Society stations on Lake Tanganyika, and also to try to foster legitimate trade in the area. It is part of the irony of human existence that this station immediately attracted from far and near, coastmen who found this a very convenient place to

---

[44] *Ibid*

[45] A plaque on the pillar beside the main door of Blantyre Church tells that on the spot Consul O'Neill made his readings from which he calculated the exact latitude and longitude of the Blantyre Mission.

[46] O'Neill to Salisbury, 19 June 1885, Private, FO 84/1709.

sell their ivory at a good price. However, at first all things went very peacefully and calmly for the station manager, L. Monteith Fotheringham, usually referred to by contemporaries as Mr Monteith.

The change for the worse came in 1887, the year of much unrest in the Shire Highlands. Three coastmen and their followers settled in three stockaded villages close to Karonga and the Stevenson Road. They were Mlozi, who was leader, and his two lieutenants, KopaKopa and Msalema. These men soon began the process carried through elsewhere at about this time, in the Congo and on Lake Tanganyika, of powerful coastmen terrorizing the local people into taking them as their chiefs in place of legitimate headmen.

There is a good deal of controversy and discussion about what lay at the root of this widespread process, but a detailed discussion of this would not be relevant here.[47] The underlying cause would seem to have been closely related to the closing of the old avenues of trade to the coastmen by the German occupation of the coast, and the general apprehension caused by this German move, as well as by the Belgian advance in the Congo and by British activity in Zambezia, Zanzibar and elsewhere.

Whether there was any general conspiracy of the Arabs to drive out the Europeans from all East and Central Africa is very doubtful; but many contemporaries firmly believed it.[48] What is certain, however, is that the activity of the coastmen at Karonga was not an isolated incident. Dr Laws, who was in close contact with the main Ngoni state of Mbelwa, informed Consul Hawes that only a savagely effective raid by Mbelwa's regiments had prevented the Bemba from co-operating with Mlozi against all Europeans on the Lake.[49] (The Ngoni had raided for their own traditional reasons and not in order to aid the mission. From their captives they presumably learned about the alliance with Mlozi.) Buchanan also said that while he was visiting Likoma he had met an *induna* of the Makwangwala who said that they had been approached by

---

[47] For details, see Hanna, *The Beginnings of Nyasaland and North-Eastern Rhodesia,* pp. 97100; Oliver, *The Missionary Factor in East Africa,* Chapter 3.

[48] Lugard, *The Rise of our East African Empire,* pp. 25-29. and R. Foskett (ed.), *The Zambesi Journal,* pp. 27 and 209.

[49] Hawes to Salisbury, 16 January 1888, no. 3 CA, FO 84/1883.

emissaries of Mlozi seeking their aid against the Company and the missions.[50]

A further piece of evidence came in March 1888, when Buchanan visited Makanjila in the company of W.P. Johnson of the UMCA. This slaver, at whose court there seemed always to have been a strong coast influence, had never been friendly to the British missionaries or traders, but now he went much further and had Buchanan stripped and beaten, shutting him up along with Johnson till they were ransomed by their boat crew the next day. Lugard[51] felt that this incident, considered along with the aggressiveness of Kawinga and Matipwiri since the beginning of 1887, confirmed the theory of a grand alliance to drive out the Europeans. Some others who had been much longer in the area, shared this view. A more likely explanation would be to say that Makanjila took advantage of the weakness of the Acting Consul's position, which had been borne home to him by the relative success of Mlozi at Karonga. Kawinga and Matipwiri and the others had reason enough to be aggressive without any encouragement from elsewhere.

The evidence of Mlozi seeking help among the Makwangwala and the Bemba is clear, but it is not evidence of an East African plot, it only points to Mlozi's good sense. He needed help if he was going to rule the north end of the Lake against the Company and the missions, who were bound to oppose him. However, Mlozi in alliance with a powerful tribe like the Bemba was danger enough to any missionary or trading establishment on the Lake, quite apart from the existence of any more widespread system of alliance.

Until a British Administration was set up and H.H. Johnston made a treaty with Mlozi in 1889, the fighting at Karonga was indecisive. The Company with its Tonga and Nkhonde allies, was never able to destroy the Arab stockades, and although the garrison was often in very bad straits, it was never defeated and forced to leave the north end. The story of this war has been clearly related by A.J. Hanna,[52] and there is no need to repeat a chronological account. However, the attitude of the Blantyre Mission to

---

[50] Buchanan to Hawes, 12 April 1888, no. 17 CA, FO 84/1883.

[51] Ibid

[52] Hanna, *The Beginnings of Nyasaland and North-Eastern Rhodesia,* pp. 79-106.

the struggle at the various stages through which it passed and the influence of the war on the campaign for a Protectorate need to be examined.

The Karonga garrison's constant need was for supplies of food and ammunition and, when the strength of the Arab stockades was discovered, for artillery.[53] These supplies could only come up the Zambezi and Shire through Portuguese territory. The pressure of the Arabs on the British at the north end of the Lake thus gave to the Portuguese a hold on the situation they had not had before and which they were now in a mood to exploit. So the two threats that the ALC and the missions had feared all along were pressing in on them with a force that seemed too strong for either the African people or the British groups in the area to successfully resist.

In February 1888, during a lull in the fighting at the north end, Hawes sent a long dispatch to Lord Salisbury describing the state of affairs and complaining of the conduct of Consul O'Neill, the Moirs and Clement Scott.[54] He reported that he had remonstrated with the Moirs for preparing an expedition to renew hostilities with Mlozi. Their reply was that they could not let down the Nkhonde. Hawes was even more angry when he found out that O'Neill was going to head the expedition, although as a private individual. He included copies of his formal protests to the ALC and to O'Neill. A strong point in his letter to the ALC was that the Company's actions now opened the way for any trader who was strong enough to make war when and where he liked.[55] On returning from Karonga to the south he had consulted Clement Scott, who had agreed with him that a further ALC expedition would not be a good thing. Hawes then went on to express anger that soon after, at a meeting of the Blantyre Mission staff, the new expedition was voted as one worthy of the mission's support, Scott voting with the majority.[56]

---

[53] Lugard, *The Rise of our East African Empire,* pp. 25-29. and R. Foskett (ed.), *The Zambesi Journal,* pp. 119.

[54] Hawes to Salisbury, 10 February 1888, no. 14 CA, FO 84/1883.

[55] Ibid

[56] Ibid

The explanation of Scott's apparent inconsistency is to be found in the high regard in which O'Neill was held by the missionaries, notably by Scott himself. In October 1886 the Church of Scotland Foreign Mission Committee had sent to Lord Salisbury a formal letter attesting to the high regard in which the Scottish community in the Shire Highlands held Consul O'Neill. This letter was sent at the instigation of Clement Scott.[57] The suspicion with which the ALC's political ambitions were held by the mission has already been noted and Scott's initial agreement with Hawes is consistent with that, but when O'Neill became the head of the expedition the situation was immediately changed for Scott. Now the expedition was led by a British official, a well-trusted one, in place of the mistrusted Moirs. Hawes naturally did not see these events in this light.

Hawes then departed on leave and his deputy Buchanan decided to go to the north end with the expedition because the Moirs guaranteed their peaceful intentions.[58] Buchanan failed to negotiate any settlement and after his departure from the north end, the Lakes Company saw no alternative to resuming the attack on Mlozi. Fred Moir was seriously wounded in the brave but unsuccessful assault on the slaver's stockades. With the Karonga garrison again driven back on to the defensive, the Lakes Company began yet again to prepare an expedition for the north end. O'Neill, then back at Mozambique, encouraged a soldier whom he felt could successfully end the affair, to go to Blantyre and offer his services to the Company. This was Captain F.D. (later Lord) Lugard.[59]

Buchanan, though at first unhappy about the fresh moves by the Company[60] in the end supported the new expedition under Lugard. Clement Scott played an important role in gaining his support. Scott was also still suspicious of the long-term aims of the Lakes Company, but when an officer, who personally impressed him and who was recommended by O'Neill, was appointed to head the Company forces his attitude was changed. He wrote to Buchanan and arranged meetings

---

[57] McMurtrie to Salisbury, 14 October 1888, Convenor's Letter Book, M.1.

[58] Buchanan to Hawes, 18 February 1888, no. 14a CA, FO 84/1883.

[59] Lugard, *The Rise of our East African Empire,* pp. 25-29. and R. Foskett (ed.), *The Zambesi Journal,* p. 18.

[60] Ibid, 48.

with Lugard and the vice-consul at Blantyre Manse.[61] It is clear from the letter he wrote to Buchanan that it was the presence of first O'Neill and then Lugard that persuaded Scott and the others at the Blantyre Mission to back the Company war at Karonga. Scott wrote:

> The present conditions of affairs seems to us, members of the British community here, to be most serious; and in the presence of Captain Lugard, who has expressed himself willing to take command of the expedition at present formed by the Lakes Company, if called upon to do so, it seems to us that an opportunity presents itself of keeping the expedition on the same lines as those to which the missionaries at Blantyre a short time ago gave their countenance to the action formerly proposed, and of lifting the expedition into the sympathy and moral; support of the whole community.[62]

Scott was quite clear about the threat posed to the missions by Mlozi, but his lack of confidence in the intentions and capabilities of the Lakes Company prevented his giving wholehearted backing to the ALC policy at Karonga, except when the whole affair was being headed by someone Scott held to be trustworthy like O'Neill or Lugard. This was a decidedly different attitude from the other two missions in the area of the Lake.

The UMCA apart from loaning their steamer to Consul Hawes at the time of the initial troubles, remained throughout the period, unhappy about the war; while the Livingstonia Mission, nearer to the danger and whose supporters in Scotland included the directors of the Lakes Company, was unswervingly in support of the war throughout.[63]

In Scotland, the authorities of the Church of Scotland showed no such hesitation as did Scott in the field. They were already closely involved with the Free Church and the African Lakes Company, forming a united pressure group on the Foreign Office. The alliance had come about in response to the threat posed by the Portuguese advance into the Shire Highlands and towards the Lake. In December 1886 they had sent a deputation to the Foreign Office, requesting the help of the Government. They wished the British Government to approach the Portuguese in

---

[61] *Ibid,* 48-9; also Buchanan to Hawes, 20 May 1888, no. 26 CA, FO 84/1883.
[62] Enclosed in Buchanan to Hawes, 20 May 1888, no. 26 CA, FO 84/1883.
[63] Hanna, *The Beginnings of Nyasaland and North-Eastern Rhodesia,* pp. 79-105.

order to obtain their co-operation with the Scottish interests in the Lake Malawi area. First, they wanted the Portuguese to declare the River Ruo as the boundary of their sphere of interest, and second, they wished the Portuguese Government to agree to a uniform three per cent tariff on all goods passing through their territory en route to Nyasaland.[64]

In February another joint deputation went to the Foreign Office, again to ask the Government to put pressure on the Portuguese but also to find out about the British Government's attitude to the Karonga affair.[65] At the Foreign Office they were received by Sir Percy Anderson. He assured them that the Karonga difficulties were over. On the Portuguese question, though, Anderson's response was less satisfactory. He seemed to have little to say except to deplore again the fact that the Scottish interests were in the hinterland of a Portuguese controlled coast.[66]

It was that month of March 1888 that the Portuguese-Arab nutcracker really began to press on Malawi. Just when, because of the North End War, the lines of communication were supremely vital, the Portuguese chose to close them. This they did by confiscating the ALC steamer at Quelimane and giving the Company four months to transfer it to a Portuguese owner. There was to be no commerce on the Zambezi except for Portuguese commerce. What freedom of navigation there had been was now gone and all were apparently left to the mercy of Mlozi and the Portuguese. In Scotland the response was instant. The Churches and the Company together called a meeting in London of all the Scots members of both Houses of Parliament.[67]

The three points put by the group to the meeting made clear their aims and showed that in two years there had been a definite change of emphasis. The three points were, first, a request for the guarantee of the freedom of navigation in the Zambezi; second, a statement of the facts of the continuing slave trade; and third, a request for the inclusion of Malawi, north of the Ruo as a sphere of British interest. The third point is a definite change from the aims of 1886: the British were now required

---

[64] McMurtrie to Dr Rankine, 22 December 1886, Convenor's Letter Book, M.1.

[65] McMurtrie to Hetherwick, 15 February 1888, Convenors Letter Book, M.1.

[66] Ibid

[67] McMurtrie to D.C. Scott, 14 March 1888, Convenors Letter Book, M.1.

to play a positive role and not simply to exclude the Portuguese. What exactly was meant by the request to be included as "a sphere of British interest" is not completely clear.

Was some kind of situation similar to what existed in the Indian princely states intended, or an actual British Protectorate? A Crown Colony may have been in the back of some minds in the group of Scots that planned the meeting, but there is no definite indication in the records. The result of the meeting was the granting of an interview by Lord Salisbury to a delegation from this Scottish pressure group. Dr McMurtrie and Lord Balfour of Burleigh (himself a Conservative politician, here acting as a Kirk elder) were the Church of Scotland representatives.

Of this appeal to Salisbury, Robinson and Gallagher have written that the Scots "were appealing to a stone".[68] At that time Salisbury was bent on securing southern Zambezia as a hinterland development from Cape Colony, and for this he was willing to leave all of northern Zambezia to the Portuguese, though the same authors say:

> His over-riding aim in attempting to settle the whole question of Zambezia with Lisbon was to obtain recognition of the British sphere in southern Zambezia. But his religious sentiment and his sense of diplomatic finesse made him try and stretch the bargain, to save the Protestant missions in the Shire Highlands from falling under Catholic rule.[69]

McMurtrie wrote a very full report to Clement Scott on the interview with Lord Salisbury.[70] Salisbury told them of the arrangements with Lobengula, Paramount of the Ndebele, which brought the British sphere of influence up to the Zambezi and enabled the Government to insist on the free navigation of its waters. McMurtrie then went on:

> But in regard to our demand that the British Government use force to repel the Arabs, he held out no encouragement. (This need not go abroad as it would encourage the Arabs.) He said that if the British arms met with a repulse it must be revenged, and there would be a

---

[68] R. Robinson and J. Gallagher, *Africa and the Victorians: the Official Mind of Imperialism,* (London, Macmillan, 1961), p. 224.

[69] *Ibid*, p. 225.

[70] McMurtrie to D.C. Scott, 10 May 1888, Convenors Letter Book, M.1.

> Gordon and Khartoum business. But, he said (and this is very private), "why not do it yourselves?" - i.e., employ force in self-defence against the Arabs. Lord Balfour said our missionaries felt that their strength lay in the natives seeing that they did not use physical but only moral force. IA. Salisbury replied, with a twinkle in his eye - "most creditable to the missionaries and creditable to their calling, but there does not seem to me to be a great difference between doing it yourselves and asking us to do it for
>
> I might tell you everything - but you, I know, will not fight except in the last resort. Certainly the Govt. would seem committed to look favourably on any measures of force which the trading companies and the missions should be driven to.[71]

The Scottish interests were back where they had started when they first began to request some sort of British aid: that is, they were on their own. We have seen that by the time Consul Hawes went on leave, the futility of the British consular presence had become obvious to all. But Lord Salisbury still seemed to think it might just do the trick, for in the same month (May 1888) he wrote a most revealing minute.

> I feel that a consul represents a compromise between the desire of the missionaries to obtain Protection and the desire of the Home Government not to be involved in expensive operations. To please the missionaries we send a representative of the Govt., to spare the taxpayers we make him understand that he will in no case be supported by armed force. The only weapon left to him is bluster.[72]

Poor Hawes had been left to find over the years that bluster was his only weapon and the process nearly broke him. The missionaries and the Company were not yet broken, however, and in northern Zambezia they continued to make their stand against Portuguese and Arab encroachments and in the UK to campaign for British support.

Clement Scott's reaction to the detention of the ALC's steamer by the Portuguese and their interruption of the flow of arms and ammunition was typical. Instead of being floored by this move which, if the

---

[71] Ibid

[72] Quoted by Robinson and Gallagher, *Africa and the Victorians*, p. 224.

Portuguese had followed through, would have meant the end of the Scottish influence in the area, he wrote:

> Portugal's detention of the Lakes Coy's steamer, her inordinate and most impolitic raising of tariff, her repeated stoppage of ammunition, at a time when it is needed for the safety of life and property, and when it is known that a considerable part of the Quelimane revenue depends upon its importation, must tell powerfully against her in civilised circles whenever such things become known.[73]

In this article he went on to make clear that direct British rule was not a first consideration, but that what was wanted was a holding of the ring by Britain to stop Portuguese interfering. He says,[74]

> It is hoped we shall get the Zambezi free for trade and some delineation of Portuguese advances, even although we do not yet ask for British annexation.

The Portuguese pressure went on through the rest of 1888 and into 1889. The missionaries and the ALC still sent their letters home, hoping to influence public opinion to support some kind of British intervention. The officials of the Company and the two churches at home also persevered with their efforts despite Salisbury's firmness in the interview in May of 1888. In December 1888 the expedition of the Portuguese under the command of Lt Cardozo was on the borders of what the Scots thought of as Nyasaland. Scott had heard, quite correctly, that the expedition was supposed to be coming to defend the British missions on the Lake.[75] This had been the constant theme of the Portuguese for some years, that they had a duty to protect the missionaries and traders. Who could prevent them if the British Government would not?

The situation was by then desperate, the Portuguese were poised on the border and the struggle against the Arabs in the north was like a running sore draining the strength of the Scottish community. Scott had himself published a letter in the Blantyre magazine, from one of the Karonga

---

[73] *LWBCA* August 1888.

[74] *Ibid*

[75] *LWBCA* December 1888.

garrison which summed up the situation. The writer, after describing some hard fighting went on:

> I do not think it is exactly fair to ask men either white or black, to face such fearful odds. Most of us came to this country with anything but fighting ideas in our heads. We are now no nearer the end than we were when the Arabs first broke out. It does seem a hard thing to think of giving up Lake Nyasa to the Arabs, but that is what will happen shortly unless help comes from outside. I do not see how the African Lakes Company can possibly stand the brunt alone.[76]

In the early months of 1889, the column of Zulu riflemen under Cardozo were seen as a threat to all that Blantyre, Mandala and Livingstonia hoped for in Malawi, yet they also seemed the only hope of help against Mlozi and the other slavers. The pressure of the Scots on Salisbury's administration had led to no action at all and appeared to have little chance of doing so. The campaign by the Scots, begun as early as 1882 by Free Church leaders, to gain some kind of British Protection could be judged a failure, as Robinson and Gallagher point out.

> Salisbury in 1888 was at one with his predecessors in thinking that these missionary concerns were no good reason to extend British rule over Nyasa.[77]

In his report to Scott about the interview with Lord Salisbury, McMurtrie had concluded that he felt that Salisbury would do nothing but would not mind "if some new Rajah Brooke 'Sarawaked' Nyasaland"[78] and thus solved the problem. This was, in fact, the way in which the situation did change and change completely. In Cecil Rhodes there appeared a man on the scene with an even greater imperial drive than Rajah Brooke, whose aim was not to "Sarawak" little Malawi alone, but a vast swathe of Africa, from Cape to Cairo. With his coming into the game, the Scottish pressure group was able to play a role of some significance in Malawi's future, which otherwise would have lain in the hands of Mlozi and Cardozo.

---

[76] *LWBCA* August 1888.

[77] Robinson and Gallagher, *Africa and the Victorians*, p. 223.

[78] McMurtrie to D.C. Scott, 10 May 1888, Convenor's Letter Book, M.1.

Chapter 5: Mission and Boma, 1889 - 1914

During the last critical years of the 1880s, the Scots in the Shire Highlands did not show any realization that their campaign to obtain British intervention in Malawi against the threat from both Mlozi and the Portuguese was a failure, although by the early months of 1889 they were somewhat depressed. At that time D.C. Scott wrote of O'Neill's transfer from Africa in a suspicious, aggrieved tone which betrayed this.

> Consul O'Neill is to leave Mozambique; he is transferred to Leghorn. It is strange that this should happen at this time, especially when his experience and counsel are so much needed; but one reads the means and motives clearly enough in the events of the past Lake troubles.[1]

In the same article Scott wrote in such a vein that it is clear that for the first time the hollow nature of the Lake Nyasa consulship had come home to him. The days of Palmerstonian support for missionary and humanitarian penetration of Africa were over, though a facade was kept up to a degree, of which the Nyasa consulship was part.[2] For some time Salisbury had seen it simply as bluff to keep the humanitarian lobby quiet.[3] It is not usually easy for contemporaries to see what is clear to those with the advantage of hindsight, so that it was only in 1889 that Scott complained:

> We seem to have grounds of complaint that the consulship had become of such little real good. We are accredited with a consul and a consulate without possessing either. A consul who leaves his post and either does, or is compelled to, tie the hands of his representative so that no help can be given in most serious emergencies, while at the same time various interests in the country

---

[1] *LWBCA* February 1889.

[2] Baikie's Niger Expedition and Livingstone's Zambezi Expedition were the high spots of this policy of combining humanitarian, missionary and government interests in the opening up of Africa to European influence. They represented a liberal" imperialism which did not visualize European rule in Africa, but the development of "western" type African states.

[3] See Chapter 4.

> have to do battle not only against the natural difficulties of the situation, but what seems unfriendly criticism, is scarcely a hearty aid to the community.[4]

Scott can be forgiven for not knowing that even when aid had been at its "heartiest" in the days of Consul Foot, things had been no different; in the last analysis neither Foot nor Hawes had any real power.

O'Neill's role was highly personal and stemmed from the fact that he was an humanitarian imperialist, the kind of person who continued to hold the ideas underlying the Zambezi Expedition, and who did not appreciate the change that had come over British policy. Before the utter weakness of their position had been made clear to the Scots, both in Malawi and Edinburgh, Rhodes' coming on to the scene had changed the situation again.

In this new era Malawi was to be dominated by H.H. Johnston, who, in November 1888, was appointed to succeed O'Neill at Mozambique. Before he left the United Kingdom to take up his post, Salisbury sent him on a mission to Lisbon. He was instructed to negotiate a preliminary agreement on the basis of which a treaty could be concluded with Portugal clearing up the difficulties with her in Zambezia. This was an extraordinary task to entrust to a comparatively junior official, even though a brilliant one, and exactly what Lord Salisbury really intended is not clear. Most authorities[5] are agreed however that Salisbury's ultimate aims were still the same; first, that southern Zambezia was to be a British sphere of influence, and second, a more negative aim, that the Portuguese should remain outside the areas claimed by the Scottish missions in Malawi.

Despite this, the draft agreement reached by Johnston was one which gave all of northern and southern Zambezia to Britain, except for

---

[4] *LWBCA* February 1884.

[5] See Hanna, *The Beginnings of Nyasaland and North-Eastern Rhodesia,* Oliver, *The Missionary Factor in East Africa,* and Robinson and Gallagher, *Africa and the Victorians.*

southern Malawi, notably the Shire Highlands, which went to Portugal.[6] On his return to London, Johnston pressed for his draft's acceptance and was supported by some of the permanent officials in the Foreign Office, notably Lister, who minuted his support on Petrie's original report before forwarding the draft to Lord Salisbury.

This episode is an interesting one both for the study of Johnston and for the study of Lord Salisbury's diplomatic techniques. Its main importance for us was that it set alarm bells ringing in Scotland and among the Scots in Malawi. This alarm created by Johnston was an important factor in the future relations between the Blantyre Mission and the British Administration of the Protectorate carved out of Malawi under the authority of Johnston. Lord Salisbury gave to Johnston himself the thankless task of selling to the missionary authorities in Scotland the situation visualized in his draft agreement Whether Salisbury had serious intentions of acting on this draft is to be doubted; Johnston's trip to Edinburgh seems to have been designed more to arouse further Scottish feelings than to calm them.[7] W.P. Livingstone's account of the Johnston visit to Edinburgh and its aftermath seems to point in this direction.[8] Lord Balfour of Burleigh's role in the whole affair seems further to confirm this impression. He was a leading Tory politician, one close to Salisbury, yet he chaired many of the large protest meetings in Edinburgh which called on the Government to intervene in Malawi in order to protect that land from the Portuguese. W.P. Livingstone believed that Balfour was primarily Salisbury's go-between with the Scots and this would seem to be supported by a letter from McMurtrie to D.C. Scott:

> In a conversation I had with Balfour, his Lordship spoke very guardedly, as was right in his position, but he left the impression on my mind - which I state to you in confidence - that Lord Salisbury is really bringing pressure on Portugal and that Portugal will retrace her

---

[6] Johnston's memorandum setting out the basis of the agreement was forwarded by Petrie in a dispatch. Petrie to Salisbury, 9 April 1889, no. 39 Africa, FO 84/1965.

[7] M. Perham, *The Diaries of Lord Lugard*, (London: Faber and Faber, 1959-1963), vol. 1, p. 144.

[8] W.P. Livingstone, *A Prince of Missionaries*, pp. 50-52.

steps. Be good enough to withhold Lord Burleigh's name as confidential.[9]

Word of Johnston's terms of agreement with Portugal soon got out to the missionaries. D.C. Scott just could not believe the report to be serious, the terms contradicted so preposterously all for which Scottish missionary circles had been pressing throughout a whole decade. Scott wrote:

> Rumours from home reach us of a division of territory between Portugal and Britain in which the Shire is the boundary line. This is disastrous if it is true: it is indeed keeping the shell and giving the Portuguese the kernel. We must hold fast to this stronghold and gateway of African civilisation whatever comes, and in the face of what Lord Salisbury and the home authorities know of the Shire Highlands, we feel persuaded enough to say of the possibility of its eventually becoming Portuguese, that we don't believe it.[10]

Scott's confidence in Lord Salisbury was not misplaced because his Lordship rejected Johnston's draft agreement. Cecil Rhodes was by then in Great Britain and was willing, in return for a Charter, to take on all of northern Zambezia including Malawi, as well as southern Zambezia. Indeed in July he specifically offered to pay for the cost of pacifying and administering Malawi even though it was not to be included in the Charter - at least at first.[11]

Salisbury was now free from the trammels of the Treasury and was able to begin negotiations in earnest with the Portuguese. An additional help in these negotiations was the discovery by D.J. Rankin in January 1889 of the Chinde mouth of the Zambezi. This meant that there was no need to touch Portuguese soil en route to Malawi, an uninterrupted waterway then existed all the way into the Makololo country and so the Zambezi could seriously be claimed to be an international waterway.

The Makololo country had become at that time the flash point in Anglo-Portuguese relations. To Salisbury his course of action was no longer in

---

[9] *Ibid*

[10] *LWBCA,* June 1889.

[11] Cawston to Herbert, 1 July 1889, FO 403/111.

doubt, what remained was careful negotiation both with Rhodes and his British South Africa Company as well as with the Portuguese Government, so that the best bargain possible could be struck from his point of view. However, to people on the spot the situation was extremely tense. A Portuguese expedition of well-armed Zulu *askari*[12] led by Serpa Pinto was encamped on the Ruo, the border of what the Makololo thought was their territory and which the Scottish mission also held to be the limit of the Portuguese sphere. Poor Buchanan, the acting-consul, was at a loss: the Makololo looked to him for advice; what was he to do? Was he to repeat the irresponsibility of the past, when the Makololo had been encouraged to resist by people who had neither the means nor the intention of backing them?[13]

At this point Johnston arrived and brought his sharp decisive personality to bear on the dilemma. Within a few days of his arrival at his post at Mozambique, he had embarked on the gunboat *HMS Stork* and sailed across the bar at Chinde into the waters of the Zambezi and then up stream as far as the *Stork* could go. Disembarking on to her steam launch, he proceeded up stream till he joined an ALC steamer which conveyed him to Chiromo and Makololo territory, thus insisting on the reality of the Zambezi/Shire route as an international waterway. He arrived at Blantyre in the middle of August 1889.

He had meanwhile sent an elephant hunter, Alfred Sharpe, on a treaty-signing expedition towards the Luangwa. Leaving Blantyre he set out himself on such a trip along the Lake shore. Johnston's treaty-making included an agreement with Mlozi and the other Swahili at Karonga which brought a cessation of hostilities there, but its primary aim seems to have been the creation of a corridor of British territory reaching out towards Uganda.[14] Before he could go beyond Lake Tanganyika with his treaty-making he felt he had to return to Mozambique because of the continuing crisis of Anglo-Portuguese relations. He arrived back in Mozambique only six weeks after his departure.

---

[12] *Askari* is the Swahili word for soldier, commonly used in Eastern Africa.

[13] See Chapter 4.

[14] R. Oliver, *Sir Harry Johnston and the Scramble for Africa,* (London: Chatto & Windus, 1957), pp. 155-168.

His initial arrival at Blantyre had been taken by the missionaries and the traders who lived nearby, to mean that the Makololo country and the Shire Highlands as well as more territory to the north, was going to be declared to be under some kind of British protection or authority. Hetherwick wrote:

> Meanwhile the Consul reached Blantyre, and at once preparations were made for declaring the country under British protection. The manse dining-room at the mission became a factory with half a dozen sewing machines for the manufacture of Union Jacks - made of calico, red, white and blue - for presentation to the chiefs of the district who gladly welcomed these tokens of protection from the Portuguese menace.[15]

While Johnston was away in the north, because of the increased threat of invasion by Serpa Pinto's column, Buchanan declared the Makololo territory and the Shire Highlands to be under British protection. He did this formally at a special ceremony on the banks of the Mudi River between Blantyre and Mandala. This ceremony was on September 21, 1889. However, it should be noted that Buchanan had already stated that these same territories were under British protection in a letter to Serpa Pinto on August 19. Neither of these gestures checked Serpa Pinto nor calmed the Makololo and the fighting, which had begun in the first few days of September, still continued with the Makololo being worsted. They were then persuaded to retire and the chiefs with their households came up into the Highlands in October and stayed either at the mission or at Mandala.

The Portuguese advanced up the Shire as far as Katunga's, the port for Blantyre, and only thirty miles from the mission. The news of this advance provoked London into issuing an ultimatum which the Portuguese Government accepted. Lisbon then transmitted to Mozambique in February 1890 instructions to their forces to withdraw to the Ruo River. That month Pinto's Zulu *askari* withdrew from Katunga's, but the Portuguese threat was not over. In May 1890 there still existed a Portuguese official whose title was Governor of Shire, who maintained a

---

[15] Hetherwick, *The Romance of Blantyre*, p. 69.

threat to the peaceful life of the Scottish interests in Malawi. Scott wrote:

> Coutinho, so-called Governor of Shire, has threatened an advance on Blantyre, and troops are being collected. His attack upon Baird and the rumoured threats in which he has indulged are internationally most unjustifiable. Neither can one understand how in the face of their own orders the Portuguese dared to fire across the bows of the Lakes Co's steamer and search her.[16]

Worse was still to come:

> The Portuguese have at length done what must put an end to all timid policy. They have captured the river steamer and captured the crew. The point at issue is whether the Zambezi is an open highway or whether the Portuguese have a right to harass, search and delay traffic as they have been doing, under the claim that the Shire below the Ruo is "Portuguese waters". Mr Joseph Thompson was under Portuguese fire for a considerable time and in imminent danger; Mr Frere's caravan, simply for starting overland was also fired at ... to our minds it is tantamount to a proclamation of war.[17]

In August Buchanan sent a full report on these matters to the Foreign Office.[18] In it Buchanan emphasized the tenuous control that Lisbon had in her East African territories, other than near the ports. Inland the *prazo* owners were still the real authority.

After this time, although it was not until July 11, 1891 that an Anglo-Portuguese Convention was concluded, the Portuguese began to behave more and more reasonably. This may have been because of the increased pressure by the "Pioneers" of the British South Africa Company south of the Zambezi, especially in Manicaland.[19] At the end of October, Major Forbes had entered Manicaland and arrested the leaders of the Portuguese expedition there, but a reprise of the trouble on the Shire/Zambezi route was probably only prevented by Salisbury stationing

---

[16] *LWBCA May* 1890.

[17] *LWBCA* August 1890.

[18] Buchanan to Salisbury, 4 August 1890, no. 45 CA, FO 84/2021.

[19] See Philip Mason, *Birth of a Dilemma: the Conquest and Settlement of Rhodesia*, (London: Oxford University Press, 1958), pp. 150-151.

two British river gunboats on it to preserve its status as an international waterway.[20]

In December 1889, Johnston had passed through Blantyre on his way back to his post at Mozambique, where he did not stay very long. In May 1890 he returned to London, officially to recover his health damaged by the strain of his rapid journey to Tanganyika, though the visit was presumably not unconnected with the peculiar state of affairs in northern Zambezia, and the need to work out the boundaries of the British sphere and the future relations of this sphere to both the United Kingdom Government and the British South Africa Company.

Tension remained high in Blantyre, not only because of the continued Portuguese troubles, but because of the pressing question of the nature of the "protection" they had now received. It was true that the Portuguese menace was being cleared away, that Mlozi had signed a peace treaty and that many other chiefs, Tonga, Yao and Makololo had also signed treaties accepting British protection. On the other hand the sole British official presence was still the vice-consul John Buchanan. No new positive development had yet taken place, and the nature of any future development was by no means clear. The new chartered company was known to be related to their future, but the point was, in what way? All od this meant that the jubilation of the Blantyre missionaries was tempered by apprehension and doubt, which was expressed by Scott in an article he wrote in the same week as the flag-raising in Blantyre.

> This month there has dawned a new life upon this land. British Protection was what we had hardly dared hope for; the utmost we had been taught to expect was that we would not be driven out of the country by the Portuguese. We do not say that everything has been accomplished, we only say that the possibility of doing effective work has been secured. The work itself has yet to be done.... We wait anxiously to see the next step proposed. The legislation to follow may be either wholly in Government hands, or in the hands of a chartered company under Government supervision. We hope for the former, and for the establishment of native rights and missionary appeal.[21]

---

[20] Hanna, *The Beginnings of Nyasaland and North-Eastern Rhodesia*, p. 171.

[21] *LWBCA* September 1889.

This disquiet grew during the long months before it became known what was to happen. Eleven months after the flag-raising ceremony it was still not known in the Shire Highlands what the future was to be. It was then August 1890 when Scott wrote to a friend in Scotland on this matter. The letter shows how deep Scott's concern was over the possibility of rule by Rhodes' company.

> We have heard nothing of any sort of government for this place beyond the Chartered Company. If we have no independent Commissioner to whom to appeal for the natives' sake and for the mission, then I fear we may look forward to years of darkness from which the only escape will be in agitation and political revolution. When government bars the way with legislation, it really means political revolution to get it removed: we want help before that legislation bars the way.[22]

The staff in Blantyre had every right to be perplexed. There was talk of the chartered company exercising the "protection", there was talk of direct imperial rule, there was even talk of being ruled from the Cape.[23] They would have been more perplexed and alarmed if they had heard the answer given to their old friend Captain Lugard by the Foreign Office, when in October 1889 he enquired about H.H. Johnston's role in Malawi's affairs. Sir Percy Anderson and Sir Villiers Lister refused to admit to him that Johnston was an accredited agent of government: He was travelling, "being an excellent traveller", just to see his consular district and his relationship even with Buchanan seemed to be vague.[24]

Did the Foreign Office view Johnston then as primarily acting for the chartered company on this expedition? It was only the famous all-night meeting with Rhodes at the Westminster Palace Hotel that had made the journey and the treaty-making possible.[25] The morning after it, Johnston had a very important interview with Salisbury.

---

[22] D.C. Scott to James Robertson, 18 August 1890, EUL Ms. 717/10.
[23] *LWBCA* August 1890.
[24] Perham, *The Diaries of Lord Lugard,* vol. 1, p. 158.
[25] H.H. Johnston, *The Story of my Life,* (London: Chatto & Windus, 1923), pp. 234-238.

the immediate issue which, in view of the Portuguese expedition under Serpa Pinto, could not wait upon the prolonged negotiations involved in obtaining a Royal Charter, was whether Johnston might not be allowed to conclude the necessary treaties at Rhodes' expense, on the understanding that the areas so ceded would be included in the sphere of the Company's charter. It was a momentous decision but Salisbury took it without hesitation. "It would be preferable", he said, "that the Foreign Office should pay your travelling and treaty making expenses in Nyasaland, as we do not want to commit ourselves to handing over the region to a Chartered Company. Outside its limits I see no objection to Mr Rhodes paying your expenses and meeting the costs of negotiations."[26]

All expenses inside and outside the limits of "Nyasaland" were paid by Rhodes and so the territory may not have been explicitly promised him, but it was in no way denied him.

The ambiguity thus created about both the status of the new Protectorate and its Commissioner was not quickly resolved. The British Cabinet was powerless to finance the new administration because of the stringent Treasury doctrine of no money for new ventures in Africa; this doctrine also left them with no clear hope of being able to do anything different in the future, though that did not force them into the logical step of agreeing to the territory becoming part of the new chartered company's domain. Instead, they simply allowed the extraordinary situation to drift on of the Company's paying for an imperial administration. Poor Johnston was left the servant of two masters, neither of whom fully understood the other, nor did either share an agreed policy and so constantly they threatened to pull him in two. The contrary pressures did reach breaking point in the last months of 1893 when the negotiations for an extension of the subsidy system took place. A basic agreement was achieved by Rhodes and Johnston at a meeting in the Cape. Afterwards a draft altered by the Foreign Office was repudiated by Rhodes, who then allowed the Company Secretary, Harris, to inaugurate a campaign of unpleasantness against Johnston.[27] Johnston

---

[26] Oliver, *Sir Harry Johnston*, p. 155.

[27] The whole rather unpleasant story is told in Hanna, *The Beginnings of Nyasaland and North-Eastern Rhodesia*, pp. 245-260.

wrote to Rhodes and after listing the tremendous amount of work, much of it unpleasant, he had put in on behalf of the company, said that it might seem similar to the work of many Anglo-Indian officers,

> but the Anglo-Indian official, to begin with, is much better paid, he leads a far more comfortable life, he has not such a crushing sense of responsibility, and, above all, he does not have to serve two masters and please them both. I was willing to endure all these miseries so long as I felt that I was really doing good work in Africa, and that that work was being appreciated by the Foreign Office which employs me, and the British South Africa Company which finds the funds for my administration; but the position had now become too intolerable to be further supported.[28]

What made the situation so utterly impossible was summed up by Rhodes himself in a telegram to Dr Harris.

> Of course the difficulty is that Johnston, an Imperial officer and paid by the Imperial Government, should be a servant of the Company ... In the proposed settlement I see he tried to get the Sphere added to the Protectorate and to be independent of us in both. We understood the agreement to be that the Protectorate should be added to the Sphere and that he should be under us in both.[29]

This was in November 1893 and shows how much Rhodes distrusted Johnston by this time, despite the fact that in a long communication in June of that year Johnston had still talked in favour of Company rule in the Protectorate.[30]

The situation which created this distrust between the two men and caused such very bitter exchanges, sprang from the same seed as the distrust that first sprouted in the minds of D.C. Scott and his colleagues in 1889-1890. Though an Imperial Commissioner, Johnston was hardly the

---

[28] Johnston to Rhodes, 8 Oct. 1893, enclosed in Johnston to Roseberry, 8 Oct. 1893, FO 2/55.

[29] Quoted in Oliver, *Sir Harry Johnston*, p. 237.

[30] Johnston to Rhodes, 7 June 1893, Salisbury Rhodesia Archives CT/1/16/4/1. The contents of this long letter were summarized and sent to me together with extensive quotations from the text, by Dr K.J. McCracken formerly of University College, Dar-es-Salaam.

"independent" Commissioner Scott held to be vital for the political health of the country.

In 1885-1886 the Blantyre Mission had successfully opposed any idea of vesting civil authority in the ALC by the United Kingdom Government.[31] This was done although the ALC was an institution sympathetic to the aims of the Scottish missions in the country; a company indeed whose home constituency was a part of the Free Church.[32] All the more then were the Blantyre missionaries opposed to the idea of civil authority being exercised by what they called a "Cape" company. From the first clear indication of the possibility of such rule they campaigned vigorously against it. The information was not unfounded rumour or inspired guesswork but hard fact. John Moir, whose company, the BSA Company, was trying to buy in order to find an acceptable channel through which to exercise its Charter in Malawi, passed on to D.C. Scott, Johnston's report to the BSA Board of Directors on his scheme for Company rule in Malawi.[33] From that moment in 1890, Scott and Hetherwick campaigned against Company rule. They also conceived a deep suspicion of Johnston. After all, he had wanted to hand the Shire Highlands over to the Portuguese; he had talked of subsidizing Swahili leaders in Malawi like the Jumbe of Nkhotakota, to the missionaries a notorious slaver, and now he seemed to be an advocate of Company rule although an imperial official. Johnston was the servant of two masters, a thing held to be impossible in the Bible. Which master did he really serve was the pressing question for the missionaries.

During the years 1889 to 1894 Johnston appeared to swing back and forth in his loyalty between Downing Street and Groote Schuur. Professor Oliver is extremely persuasive in his argument[34] that this was only an apparent inconsistency. He insists that at all times Johnston was committed to the pursuit of a single vision of British power in Africa. However, in reply, it must be said that even if this had been explained to D.C. Scott it would have been no help. The very fact that Rhodes and the

---

[31] See Chapter 4.
[32] All the directors of the ALC were Free Church men.
[33] Johnston to Rhodes, 7 June 1893, Sal. Rhod. Archives, CT/1/16/4/1.
[34] Oliver, *Sir Harry Johnston,* Chapter 6.

Cape were possible parts of Johnston's vision for Malawi's future meant that these two men, Scott and Johnston, with their genuine and at times possessive love for the country of the Lake could never really be in agreement. Scott and his colleagues could accept neither Cape colonial attitudes nor Chartered Company rule; a combination was unthinkable.

Throughout their campaign to maintain a direct link between the Protectorate and the UK Government, the missionaries hammered away at these two themes. Their attitude can be summed up by two extracts from articles by Clement Scott:

> a Chartered Company is not a government and never can be. To be ruled by such is to be ruled for commercial ends by absentee directors and shareholders whose real interests are only served by tangible dividends.[35]

> Very little ground in Cape Colony belongs to the natives and no advance has been made without some Kaffir war. We have here very different antecedents and very different relations, and we look forward to the settlement of questions in this land without wars and without bloodshed.[36]

Possibly the lobbying and protest mounted by the missionaries and their friends in Scotland would not have succeeded but for the fact that Salisbury, as we have seen, was not in any case very enthusiastic about the Company having anything to do with the Protectorate. Be that as it may, the Order in Council of May 14, 1891 set up the Nyasaland Districts as an Imperial Protectorate separate from the Chartered territory in northern Zambezia. Admittedly this was a Protectorate financed by the Company but it was not in its control.

Johnston saw this decision as a victory for the Blantyre missionaries:

> remember that it was mainly Scott and Hetherwick who balked the scheme in 1890 of all British Central Africa coming under the Company's Charter.... In August-October 1890 I proposed to place the whole of British Central Africa under the Company's Charter, to be governed by an Anglo-Indian officer as the Company's administrator,

---

[35] *LWBCA*, October 1890.
[36] *LWBCA* August 1891.

> the Crown or Foreign Office exercising a supreme control over the Administration in a manner similar to that exercised south of the Zambezi.... Somehow or other this memorandum on the future administration of B.C.A. got communicated to John Moir who promptly showed it to the Scottish missionary bodies. They took flame at the idea of being governed by a wicked Company and at once commenced to worry the F.O. with the result that Lord Salisbury decided to cut off Nyasaland into a special protectorate - he even had leanings towards making the whole of British Central Africa a protectorate.[37]

In awarding this accolade to Scott, Johnston would seem to be clearly affirming that he had been in favour of Company rule at that time. It was certainly as a Company man that he was seen by the missionaries when he arrived back in Malawi in July 1891. This did not augur well for the future relations of the mission and the Boma, as the Administration of the Protectorate came to be known in both Nyanja and the Protectorate slang, despite the frenzy of Union Jack-making in the Blantyre manse in 1889. The relationship between the two institutions up to the departure of D.C. Scott in 1898 were epitomized by Sharpe when acting Commissioner in 1894. He wrote to the Foreign Office:

> Mr Commissioner Johnston in his dispatches advised that there would be no permanent and satisfactory state of things with regard to this mission until two missionaries, the Rev. D.C. Scott and the Rev. Alexander Hetherwick were removed from the country ... I am sorry to say that this mission has entirely returned to its old practices ... the missionaries are taking a course that makes them appear in the eyes of the natives of this Protectorate as an Opposition Party to H.M. Administration.[38]

Whether as "Opposition" or in any other role, the influence of the Blantyre Mission was felt only in what is now the Southern Region of Malawi and the Ntcheu District of the Central Region. However, since it was not until the turn of the century that effective control by the Boma came into being beyond this area, Sharpe's statement holds good.

---

[37] Johnston to Rhodes, 7 June 1893, Sal. Rhod. Archives, CT/1/13/4/1.
[38] Sharpe to Kimberly, 31 Oct. 1894, FO 2/67.

This opposition to the Administration on the part of the mission has been described by Professor A.J. Hanna in his book, *The Beginnings of Nyasaland and North-Eastern Rhodesia*. However, in his discussion he concentrated on a few months in 1892-1893, when the atmosphere can only be described as hysterical and certain charges against individuals in the Administration, and the Administration it-self, were made on the basis of rumour, and were clearly refuted by Johnston, though even in that period by no means all the complaints or the rumours were refutable. Professor Roland Oliver in his biography of Johnston,[39] also discusses this conflict with a little more sympathy for the missionaries' point of view, though he too tends to dwell on that particularly hostile period. This is accounted for, at least in part, by the fact that in the official papers in the Public Records Office, it is this period which is most clearly reflected, and neither author consulted the mission material in Edinburgh and Zomba. This prevented them from appreciating the long-term nature of the mission's critical approach to British authority. Above all, these two authors do not take seriously enough the reality of the threat of Company rule, nor Johnston's support for it.

As we have already seen Johnston planned a Company administration for all British Central Africa in 1890 and regretted its failure to achieve fruition. In 1893 in the April edition of *Life and Work in British Central Africa,* Scott reported a speech of Rhodes in the United Kingdom in which he said that he had an understanding with the British Government that the Company would gradually relieve them of their responsibilities in the Protectorate.

In the early months of that year Johnston was again moving in favour of such a transference. At least that is what he seems to be saying to Rhodes in a long letter sent from Chinde in June of that year. This letter was not included in any dispatch to the Foreign Office, and I can find no reference to it by either Hanna or Oliver. He begins:

> I don't think you have ever realised the bitter hatred borne you by these Scotch missionaries of Blantyre. They hate you because you are an Englishman, because you threaten to overshadow their own petty meddling and muddling with grander schemes that will outshine

---

[39] Oliver, *Sir Harty Johnston,* Chapter 6.

mission work in popular favour. Remember that it was mainly Scott and Hetherwick who balked the scheme of 1890 of all B.C.A. coming under the Company's Charter. They are now up and at it again and are the most serious enemies you possess.[40]

He then goes on to review the attitudes of the other missions saying that Livingstonia was neutral; the London Missionary Society, friendly neutral; and the Universities' Mission, the Dutch Reformed Mission (from Cape Synod) as well as the Roman Catholics were classed by him as friendly to the Company. However, he warns Rhodes that Blantyre can influence the Foreign Office more than all the others together because they are the only people with a newspaper in the whole of British Central Africa. He then goes on to rehearse the policies he has pursued and their carrying out from 1890 onwards. He says that at different times he has felt first the Company and then the Foreign Office was best suited to rule. His most recent decision he says is that Company rule would be best for the future of British Central Africa. How to deal with Blantyre was the problem, and then follows the most extraordinary part of the letter:

> A reconciliation with Scott and Co. is hopeless. From December to March I tried every means of making friends with him and Hetherwick, but it was all of no avail and they are now worse than ever because the idea of the Company extending itself over the Protectorate is coming over them as a grave possibility. Therefore if the Government accept the agreement which you and I were agreed as the result of our conference, I must propose to meet the hostility of the Blantyre missionaries ... I intend to fight them in two ways: by starting my own newspaper *The British Central Africa Gazette* (not ostensibly a Government organ but used as the drain [?] for all Government communications) and by affecting a religious cleavage at Blantyre. You will notice in a paragraph I have marked in the May number of the Mission paper that Blantyre Mission is already beginning to quarrel with the other Scotch mission - that of the Free Church. I propose however to seek for support rather with the already friendly Universities' Mission ... Accordingly the other day I sent (partly from Administration funds) a cheque for £35.7s.0d. to Archdeacon Maples towards the building fund of Likoma Cathedral. This I made up as follows:

---

[40] Johnston to Rhodes, 7 June 1893, Sal. Rhod. Archives, CT/1/16/4/1.

£25	from the Honourable Cecil J. Rhodes
£1.1.0.	Dr Rutherford Harris
£1.1.0.	Sir Charles Metcalfe

besides a sum of £8.3.0d. composed of small subscriptions most of which were collected by me. About £30 of this amount is really contributed by the Administration, but to send it as a plain donation from that source would look rather too much like a bribe so I have attributed the main origin of the money to C.J.R. [Cecil Rhodes] and others. Please explain to Harris and Metcalfe so that they may not be surprised at being thanked for their guineas.

But I am going to do more than this provided the F.O. accepts our arrangement of May 8 and we have to fight the Blantyre Mission. I am going to build an English Church at Blantyre at a cost of about £600, which I can raise by subscription local and external and establish the Universities Mission here.

The threat of Company rule was always real until 1894 when the final break between Rhodes and Johnston came. The British Treasury finally decided in July of that year to begin the support of the Administration of the Protectorate by grants-in-aid.

The decisive change, however, did not mean the end of tension between the two institutions, because although the fear of Company rule was a serious element in that relationship, there was from the beginning another very deep cleft between Boma and the mission. This was a divergence in their understanding of African society and the relation of Europeans to it.

The personality of David Clement Scott dominated the mission during this period and though his influence waned after his departure in 1898, Alexander Hetherwick, his successor, never quite shook free from it.

As we have seen[41] Scott came to Blantyre still firmly committed to a view of Africa and the task of Christian missions there which was essentially old-fashioned. His ideas were much more typical of the Palmerston era, closely related to those David Livingstone and Henry Venn, the great secretary of the Church Missionary Society. The attitudes of that age have been summed up by Ronald Robinson and John Gallagher thus:

---

[41] See Chapter 4.

the trader and missionary would liberate the producers of Africa and Asia. The pull of the industrial economy, the prestige of British ideas and technology would draw them also into the Great Commercial Republic of the world. In time the "progressive" native groups within the decaying societies of the Orient would burst the feudal shackles and liberalise their political and economic life. Thus the early Victorians hoped to help the Oriental, the African and the Aborigine to help themselves. Many would be called and all would be chosen: the reforming Turkish pasha and the enlightened mandarin, babus who had read Mill, samurai who understood Bentham, and the slaving kings of Africa who would respond to the Gospel and turn to legitimate trade.[42]

This very attitude had strong elements of arrogance in it, yet it did very often lead to reasonably good relations between men of European and other stock, since the others were all seen as potential English gentlemen. Professor Ajayi[43] and Messrs. Robinson and Gallagher[44] chart a decided change in British attitudes from about 1870 onwards. The view grew that perhaps people of the other continents were essentially different, or at least were much more deeply different than had been thought. This could have been a healthy attitude but for the fact that it was almost always combined with the concept of the inferiority of these different peoples.

Perhaps Scotland is always a little behind the times, for not only did Scott hold the older attitude, but it seemed still strong in Scotland in the mid-nineties. This is seen in Scott's writing about Mungo Chisuse's two years training in the printing works of Edinburgh's famous House of Nelson.

> The Messrs. Nelson received Chisuse into their well-known printing establishment, and treated him with kindness for which we cannot be grateful enough. He was introduced not only to the beautiful touch of the great firm's workmanship, but to the stalwart band of Scottish workers who took to Chisuse as he took to them. This fine manly intercourse is especially good for our mission material. It

---

[42] Robinson and Gallagher, *Africa and the Victorians,* pp. 3-4.
[43] J.F.A. Ajayi, *Christian Missions in Nigeria, 1841-1891,* (London: Longmans, 1965), pp. 233-273.
[44] Robinson and Gallagher, *Africa and the Victorians,* pp. 1-26.

brings about an inter-racial communion without in any way the dispensational difference and respect. Mutual respect is the lesson we so much need to learn at this time - and we say nothing in the inter-relation of races as to which side holds most of the dispensation power.[45]

However, in 1914 we find a friend of Hetherwick warning that racial feelings were by that time so strong in the cities of Scotland that it would not be a good policy to continue bringing Africans to Scotland for training as it would be a hurtful and not a helpful experience.[46]

From 1881 when Scott arrived in Malawi until the day he left, he attempted to work on the principles associated with Venn, which already had received in West Africa severe set-backs within the area of the work of Venn's own society. The Niger River Diocese[47] and the Sierra Leone Native Pastorate,[48] the most outstanding pieces of work based on Venn's belief in the capacity of Africans to be independent and assume authority, had ended disastrously. There were other factors involved in these failures, but the, by then widespread, idea in Britain of the inferiority of African people was the key factor.[49]

D.C. Scott saw Africans as people. He saw African society as something valid; something to be built on and not something to be destroyed. He believed individual Africans to be capable of absorbing Western culture which was neither essentially alien to them nor something that could only be open to their distant descendants. In the August and November issues of the mission magazine in 1888, Scott wrote of the future as lying with the development of "native power" towards a civilized Christian

---

[45] *LWBCA*, December 1897.

[46] F. Morrison Bryce to Hetherwick, 4 April 1914, Hetherwick Files, Malawi Archives.

[47] Ajayi, *Christian Missions in Nigeria, 1841-1891,* Chapter 8.

[48] H. R. Lynch, "The Sierra Leone Native Pastorate", *Journal of African History,* vol. 5, no. 3, pp. 395-413.

[49] Neill, *A History of Christian Missions,* pp. 259-260, 377-378. K. Latourette, *A History of the Expansion of Christianity,* (New York: Harper and Row, 1937-1945), vol. 5, pp. 37-45. Both these modern histories of missions fail to deal with the existence of this growing racial feeling and its impact on Christian missions.

society, and emphasized that this growth was to be "a growth of the community upon its traditional base." Western civilization and Christianity were to be brought into a creative relationship with African society and not simply displace it; a new Africa was to be the result. He saw the role of the white man to be that of a helper to aid the African people forward in that direction. These ideas are of a piece with those described by Robinson and Gallagher.[50]

This view of the role of Europeans in Africa received its most explicit statement by Scott when the Commissioner talked of introducing Indian settlers to fulfil roles he believed the African incapable of fulfilling. Of this D.C. Scott wrote:

> we believe it to be fatal to the true interests of the country and of the people who live in it both black and white. Africa for the Africans has been our policy from the first, and we believe that God has given this country into our hands that we may train its peoples how to develop its marvellous resources for themselves.[51]

To most Europeans in Zambezia, Africans were "niggers" or "Kaffirs", so Scott's appeals for brotherliness and oneness in the Church, which the mission magazine published again and again in the 1890s, seemed to them just nonsense. There were some more reasonable Europeans in Malawi, Commissioner Johnston being one of them, though his attitude was still very different from Scott's. Johnston believed that in three generations it might be possible for the African to assimilate modern culture. He admitted that the "clothed negro" was, from the Administration's point of view, an improvement on the untutored tribesman, but was otherwise scathing about the products of the missions. He could accept that a man like Mungo Chisuse could become a printer, but could not accept the reality of his Christianity or his moral integrity.[52]

More important from the point of view of immediate policy was the fact that this difference in attitude extended to African society as well as to

---

[50] *Ibid*

[51] *LWBCA* January 1895.

[52] H.H. Johnston, *British Central Africa*, (London: Methuen, 1897), the chapters entitled "Missionaries and "Natives of British Central Africa".

African individuals. By 1891 the Scottish missions had lived with the chiefs and people of Malawi without the benefit of a European administration for fifteen years - Scott personally for ten years. The missionaries had found this possible primarily because, as Scott said, the people were a "constitutional" people, working out their social and communal problems through the *mlandu* according to their traditions. To Scott and his colleagues it was the Arab and Swahili visitors who were the real source of trouble. To Johnston, however, the Yao chiefs were "robbers" and "inveterate slavers", to be dealt with before the Protectorate could be made real. Indeed, while only his first visit to Malawi, when still Consul at Mozambique, he made up a list of chiefs that would have to be dealt with by any administration.[53] These were nearly all Yao, many of them well known to the Blantyre missionaries for over a decade; the very men from whom the Scots got their ideas of African constitutional behaviour. Johnston later in his dispatches did not see this at all and is scathing about Hetherwick's calling Mitochi of Chiradzulu "an old friend". He raked up the old pre-MacDonald clash with Mitochi as evidence of enmity and said that the missionaries are simply employing any stick with which to beat the administration.[54] Despite the clashes in the past with Mitochi and Chikumbu, relations had been built up by the missionaries on the basis of traditional *mlandu* with most chiefs in the Southern Region, including these old enemies as well as with the Maseko Ngoni. D.C. Scott felt that this way of the *mlandu was* the only possible route the Administration to pursue, especially as it was so weak militarily.

In the dispatch about Mitochi and in others, Johnston reiterated his ability to get on with the other missions as proof of the peculiarly bad character of the Blantyre Mission. But it must be pointed out that, throughout the period of his Commissionership, his authority was only nominal in the areas worked by the other missions; it was only the Blantyre Mission that was in day to day contact with the Boma, and had any direct experience of its administration. Dr Eric Stokes has argued convincingly that even had the Yao chiefs not in many cases been guilty

---

[53] Johnston to FO, 29 December 1891, FO 84/2114,
[54] Johnston to Lister, 4 June 1893, FO 2/54.

of slave trading, Johnston would have destroyed their authority.[55] Johnston's aim was the creation of a Crown Colony form of government whether under Company or Imperial auspices.

> His view was put most clearly in a memorandum he submitted on the future of the Oil Rivers Protectorate which he was to cite a few months later as a rough model for Nyasaland.[56]

Apart from this evidence there are several references in Johnston's dispatches about the Protectorate soon becoming a Crown Colony.[57] The authority that Johnston was given by the United Kingdom Government was limited and his instructions were not phrased so as to leave him free to develop them.[58] Officially Johnston had no more than control over the external affairs of the chiefly states, and general authority over all British citizens and other foreigners in the area. The internal administration of the tribes was to be left to the traditional authorities. This was in fact the kind of "protection" for which the missionaries had been campaigning, as well as being the sort of rule in Africa that the radicals in Britain supported, people like Mary Kingsley and E.D. Morel. It was still in effect the Palmerstonian approach to British influence in Africa.

Despite this, almost immediately after arriving as Commissioner, Johnston began his campaigns to knock out the Yao chiefs. Each campaign was explained on the grounds of the needs of destroying the slave trade. Sometimes it has been suggested that the Blantyre Mission's criticism of these campaigns applied only to actions against Yao chiefs who were in some sense their clients.[59] But from a careful perusal of *LWBCA* it is clear that they were in some degree critical of all Johnston's campaigns except those against Makanjila, Kawinga and Mlozi. Many of the chiefs such as Mitochi and Chikumbu could by no stretch of the

---

[55] E. Stokes, "Malawi Political Systems and the Introduction of Colonial Rule", *The Zambesian Past,* E. Stokes and R. Brown, (eds.), (Manchester: The University Press, 1965).

[56] *Ibid*

[57] E.g. Johnston to Roseberry, 31 January 1893, no. 6 CA, FO 2/45.

[58] FO to Johnston, 24 March 1891, FO Pr. 6178, no. 9.

[59] E.g. in the discussion on the papers presented to the Lusaka Conference on the history of the Central African Peoples in 1963.

imagination be thought of as clients of the mission, and later as in the case of the Boma campaigns against Chikuse and Mpezeni, there could be no such claims made.

However, it was not only the Blantyre Mission that was sceptical about these campaigns. Dr Wordsworth Poole was a medical officer with the Administration, and excerpts from his journals and letters have been put together by Dr Michael Gelfand. One such extract shows a mocking scepticism which Gelfand seems not to notice. Poole says:

> In six more days the expedition starts and I'm going with it - Hurrah! it is going to be a great show. That is, whether it actually is or is not a great show, it will be made out one on paper. Reams will be written about it and it will be boomed at home. Why a private secretary and his typewriter are going with us. What does it matter what really happens? Nobody at home knows. A fine report is sent in. The Foreign Office says what a smart little chap the Commissioner is. The Indian Army officials say: Well that chap Edwards must have something in him. What terrible odds. So he gets a D.S.O. and brevet majority and we all get medals.. [60]

And again, in a letter to his aunt, he says of the campaigns and the dangerous threat of Yao power that made them necessary: "Yet after capturing 50 towns and combating many thousands, the fact that five of our men were killed gives the show away in the end doesn't it?"[61] This attitude is even more clear in the parts of the Poole papers which Dr Gelfand did not include in his edition, though they are quoted by H.A.C. Cairns in his book *Prelude to Imperialism*.

> [Poole] wrote that if the Africans refused to pay hut tax for protection they did not want "there is war, and we kill their men and burn their houses and collar their cattle and ivory and cloth and beads and their women whom we call slaves and to whom we give papers of manu-mission, which papers are found again afterwards thrown away in heaps, for obviously a paper saying so and so has

---

[60] M. Gelfand (ed.), *Doctor on Lake Nyasa*, (Salisbury: privately printed, 1961), p. 40.
[61] *Ibid*, 57.

been freed by me this day - signed so and so, is not really much use to a free woman."[62]

This sounds like one of the "hysterical and unfounded" Blantyre complaints but in fact it was made by a member of Johnston's staff. Indeed, Johnston himself says something very revealing in a dispatch when he was complaining of the behaviour of the *askari* of a German anti-slavery expedition passing through the protectorate.

> Of course to call this an Anti-Slavery Expedition is one of the many hypocritical devices which it seems necessary to use now-a-days amongst all European nations for any attempt at the conquest of savage countries.[63]

Whether it would have been possible for a Commissioner to carry out his task along the lines of Johnston's original instructions appears not to matter, since the Commissioner seemed intent on destroying the Yao "robber" chiefs and setting up a form of administration similar to that outlined in his memorandum on the Oil Rivers Protectorate.

These operations led to the Commissioner taking the land of the defeated chiefs as Crown land. This land was then held to be leasable by him to planters or others. It was both the campaign against the chiefs and the resulting land decisions that provoked Scott's protest. Although Scott exaggerates when he speaks of settling matters "without striking a blow", his concept of what the Protectorate's administration should be like was closer to Johnston's legal remit than was the Commissioner's behaviour.

> Our contention is that if the Europeans take the land they practically enslave the native population. There is no law to help the native in his distress; but there is power to put into the European's hands to force the native to work. We have heard it said, "a good thing too", followed by invective against the native character but we beg to say that the native does work and work hard, and that the invectives are cowardly and untrue; and we uphold that no civilised power can come into a country more especially under Christian promises, and turn the natives into slaves in their own holdings ... we cannot treat

---

[62] Cairns, *Prelude to Imperialism*, p. 237.
[63] Johnston to Anderson, 21 January 1893, Confidential, FO 2/54.

> the land as conquered country, and we must in every case of confiscation or annexation have the very best proof to show that no other way than fighting the natives was possible. We have all along believed and believe still that the British Government could rule and develop this whole African Empire in all questions really native, without striking a blow.
>
> We grant that it needs endless tact and patience and a real grip of native language, life, customs and history, but this is obtainable; Africa won't be ruled without trouble and much "palaver, but what country is?[64]

This was no repetition of some rumour about the morals of an administrative officer or complaint about an illegal arrest, of which Johnston makes the mission opposition appear to consist. It has to be admitted that such inaccuracies did creep into the exchanges in 1893 notably in the May issue of *LWBCA*. However, these were aberrations in the main mission argument. The Commissioner's own integrity and judgement could also be impugned if the only knowledge of his thoughts and attitudes were some quotations from his dispatches in that tense year. Professor Oliver says that,

> He did not confine himself, like Lister, to the comment that "a duty on missionaries would be useful - Scotch ones to pay double, with an extra tax for Presbyterians in any form"; and even in counter attack his shafts went nearer the mark than those of his opponents.[65]

Some shafts can hardly be called "near the mark"; for example, when he referred to Scott and Hetherwick saying,

> These men quarrelled with and harassed Consul Foot, Acting Consul Goodrich, Consul Hawes, Acting Consul Buchanan and have from the earliest days of my administration pursued me with the same animosity. The reason being that they do not care a scrap for the spread of religion, but aim at making themselves great political powers in the land. Foolish partisans at home puffed up Mr Scott with the idea that he was going to be made Commissioner for

---

[64] *LWBCA* December 1894.
[65] Oliver, *Sir Harry Johnston*, p. 211.

> Nyasaland and he never forgave me for receiving the appointment instead.[66]

The attack he is specifically complaining about in this dispatch was in the mission magazine of April 1893 and was, in fact, an attack on the continuing threat of Company rule and directed primarily against Rhodes and his claim to the reversion of Nyasaland. Johnston appeared only in the article in so far as he was Rhodes' agent - which he indubitably was - though he was not simply the tool of Rhodes that the missionaries feared. Surely if Goschen, the Chancellor of the Exchequer in the Government which appointed him could complain that he was never clear what Johnston did for Rhodes and what for the Crown,[67] Scott deserves some sympathy for his suspicions.

Professor Oliver in his discussion of Johnston's relations with the mission shows that, like many observers he has misunderstood the attitude of Scott and his colleagues when he says:

> And yet if their attitude had been more responsible and more constructive, there is little doubt that the Blantyre missionaries could have pointed out and helped in the solution of some real injustices in the operation of the new regime.[68]

The nationalist parties in Zambia and Malawi replied to their white-liberal critics in the 1950s who complained that they did nothing to help make the Federation a more just and liberal state, that their opposition was totally against Federation per se, so these questions were peripheral to their objective of ending Federation. This is a close parallel to the Blantyre attitude towards the administration in its early years. They wanted a totally different style of administration. The whole structure of the life of the Shire Highlands, within which the mission had begun to set roots, was being torn apart by the new Administration with its policy of "dealing" with the Yao "robber" chiefs. The mission had pressed for a Protectorate to defend the Shire Highlands from the Arab and the Portuguese but the protector was becoming a destroyer from their point of view. Clement Scott summed up the mission attitude succinctly in his

---

[66] Johnston to Lister, 4 June 1893, FO 2/54.

[67] Robinson and Gallagher, *Africa and the Victorians*, p. 249.

[68] Oliver, *Sir Harry Johnston*, p. 212.

review of Johnston's book, *British Central Africa, in* the mission journal. The review was favourable in the main but for Johnston's chapter on "The Natives of British Central Africa", which Scott felt to be "slanderous". But the most significant comment was that made on the author's description of the pacification of the Protectorate. Scott said,

> To our mind Sir Harry's "wars" were not always so absolutely necessary. The country was and had been steadily progressing without them. It was not to make a state that Sir Harry Johnston was sent out but to deliver from Portuguese occupation a state already made.[69]

Taken out of the context of Scott's thought expressed in his correspondence and in the mission journal, that phrase might be taken to mean he wanted a missionary theocracy; but it is clear that was not what he meant. He meant that slowly and painfully a new African society was emerging out of contact with the missionaries and other European agencies, and that it could have continued to grow if only Britain had held the ring to keep out both the Portuguese and the Swahili Arabs. Perhaps this idea which we have called the Pahnerstonian concept of African development, was about thirty years too late, but it was Scott's passionate belief.

This suspicion of the Administration's wars continued because of a difference of principle and not because of personal pique. When the Maseko Ngoni were crushed and Nkosi Gomani executed in 1896,[70] and again when the Ngoni of Nkosi Mpezeni were "pacified" by the Administration's forces two years later, the Blantyre Mission through its magazine queried the Administration's policy. In both cases they agreed that at the end a situation had been created that meant force was inevitable as a solution, but they asked if that situation need have been created at all, and why was Gomani killed like a criminal?[71] Two years earlier, when the Mulanje chief Mkanda had to be "dealt with" at the time of the BSACo attack on the Ndebele in Rhodesia, Scott linked the two together in an article in the mission magazine. His scepticism

---

[69] *LWBCA* August-December 1897.

[70] *LWBCA* December 1896.

[71] *Ibid*

harmonizes with that of the Administration doctor, Poole, and with that of liberal observers of the BSACo relations with Lobengula:

> We do no find in history a people who loved their conquerors, it would be unnatural, and we do not look for it to be reversed in Africa.
>
> Can we thrash a man and expect him to thank us for it, and have we not practically thrashed the native out of power and possession, and for no tangible reason; our war-cry is the slave-trader, but the slave-trade has little to do with it; the real motive power is gold thirst and land grabbing.
>
> The unjust scene of blood in Matebeleland was to protect the Mashona slaves. Our late attack on Mkhanda was reported at home as an attack on the slave trade. Where then are our merits for gratitude which we grumble at not getting?[72]

This terrible sense of "let-down", of having encouraged something which has turned sour on maturing, runs through the mission's opposition to the early taxation policy of the administration. Hetherwick, in a very careful article, pointed out that at six shillings per person it was economically outrageous.[73] What was more important, he insisted, was the fact that no attempt had been made to explain the tax and to gain popular consent. He reiterated Scott's principal theme that the way of the *mlandu* would have to be followed if there was to be a peaceful and happy development. There was also, in the opposition to these taxes, the fear that the mission would lose its good relations with many of the chiefs, who bitterly resented these impositions by an administration they had often been persuaded to accept by the mission. The taxation applied only to the Highlands and the Makololo country, so that it did bear heavily on Blantyre alone. This dilemma was clearly expressed in Henry Scott's[74] reply to the Zomba Collector over Malemia's refusal to pay taxes. H.E. Scott wrote:

---

[72] *LWBCA* September 1896.

[73] *LWBCA* November 1891.

[74] The Reverend Dr H.E. Scott, doctor and minister, successor to Hetherwick as head of Domasi Mission, later founder of the Zomba station of the Mission and in 1908 successor to D.C. Scott at Kikuyu, Kenya.

> In 1889 the then head of this mission station was present when Mr Buchanan, acting for H.M.G. urged upon this chief and his people to accept the English flag in lieu of the Portuguese. At the same time Mr Buchanan laid much stress upon the promise that the former did not involve taxation ... The Domasi Mission thus gave a pledge based on the assurances of the representative of H.M.G. that they, Malemia's people, would not be taxed.[75]

In this field of taxation, a small victory was gained of the kind asked for by Professor Oliver, when the next year the tax was cut by Johnston to three shillings; also when in 1892 the Commissioner held conferences in Blantyre and Zomba at which planters, missionaries, chiefs and headmen could hear the Boma's case and put forward their ideas and complaints.[76] Dr Hanna, in his discussion of Johnston's taxation policy, emphasized the need for some check on his rule:

> Most important of all, the need for Foreign Office approval was salutary as the only existing check on what would otherwise have been, however well intended, a personal autocracy.[77]

It was this kind of check that through their "opposition" role the Blantyre Mission tried to carry out. By 1898, what had the "opposition" of the Mission achieved? We have seen that Johnston thought that their opposition had been decisive in keeping the Company out of Malawi, both in 1890-91 and later. This would probably not have been the case but for Salisbury's own feelings; but this can be called a real success and one of permanent value.

To this we must add the minor but real gain of having the rate of taxation cut by fifty per cent. The attempt the Commissioner made to consult with, and not simply to dictate, to the chiefs and headmen in 1892 and 1893 over taxation policy was also a small gain.

However, by 1898, the main plank in the platform of Scott and Hetherwick was clearly lost. There was by then no chance at all of a "Pahnerstonian" form of Protectorate; Johnston had brought the area

---

[75] H.E. Scott to Cameron, Asst. Collector, Zomba, 19 August 1892, Hetherwick Correspondence, Mal Arch.

[76] Johnston to Roseberry, 12 January 1893, no. 21 CA, FO 2/54.

[77] Hanna, *The Beginnings of Nyasaland and North-Eastern Rhodesia*, p. 224.

that was effectively in the Boma's control under a form of Crown Colony government, though that legal status had not been achieved.[78] The role of the Blantyre Mission as an opposition to the Boma changed after 1898.

This was for a number of reasons. First, the Administration expanded its sphere from 1898 onwards and began to operate effectively in what is now the Central Region of Malawi and after 1904 in the Northern Region. Thus the relationship between the two institutions was no longer the simple one it had been up till then when the only effective power of the Administration was in the area worked by Blantyre. Second, in 1898 David Clement Scott was forced by ill-health to resign and leave Malawi for good. The headship of the mission then passed to Alexander Hetherwick. This was not simply the interchange of two men. The end of 1898 marked a profound change because most of the staff who had been peculiarly D.C. Scott's followers, both in their approach to their work and their attitude toward the African people, had also left the scene, notably, Henry Henderson, Dr W.A. Scott and Dr John Bowie. There still remained H.E. Scott, John McIlwain, the carpenter and Dr Neil Macvicar who were close to D.C. Scott, but none were really in a position to challenge Hetherwick, who indeed, soon got rid of Macvicar.[79] The other members of staff until the arrival of the Reverend Robert Napier in 1910 were all secondary figures.

Hetherwick was D.C. Scott's right-hand man, but after Scott's departure the real differences between the two men became more clear. Hetherwick never achieved the close personal relations with Africans that Scott did,[80] and never was so passionately and understandingly negrophile as was Scott. Now that active resistance to the Boma was ended, he continued in the role of being a spokesman for Africans who had no very effective way of speaking for themselves, but this was, in Hetherwick's case, very much a matter of knowing what was good for the African even if the African did not.

---

[78] See Stokes, "Malawi Political Systems and the Introduction of Colonial Rule", Stokes and Brown, (eds.), *The Zambesian Past,* pp. 352-375.

[79] See Chapter 6.

[80] see Chapters 4 and 6.

Hetherwick was a man of integrity with a passion for justice, but he lacked the imaginative sympathy which was so dominantly a characteristic of D.C. Scott. Hetherwick, in a letter at the time of Scott's death,[81] is critical of Scott's being too trusting towards Africans. This criticism is symbolic of the difference between the two men. Scott's thought was poetic and imaginative in form and not at all schematic. It is, therefore, difficult at times to understand in precise detail. His use of the image of Ham for the African, as, for example, in his specially published sermon on the anniversary of Blantyre Mission in 1901,[82] did not mean that for him the African was destined by God to any inferior role in the world; the whole mass of his writing in *Life and Work in British Central Africa,* and such of his letters and sermons that survive show this. Three examples of his writing can be taken to characterize his extraordinary vision of the African and his role in the world. First, there is an extract from the anniversary sermon of 1901 where he is mentioning individuals whom he knew and were for him representatives of the Church in Africa,

> [Chisuse],[83] the civilised, the best fitted to meet and interpret the incoming civilisation ... Cedric Kalaliche, scholarly and capable, Miss Beck's right-hand man, a perfect teacher. John Gray Kufa,[84] the physician, Dr Macvicar's ideal of a man. Brave, he stood unarmed in the mission gateway in Lomweland against a yelling crowd of natives with their spears and guns.[85]

J.G. Kufa is an ideal man, not an ideal mission product or an ideal African.

Second, from his long review of Johnston's *British Central Africa in* the August/December 1897 edition of the mission magazine, two poems he wrote in his highly personal "metaphysical" style as counter to Johnston's chapters on the peoples of Central Africa and their customs can also be taken to illustrate his attitude.

---

[81] Hetherwick to F. Morrison Bryce, 1 October 1907, Hetherwick Files, Mal Arch

[82] D.C. Scott, Livingstonia, Blantyre Anniversary Sermon, 1901.

[83] See chapter 3, note 34.

[84] Later hanged by the British for his relationship to John Chilembwe in 1915.

[85] Source lost.

The Kaffir

There's a soupcon of centuries old
That unravels the mystery
Of a Kingdom once bought and sold.

For his smile is of beaten out gold
And in gold that is brave and free
There's a soupcon of centuries old.

He's a chalice of kingly mould
Lily wrought; hieroglyph see
Of a Kingdom once bought and sold.

Though the judgements that on him rolled
And engulfed him in misery
There's a soupcon of centuries old.

No robes on his shoulder fold
But the earth yields him tribute free
Of a Kingdom once bought and sold.

He's a king, though no more he hold
The sceptre; in him we agree
There's a soupcon of centuries old
Of a Kingdom once bought and sold.

Is the African a Sphinx?

Mysterious? Across the sand,
In noon-tide glare, by hot winds fanned,
There gazes motionless, the Sphinx,
No Angel guesses what she thinks,
From God's gates to Samarkand, Mysterious.

Dark Ham, by fifty centuries tanned,
Stands tried, sublime. His race has spanned
The age-long world. The world's sun sinks
In desert deeps; they light their links
And smile, ranked in God's starry hand, Mysterious.

Having lived through the experiences he did in Africa, D.C. Scott was not indulging in naive dreams of the "noble savage"; yet in these poems there is a hint of glorying in Africanness that is reminiscent of the "negritude" poems of Senghor.

The third example of his writing is one which is extremely daring theologically and yet, I believe, it enshrines the idea which, though never rationally worked out, underlies all his work.

> But in order to put down the slave trade you must have a proper doctrine of humanity, a true appreciation of the slave. Just as Christ took upon Him the form of a slave long ago, so He takes upon Him the form of Africa today. Africa bears the sins of the world's rulers. How long are we as a nation going to lay our selfishness, our meanness, our falsehood, our lusts, yea, and the whole burden of our sins upon this Lamb of God?[86]

The African as a Christ figure is a daring theological concept indeed; yet it is, I believe, central to any understanding of Scott. This difference between D.C. Scott and Hetherwick led to a decisive alteration in the relations of the mission to the Administration. This difference was not simply one which followed automatically from the new, stable political situation. The change was much more profound and meant that the mission was now part of the imperial establishment.

The mission continued to criticize actions of the Boma, to press for recognition of African rights in many spheres, and what was new, it did so with an increasingly close co-operation with Livingstonia. However, the "opposition" that Sharpe complained of in Scott's day[87] became more of an acceptable "Loyal Opposition", basic criticisms of the whole colonial structure no longer being part of its function. The role that the mission came to play under Hetherwick's leadership was much more the role that Professor Oliver criticized them for not playing in the 1890s: that of accepting the overall pattern of affairs and striving to correct specific injustices within it.[88]

---

[86] *LWBCA* August-December 1897.

[87] *Ibid*

[88] Oliver, *Sir Harty Johnston,* p. 212.

From the departure of D.C. Scott in 1898 till the end of our period in 1926, Alexander Hetherwick was in a sense the Blantyre Mission. Apart from Robert Napier who came to Blantyre in 1910 and was so tragically killed by German *askari* in 1918, there was no one on the staff who had any kind of status or position independent of this veteran missionary. The length of his service, his knowledge of both Yao and Nyanja, his intimacy with so many of the chiefs whose fathers he had also known, gave him enormous prestige with the settlers and the Administration as well. Just how much of an "establishment" figure he was became clear in 1908, when Alfred Sharpe, who had once called for Scott's and Hetherwick's removal from the country as vital for the creation of good government, appointed him a member of the newly formed Legislative Council. The seat he took was the one set apart to represent missionary and native interests.

A more extraordinary development was the role played by Hetherwick in the setting up and working of the Blantyre Chamber of Commerce, an organisation of white settlers, both planters and traders, which was established to look after their economic and political interests, primarily by lobbying the administration.

To be fair to Hetherwick, this step was not a simple capitulation, he did not simply go over to the other side as it were. In the complicated labour and land troubles of the decade before the Great War, Hetherwick felt that the Chamber could play a role for the good of all the people in the Protectorate. He continued to be critical of many of the actions of the settlers and in turn to be attacked by them as being pronative.[89] Yet when this has been said, this was still a drastic departure from D.C. Scott's vision of Africa's future, where the role of the European was to be an aid to African development and always secondary to African needs[90] This transformation in Hetherwick's position vis-a-vis the Administration was the sort of thing that the Convenor of the Foreign Mission Committee of the Church of Scotland was thinking of in his extraordinary book, *Our Empire's Debt to Missions,* in which he wrote:

---

[89] Notably in the columns of R.S. Hynde's *Central African Times.*
[90] *LWBCA,* January 1895.

> Pioneers for Christ these missionaries were: pioneers of Empire they became, often not willingly but in the end whole-heartedly and effectively. The record of this Empire-service is one of the romances alike of modern history and modern Missions.[91]

It must be insisted, though, that Hetherwick himself never spoke in these terms and gave no sign of thinking in them. What were these land and labour problems which were the contended issues in the pre-war decade? Their roots are entwined together and stretch back to the first years of Sir Harry Johnston's rule over the Protectorate.

When Johnston arrived in the Shire Highlands as the new Commissioner, one of his first actions was to send out on July 18, 1891, a circular calling a halt to all further buying of land from the chiefs. The circular also called on all who had already bought, or claimed that they had bought, to submit these transactions to him for their official confirmation. This was a vital step because land speculation was already rife. As early as April 1890 Scott had complained of its dangers.[92] In the next eighteen months Johnston settled these claims and developed a policy on "Crown Land" that laid down the pattern for the future Protectorate.

This pattern of land ownership contained the root of most of the future difficulties over land and labour. However, the fault was hardly Johnston's. He was placed in a difficult situation where chaos could have ensued if the Government had not taken immediate action, if not to clear up, at least to tidy up the situation. This would have been a gigantic task for a well-staffed administration. In fact, Johnston had few staff and got no additional help to deal with this issue which he undertook more or less single-handed. He laid down that he would issue a Certificate of Claim for any piece of land if he were satisfied on certain points. His criteria for issuing certificates have been analyzed by B.S. Krishnamurthy,[93] and on the basis of that study can be summarized thus:

1. Had the seller the right to sell?
2. Was there another claimant?

---

[91] Ogilvie, *Our Empire's Debt to Missions*, p. 27.

[92] *LWBCA*, April 1890.

[93] B.S. Krishnamurthy, "Land and Labour in Nyasaland, 1891-1914", unpublished London University Ph.D. Thesis, 1964, pp. 86-88.

3. Was a reasonable price paid?
4. Was the claim a monopoly in the area?
5. Had the seller understood what he was doing?
6. Were there safeguards for the people actually living on the land in question?

The first question was the crux of the matter. It was a very difficult question to 'answer. It is now generally recognized that chiefs and headmen did not have the right to sell land, and at the time most of them thought that they were selling the use of land, in other words giving a kind of lease. Europeans did not understand this because of both cultural and linguistic barriers.[94] The problem of whether the chief had the right of sale or not was not discussed by Johnston, who assumed they had the right and that they had sold and not leased the land. At that point in time another thorny problem was, which chief had this right? Was it the present ruling chief, be he Makololo, Yao or Ngoni, that is one of the new conquering rulers, or was it the original chiefs of Chewa, Chipeta, Manglanja or other Malawi stock?

In another context, that of his punitive expeditions against Yao or Ngoni chiefs, Johnston made use of the distinction between the indigenous people and the incomers.[95] However, in the context of land claims he chose to ignore this distinction and the chief holding authority at the time was taken as the legal ruler, though he were a recent conqueror. At first this was not a matter of difficulty until the return to the country in 1891 of Daniel Rankin (the discoverer of the Chinde mouth of the Zambezi) as an agent for Commander Cameron's Central Africa Company. Rankin made claims to large tracts of land in the Shire Valley and cited agreements with Amang'anja headmen, not the present Makololo rulers, in defence of these claims. He did not claim that these agreements had

---

[94] A good example of this was the difficulty between Chikumbu and the Mulanje planters in 1890 when they thought that they had bought land outright from Chikumbu; so they were bitterly resentful of his demands for further payments the next year, a form of tribute he felt was due for another year's use of his land. Johnston saw this behaviour as confirming his view of the chief as a robber, but Chikumbu felt equally indignant at the white man's bad behaviour. See *LWBCA*, August 1891.

[95] Johnston to Kimberly, 24 January 1894, no. 12 CA, FO 2/66.

been made when these chiefs had ruled but on the basis of their continuing to be the rightful rulers. The claims were refused because, as Johnston pointed out to the Foreign Office, an impossible turmoil would result from an attempt to effect any kind of restitution. Even more important was that any kind of recognition of Rankin's claims brought into question the validity of the Protectorate since it was based on treaties signed with Makololo and Yao chiefs, the rightfulness of whose authority Rankin now denied.[96] Leaving this basic point of ultimate ownership aside, it can be claimed that Johnston did try to be fair to all, and was especially careful to try to protect African rights. The people living on the claim had to be protected from exploitation, so on most Certificates of Claim there were clauses protecting the "native villages and plantations" from disturbance. The effectiveness of these clauses and the relation of these villagers to the labour needs of the European plantations became a key issue in Malawi life for the future.

Before looking further into that, it should be noted that there were two notable spheres of land ownership where Johnston cannot be seen to have been applying his rules for the maintenance of fair play. These two exceptions were the creation of Crown Land in what is now the Southern Region of Malawi and the land grants to the BSACo in the Central and Northern Regions. In neither case did Johnston seem to apply his standard criteria for the granting of Certificate of Claim.

When in 1892 and 1893 Rhodes claimed enormous areas of land in the Protectorate on the basis of the old ALC Treaties of 1885-6, Johnston rightly refused to endorse them. The Foreign Office had already agreed that the ALC Treaties were insupportable.[97] He himself had reiterated this in a confidential dispatch at the end of 1891.[98] However, after the negotiations with Rhodes in 1893 about the continuance of the Company's subsidy to the Administration, the Commissioner then granted the BSACo vast tracts in Central Ngoniland, at Nkhotakota and in

---

[96] Johnston to Anderson, 21 January 1893, FO $^2/_5$4, and Johnston to Roseberry, 5 January 1893, FO 2/54.

[97] Hawes to Salisbury, 30 March 1886, no. 13 CA, FO 84/1709 with enclosed letter from Hetherwick to Hawes.

[98] Johnston to FO 5 December 1891, no. 22 CA Confidential, FO 84/2114.

the Northern Region, all based on the same old discredited treaties made by the Moirs in the previous decade. This extraordinary state of affairs was modified in 1895 when the BSA subsidy ceased and the Foreign Office began to pay for its Protectorate. Then the land grants to Rhodes in the Central Region simply became mineral exploitation rights, but the northern claim of 20,000 square miles remained. Fortunately for the future of the country the BSACo at no time attempted to exploit that grant to any extent.

In the creation of Crown Lands in the south, again expediency overcame the Commissioner's basic principles for apportioning land. By the end of 1893, Johnston had acquired as Crown Land, a great deal of the land not granted to settlers, and in all areas had gained for the Crown the right of reversion of the land. Some of this Crown Land was bought from chiefs, some was claimed because the chief had taken up arms against the Protectorate authorities, some of the land was claimed on the basis that the chief had ceded it to the Crown.

The nature of this development was desperately confused because cession and purchase were not distinguished by Johnston, nor was the problem worked out of the relation of political sovereignty over, land to the ownership of land. The ambiguity was there from the beginning and can be seen as starting in July 1891 with the treaties signed by chiefs in Thyolo and Nsanje districts. In the dispatch[99] reporting these treaties, Johnston talked of the chiefs ceding their land to keep out bad whites, the implication being that it was sovereignty that was involved. However, Johnston goes on to say that after apportioning a reserve, he would like to recruit good tenants, ominously adding, "If your Lordship should approve, I intend to endeavour to obtain similar acts of cession in other parts of Nyasaland." This dispatch is also of interest in showing how eminently pragmatic the policies pursued by the Commissioner were, since two of the signatories of this act of cession were chiefs Ngabu and Tengani, traditional Mang'anja authorities, not Makololo newcomers whose rightful authority was being so insisted upon in other contexts.

---

[99] Johnston to FO, 21 July 1891, no. 10 CA, FO 84/2114.

The legal advisers of the Foreign Office and the Colonial Office were not happy about these land deals,[100] but Johnston largely ignored what he considered their petty quibbles. He dealt with the situation in a practical and tidy way, maintaining two clear objectives: that the Crown should be able to raise money from the land and profit from its development and also the protection of the rights of the African.

In many ways the Commissioner was right to congratulate himself on his dealing with the land problem. He had stepped into a situation verging on a fever of land speculation, and with a very small staff he had quickly brought order to the situation. However, one of his main aims, the protection of African rights, was soon clearly a failure. He attempted to have protective clauses written into the agreements, but these were of little effective protection in the working out of the real situation facing the African villager and the planter in need of labour for his plantation.

Many of the first whites who came to Malawi, other than the missionaries, had been hunters. However, in the late eighties men looking for possible mineral deposits began to arrive, and there was hope of another Rand in the early years of the administration. The fact that the BSACo held on to their mineral rights when giving up their land claims in 1895 confirms the strength of this hope, despite the dearth of finds.

Agriculture, with its heavier demands on patience and labour, was not so attractive but some white settlers did come to begin plantations. The Buchanans in the 1880s had already shown on their Zomba estate that coffee, sugar and tobacco could all profitably be grown in Malawi. The combination of the lack of good roads and the tsetse fly meant that human porterage, the *tengatenga,* was the only effective means of transport, but even with that difficulty the Buchanans made a living.

Coffee was the only one of these proven ventures taken up by the planters and by 1898 the Protectorate Blue Book showed that 82% of its exports was coffee. From the beginning the European community looked to the African population as a labour pool for their activities. The people showed no great desire to become such a resource. The planters quickly

---

[100] The legal advisers at the Foreign Office pointed out that if the annexed land became "Crown Land" they could not be held to be part of a "Protectorate".

demanded to have, as of right, the labour of those people living on their estates and the help of the Protectorate authorities to recruit others to fill any gaps left, as well as to ensure an adequate supply of *tengatenga*.

Johnston resisted the planters, saying of them "the native in their eyes is simply a chattel who must be compelled to work for them whenever they require them."[101] But his attempt to protect the rights of the Africans resident on the estates, did not protect them from the pressures the owner could put on them, and his policy of taxation was a strong, if unintended, inducement to people to work for Europeans in order to gain the wherewithal to pay.

From the beginning the Blantyre Mission was aware of these combined problems of land and labour. As early as 1892 they were receiving complaints from Africans about estate owners destroying villagers' crops if they did not work as and when required. The problem was that the time when the villagers' "gardens" needed most attention was the very peak of demand for labour by the planters. In the February issue of the mission magazine of 1892, a long article dealt with the problem and pleaded with the planters to abjure the policy of force and instead to attempt to create a genuine atmosphere of co-operation. The writer then turned to the Administration and begged that, since only now was the full implication of the sale of their land becoming obvious both to the villagers and those who had their interests at heart, could not some way be found to guarantee the villagers' right to cultivate their own gardens? There was an immediate reply to this article. A planter, who was described by D.C. Scott as "a reasonable man", wrote to the editor totally opposing the mission's line on the problem. He made no attempt to deny the practices of which the planters were accused, going on to say that the people were paid, therefore there was no justification in the use of the word slavery, and in any case, he went on:

> No doubt the native is not so black as he is often painted, yet it is well to bear in mind that the light of civilisation has only been burning in the Shire Highlands for some sixteen years, and the

---

[101] Johnston to Anderson, 24 April 1896, FO 2/106.

> aborigines are therefore still like children, and we should bear in mind that good old precept - "Spare the rod and spoil the child."[102]

Scott commented that this was a "reasonable man" and what he said was bad enough; in the case of other men the situation of their tenants could scarcely be distinguished from slavery. No change for the better resulted. Indeed, taxation made the situation worse because the Administration allowed that if a landowner paid his tenants' tax he could then claim a month's work from them, a claim that could then be backed by the Boma and its police. lithe month's work demanded was, as it often was, during a key planting month, September or October, then food production was badly affected in the area and what good was a wage in cloth or calico when there was just not enough food to be got?

Two years later the issue was again raised in a major article in the mission magazine. This article relates the problem to Scott's earlier unhappiness about the constant small Yao wars that led to confiscation by the Commissioner of land, which then could be sold or leased by the Crown to planters. It was occasioned by planters turning people off their land because of a refusal to work and by the problem of planters refusing others the right to till gardens they had left unfilled for a year or so. Scott pointed out that this was common village agricultural practice and if the law let the planter do this then their tenants really had no protection at all.

> Our contention is if the Europeans take the land they practically enslave the native population. There is no law to compel them to help the native in his distress, but there is power put into Europeans' hands to compel, to force the native to work. We have heard it said, "a good thing too", followed by invectives against the native character, but we beg to say the native does work, and works hard, and that the invectives are cowardly and untrue; and we uphold this that no civilised power can come into a country, more especially under Christian promises,[103] Africa and turn the natives into slaves on

---

[102] *LWBCA*, March, 1892.

[103] This is an example of the profound unease felt by the leaders of the mission over the role they had played in bringing about an official British presence, wnich acted in ways contrary to promises made by the missionaries in persuading the chiefs to agree to British protection.

their own holdings.... We cannot treat the land as a conquered country, and we must in every case of confiscation or annexation have the very best proof to show that no other way than fighting the natives was possible.[104]

Other supplies of labour were available from the Ngoni and the Tonga in the north. Even before the formal declaration of a British Protectorate, Ngoni from Ntcheu and Dedza had come down to be employed on the building of Blantyre Church. The Tonga contact with the ALC in the Mlozi war in the 1880s continued in the nineties when the Tonga came to Mandala as workers, no longer as military levies. They soon began to go to other European employers when openings appeared. Johnston and Sharpe both attempted to guarantee them fair treatment but there was no legislation which was really effective to check bad employers, of whom there were plenty. The problems of the migrant worker, as opposed to the problems of the tenant being compelled to give labour, are not reflected to any extent in the columns of the mission magazine, though the almost constant exhortations of the European population to strive to achieve a happy community with the Africans based on a common humanity, are surely related to it.

Some of D.C. Scott's regular little "filler" paragraphs in the magazine were also directed to this issue as well as to the closely related problem of race-relations. Typical are these words:

> It was good old Dion Cassius, we believe, who once described a certain race as "an idle, indolent, thievish, lying lot of scoundrels." We have heard and read almost the same words used to describe certain tribes of our Protectorate. The Latin historian's strong epithets referred however to the English.[105]

It was only after Scott's departure, in the years 1898-1900, that the deep-seated problems of land and labour reached a peak. A multiplicity of factors came together; the rights of tenants to farm their gardens and to give or withhold their labour freely; the rights of new tenants to gardens and to withhold labour; the conditions of recruitment of migrant workers as well as their work conditions; and whether it was tolerable for people

---

[104] *LWBCA* December 1894.
[105] *LWBCA,* March 1896.

to be recruited to work outside the Protectorate. Perhaps even more important from an economic viewpoint was whether the economy of the Protectorate could ever develop with *tengatenga* the only effective means of transport. The work was physically exhausting, it was an awkward system because of the limitation of size of unit able to be transported, and it was capable of absorbing an incredible amount of men. In the planting and weeding season of 1899-1900, the major part of the available labour force was caught up in carrying loads and not in work in gardens or plantations,[106] yet thousands of loads were still badly delayed in reaching their destinations.[107]

The situation was complicated at that time by the entry into the Protectorate of recruiters for industries to the south, in Zimbabwe and Mozambique. The planters clearly were alarmed at the attempt to divert labour from the Protectorate which was suffering a shortage, and campaigned for no such recruiting to be allowed, as well as for a railway to relieve the transport problem and for the Government to aid the recruitment of labour for them.

At first the mission concentrated its campaign of agitation on the transport issue, though the sending of men south of the Zambezi was also deprecated.

> The country - its resources and the development of its productions - and the people to whom we look for this development, must grow together. Transportation of labour acts deleteriously both on the labour itself and on the soil and country which is thus deprived of it. Every pair of hands drafted south means one pair of hands less in the development of their native soil ... South Africa has so notoriously failed with its own native question that we are justified in protecting against it thus interfering with ours.[108]

The March issue of 1899 of the mission magazine reported with distress that conditions for Protectorate men in South Africa were so bad that some had gone on strike and were in prison for their pains. The editor also attacked the concept propounded by Rhodes in a speech in

---

[106] Krishnamurthy, "Land and Labour in Nyasaland, 1891-1914, p. 178.
[107] *LWBCA*, January 1900.
[108] *LWBCA* June 1899.

September 1899, which represented the countries north of the Zambezi as a pool of labour for the industries of the south. The main burden of the campaign was, however, in the area of the transport problem. The mission took every occasion to back and support petitions for railways and schemes for their establishment as a permanent solution, but it also campaigned for a change in the conditions of work of the *tengatenga*.

Four major articles[109] were written in the magazine criticizing the whole system in detail and putting forward concrete reforms. The joint conference of Medical Missionaries held at Livingstonia specifically dealt with this problem in its report, deploring especially the effect of *tengatenga* work on the immature youth, so often paid a food allowance in calico.

"Such cases in spite of what we can do, are very often fatal, the direct result of a system of porterage, worse than American slavery before the Civil War."[110] The conference endorsed the clear-cut proposals put forward by Blantyre Mission the previous year, 1900. These were that the Government should build a railway, and develop a road system capable of carrying wheeled transport for at least the major part of the year, at the same time reform of the *tengatenga* system was vital and the following proposals were suggested:

- a) Wages should be paid in money not calico.
- b) Food should be served to the men daily instead of giving calico as a food allowance as at present.
- c) Houses should be provided by the transport companies each a day's journey apart, thus securing shelter during the cold nights so common in the Shire Highlands.
- d) No native to be employed as a carrier till he reaches the age of maturity.[111]

Hetherwick concluded the article with a paragraph, whose bitter tone is reminiscent of the quarrels of the early 1890s.

---

[109] *LWBCA* issues for January, August and December 1900 and the April/June issue of 1901.

[110] Report of the Medical Missionary Conference held at Liyingstonia and quoted in *LWBCA,* April/June 1901.

[111] *LWBCA* August 1900.

> Surely if we use the native as a beast of burden, it is our duty to feed and house him. Instead to avoid trouble and lessen the cost, which means bigger dividends to the British shareholder, we trade upon his humanity by making him do the work of an ox and then forage for his food in a foodless country. Is this the British justice and equality which we pretend to uphold and fight for?

This campaign which came to the top in missionary social concern during the First World War, when demands for *tengatenga* for campaign in German East Africa led to the deaths of thousands of Malawians, had no significant success until the 1920s, when the coming of the automobile and new roads ended the difficulty. The coming of the railway in 1907, since it reached no further than Blantyre, did not radically alter the situation of the *tengatenga* though it helped planters with their export trade to some degree.

The complete failure in 1899-1900,[112] either to move all the loads entrusted to the transport companies or to effectively weed and tend the plantation crops, forced the Administration into taking further action in the matter of labour supply. In 1901 a Labour Bureau was set up to deal with the recruitment and regulation of labour, especially that coming from the north into the Shire Highlands. The District Commissioners were instructed to aid the agents of the bureau and were soon identified with them. The Administration saw this scheme as an aid to the collection of taxes. If a man pleaded poverty, he could be steered into employment which would solve his difficulty over tax. This process was carried a stage further when in 1901 Commissioner Sharpe accepted a scheme specifically linking taxation and working for a European. It was decided that the tax should be 6/- unless a man worked for a European, when it then was reduced to 3/-; the Commissioner had the right also to designate certain areas where these figures then became 12/- and 6/-.

When this new law was taken in conjunction with the traditional idea that a landowner could legally demand a month's work if he paid a man's tax, an explosive situation was created. Its roots lay in the land settlement of 1891-92. We have seen that Scott pointed out that this had

---

[112] *LWBCA* January/March 1901.

left tenants in a situation akin to serfdom, despite Johnston's attempted safeguards.

In 1901 the Blantyre and East Africa Company initiated a new ruthless policy of work or quit against their tenants, and many planters followed suit. They insisted that the Certificate of Claim guaranteed only those "gardens" or crofts being worked at the time of the issue of the Certificate. Since then, because of the techniques of traditional agriculture, most people had moved to other patches of land these original tenants by that action became no different from newcomers, many of whom were coming from Mozambique at this time, whose gardens were held only at the will of the planter.

What D.C. Scott in 1894[113] had warned would happen had happened, and all African tenants were reduced to being serfs on their own land. In the period we are considering, no satisfactory solution of this situation was found. Hetherwick pleaded in the mission magazine for the Government to clear up once and for all this matter of security of native tenure of land, which was so central to the African's way of life. Hetherwick also asked for and got an interview with the Commissioner, Sharpe, where he put the mission's plan for the protection of African rights. He reiterated that the very nature of traditional agriculture meant that land had to lie fallow for three to five years while other land was worked before coming into use again, and so the original Johnston settlement with its guarantee of only the plot which was then being worked, was of little use.

The specific proposals put by Hetherwick were fair: the first only to apply to the new land grants, and the others to apply to all estates. The proposals can be summarized as follows:

1. On the new land grant given to the railway company, each family should be given four plots of two and a half acres each, if cultivated in succession the family would be self-sufficient indefinitely.
2. The time of labour should be stated so as not to be exacted suddenly or arbitrarily.
3. Taxes should be paid directly to the Boma and not through the land owner.

---

[113] *LWBCA* September 1894.

4. A special inspection of natives on estates be instituted for they are afraid to initiate complaints themselves because they are so much in the power of the land owners.[114]

The government responded by raising a test case in court and Judge Nunan ruled that the tenancy agreements were unfair and set them aside. A Land Commission was then set up to investigate the whole matter. Its findings led up to the Native Locations Ordinance of 1904, which set up Native Reserves in the rural areas and "Locations" in the towns. Nobody liked these arrangements and in fact the Ordinance was never put into operation. From time to time the Administration made recommendations to the land owners about the relationship with their tenants, but no reform took place and the system continued as before, with tenants working for the landlord when required and paying rent in cash or in produce, a system that came to be known as *thangata*.

From 1898 when the idea was first mooted, the recruiting of labour for South Africa was the really pressing controversy for whites in the Protectorate. When the idea was suggested by Rhodes and then by Johnston in the British press, Hetherwick opposed it vehemently. Despite these protests recruiting for the mines on the Rand began in 1903 and continued for four years until in 1907 it was formally stopped, only to be resumed again after the First World War. When considering Hetherwick's role in the campaign against labour recruiting along with his activities in the closely related problem of land, we see the deep ambiguity in his position to which I have already referred. He consistently and tirelessly opposed the recruitment of labour for South Africa with many cogent arguments, founded on a sympathy and concern for the people, just as much as were his recommendations on the land problem which he submitted to Sharpe. Indeed in many of his articles in the mission journal, almost one a month for four years, a good deal of his old anti-Cape invective of the early nineties reappeared, coupled with attacks on a new foe - the capitalist.

---

[114] Notes of an interview between a delegation of the Blantyre Mission and His Majesty's Commissioner at Blantyre on March 18, 1903 contained in Sharpe to Hill, 16 May 1903, FO 2/747.

> By the latest telegrams that have just reached us, it would seem that Mr Chamberlain has yielded to the demands of the Capitalist.... It behoves all who have worked for the amelioration of the African race to be up and doing, and bring every possible force to the aid of the native who is thus to be exploited for the profit of the mine-owner and the Capitalist of the South African Colonies.[115]
>
> For the profit of the Capitalist in South Africa for the interests of the mines in a land of whose existence the native of twenty years ago was in complete ignorance, he is to have his whole social life and development thrown in confusion, and the progress of his country arrested.[116]

The particularly obnoxious aspect of the recruiting was that it was done with the cooperation of the District Collectors. As the Mission Council of Livingstonia Mission pointed out:

> The Council views with apprehension the moral results that will follow from recruiting labour in B.C.A. for the Johannesburg mines.
>
> They strongly protest against the Administration acting as a recruiting agency. Already a feeling of alarm has been created in the West Nyassa district, where the Collector to whom alone the natives can look for protection against coercion and injustice, is calling for labour through his messengers, in the case of whom the native may not distinguish a request from a command.[117]

Livingstonia was united with Blantyre over the element of compulsion in this recruiting, in fear for the physical health of the men who went, in fear of the moral disintegration brought about by the all-male barracks of the mines, and the terrible family problems presented by the absence of menfolk from the villages. However, Hetherwick went further and insisted on the need for the labour of these men for the development of the Protectorate. By this he did not mean primarily the development of any kind of peasant agriculture, but the continuing need expressed by the Protectorate's planters for labour.

---

[115] *LWESCA* February 1903.

[116] *LWBCA* April 1904.

[117] Quoted in *LWBCA* July 1903.

This element in his opposition to labour recruiting also affected his attitude on the problem of the relations of landlord and tenant. His 1903 recommendations to Sharpe on this problem would have been of enormous service to the African people, but they cannot be taken separately from his role in the Chamber of Commerce and its agitation over the shortages of labour. As a member of the Chamber he not only welcomed the 1901 Tax Ordinance, but was associated with the petition which called for it.[118] In fairness it must be added that he hoped a strict Administration would prevent this system being abused by bad planters.

This association with the planter's pressure group seriously complicated Hetherwick's role as a spokesman for the African population. The local planters were, on the whole, bad employers and were categorized as such by Sharpe in his dispatches.[119] In these the Commissioner included a number of letters from other observers in the Protectorate confirming his view. One states:

> I venture to say that our domestic animals received more attention and better treatment than our human beasts of burden, when working on our plantations their existence is almost as bad as it can be.[120]

These reports only confirm what appeared in the columns of the mission magazine from 1891 onwards in complaints about the "serfdom" on the estates, and the bad conditions undergone by the *tengatenga,* ironically enough complaints often made by Hetherwick himself.

How is Hetherwick's support for the planters' interests to be explained without calling in question the sincerity of his acting the role of representative for the interests of the African people? A role which became institutionalized when he was appointed as such to the newly constituted Legislative Council of Nyasaland in 1908?

---

[118] *The Central African Times,* March 10 1900.

[119] Sharpe to Hill, 31 December 1901, FO 2/472, and Sharpe to FO, 2 May 1903, FO 2/747.

[120] Letter from Teixeira de Maltos to Sharpe, enclosed in Sharpe to FO 2 May 1903, FO 2/747.

It can be explained in terms of the original starting point of the Blantyre Mission's understanding of its role as formulated by Scott. As we have seen, Scott worked on the understanding that the economic structure of African society had to be altered so that it was no longer one based on subsistence agriculture and the slave trade. He was following up Livingstone's hope that "commerce and Christianity" would bring a new, better life to the people. Livingstone had thought in terms of a primarily African peasant agriculture made viable by European traders; Scott never seriously discussed the economic problem, but concentrated on the social and political aspects of the change. To Hetherwick, plantation agriculture, because it was underway and was transforming the Shire Highlands, had to be given every help to continue this vital task, but along the right lines. Thus he pleaded for security of tenure for those living on the plantations, and campaigned for railways and better conditions to relieve the *tengatenga* of their terrible burdens, and yet he was a leader of the Chamber of Commerce in the first decade of the twentieth century. He believed that if plantation agriculture failed then there was no hope of development. He believed that it was good for the African people to be in paid employment, and that it was right that some Government inducement should be brought in to push the process along, because the alternatives of failure of the plantations, or the introduction of "coolie" labour, were inimical to the interests of all.[121]

Livingstonia Mission opposed the 1900-1901 scheme of tax inducements towards paid employment, and Livingstonia never opposed labour recruiting on the grounds of the needs of the planters for labour, both of which Hetherwick did. In Scott's extant writings there is no hint of any such leaning. Thus Hetherwick, in continuing the Scott tradition, added to it in a way that altered it. He saw the role of the white man, especially the planter and businessman, as a much more permanent necessity in Zambezia than Scott's caretaker view. The differing personalities of the two men, especially in their ability to deal imaginatively and sympathetically with people, added to the divergence in attitude and understanding. The difference is clearly seen in two quotations, the first from Scott, the other Hetherwick's, on the role of the white man.

---

[121] *The Central African Times,* March 10 1900.

> Africa for the Africans has been our policy from the first, and we believe that God has given this country into our hands that we may train its peoples how to develop its marvellous resources for themselves.[122]

> Central Africa ... is the home of the black man and the black man alone. He alone can develop its resources under the rule and guidance of the European ... this is his sphere. Ours is to govern and to teach him till he sees that his lot is in his own home and on his own soil and not in the mines of Kimberly or the Transvaal.[123]

Yet Hetherwick did persevere in struggling for what he thought was good for Africans and their rights. After the ban on recruiting for southern industries, no particular cause was at issue between the mission and the Administration. However, the mission did continue, through Hetherwick, to try to protect both the *tengatenga* and the tenants on the European estates. No solution was found to the problem of the rights of tenants and the rebellion of John Chilembwe was an eruption of the frustration caused by that totally unsatisfactory situation. Just a few months before the rebellion, Hetherwick wrote of this problem:

> Unfortunately, Government has begun to legislate for people on European estates and not begun on the question of land for people who are outside these estates, but who may be in a position any day of having their land leased to a European over their heads and themselves put in a position of serfdom.[124]

Two new issues were raised by Hetherwick in these years, issues which were of vital importance for the future of the people of the Protectorate. In neither case did Hetherwick get very far, but it is of significance that the issues were raised at all. The first was the idea of direct African representation on the Legislative Council. Hetherwick, in a long and very elaborate review of The Report of the Native Commission in South Africa, commended as worthy of serious consideration, the recommendation of that Commission for African elected representatives to sit on the

---

[122] *LWBCA*, January 1895.

[123] *LWBCA* August 1902

[124] Hetherwick to Morrison Bryce, 22 July 1914, Hetherwick Correspondence, Mal Arch

Legislative Council. He did not raise the issue when he himself came to represent Africans on the Nyasaland Legislative Council, yet his commendation of the idea was publicized among the growing literate African population by the mission journal.[125]

The second was one which he did pursue in the quiet years preceding the War. This was that the Administration had a duty to pursue a more constructive social policy than simply to maintain a minimum of roads and to keep law and order.[126] Hetherwick not only insisted that, because African people paid tax, they should have some socially constructive return for it, but pressed that the United Kingdom Government should also consider grants to help this sort of development of the Protectorate.[127] In the pre-war years the only response was the decision by the Protectorate government to give an annual grant of £1,000 to the missions to help them with education. This sum, when related to the number of schools (the Blantyre Mission alone had over fifty in 1908) was paltry. However, an important principle had been established.

It was along these lines that the Protectorate's future lay. D.C. Scott's vision could not be fulfilled in the ways he had conceived, yet the lines along which he had started the mission in its concern for the total life of the people was one which led to a concern with the key issues of the future education and political representation.

---

[125] *LWBCA* April 1908.

[126] *LWBCA* July 1903.

[127] Hetherwick to Macfarlane, 29 April 1912, Hetherwick Correspondence, Mal Arch.

Chapter 6: The Growth of the Church, 1891 - 1914: D.C. Scott as Leader

On May 10, 1891 the new church which he had built at Blantyre was dedicated by David Clement Scott. His closest colleague, Alexander Hetherwick and his brother, Willie Scott, also took part in the service. The solemn dedication was followed by a more African form of celebration, a feast of rice and roast ox, for all who had helped in the work and the others who had gathered for the occasion. This ceremony, taken together with his sending to the press, the previous year, of his *Cyclopaedic Dictionary of the Mang'anja Language,* marked the end of the initial task D.C. Scott had set himself.

Now that the seeds of an African Church had been sown and its language laid out in all its richness, what lay ahead? Where did Scott see the future leading? As important, what did the Foreign Mission Committee in Edinburgh see as the future of this work so well begun?

There is no record of the officers of the FMC of that period, doing any kind of long range planning or fundamental thinking about the nature of the missionary task. As we have seen, the Committee was constantly in danger of bankruptcy, and continually in despair over the dearth of suitable candidates for service. It is reasonable to suppose that these burdens had a crippling influence on the Committee, checking any kind of serious planning. Throughout the period under discussion, the Committee's policy was primarily one of reaction to what happened "in the field", and contained no element of initiative. The nature of their reactions, however, is a valuable, if indirect, gauge of the nature of their understanding of mission, of African society and of the Church.

By contrast, D.C. Scott knew exactly where he hoped to guide the Church as it grew in Malawi. His ideas[1] provoked a very strong reaction from the Foreign Mission Committee and from the local European community. This was an era in the history of Christianity which has been categorized by Stephen Neill[2] as one when the doctrine of the Church was peripheral

---

[1] See Chapter 3, p.61.
[2] Neill, *A History of Christian Missions,* p. 510.

to the thinking of missionaries, as well as to the leaders of the missionary organizations and their supporters in the "home" countries. He has summarized the characteristics of the period as being:

1. a period when, because of the great improvements in communications, missionary society committees dominated their men in the field in a way that they had not done before;
2. a time when, even among Roman Catholics, there was little constructive thinking about the doctrine of the Church; and
3. a period when the status of the majority of missionaries was primarily that of employees of a missionary society. Indeed, many clerical missionaries were given a conditional ordination: that is, ordination valid only for the country to which they were being sent and not valid universally.[3]

D.C. Scott did not in any way conform to this pattern. However, it must be noted that legally he, along with all other Church of Scotland missionaries, was an employee on contract with the Foreign Mission Committee of the General Assembly, and so legally no different from the employee of the CMS or the LMS. But those missionaries first appointed to Blantyre had full and not conditional ordination.[4]

Scott was a churchman, par excellence, holding a very high doctrine of the Church and of the vital role of Baptism and Holy Communion in the Christian life.[5] He did not see his role as that of being anyone's employee, and was always unwilling to accept any attempt by the FMC and its officials to give him detailed directions about the work in Africa.[6]

The new Blantyre church was a fitting symbol of that for which he stood and the goal to which he looked. He wanted the church to be beautiful and it was. Testimony of the impact it made on people came from a witness, usually guarded, sometimes hostile, to the Blantyre Mission.

---

[3] *Ibid*

[4] Later in 1897 J.A. Smith was given such a conditional ordination after service as a lay missionary.

[5] *L WBCA* July 1894.

[6] For his complete indifference to the recommendations of the Rankine Commission Report, see Chapter 3.

Emily Booth Langworthy[7] wrote thus on first seeing the church, after a long weary journey from the mouth of the Zambezi:

> God must like beauty or he wouldn't have made such a beautiful world. The inside of God's house ought to be beautiful too. Here in the heart of Africa, a Scotsman had made God's house a thing of beauty. I felt contentment.[8]

In the building of the church Scott also showed clearly his attitude towards the current patterns of missionary activity. His view of the relationship of the work in the field and the "home" committee was one of maximum freedom in the field and minimal interference from Scotland.

In June 1888 he began work on the building of his new church. From then until the invitations to its dedication were sent out in March 1891, there was almost no mention of this gigantic task in the columns of the mission magazine, where Scott was usually so unrestrained. Also, there was almost no mention of the work in the official correspondence with the FMC. He did raise the matter in October 1888, after the work was already well begun. Dr McMurtrie in his reply[9] said that Scott's letter had put some of the committee into a "kind of shock". He asked Scott not to continue the project, saying that it gave a handle to Blantyre's enemies, who were continually complaining about over-spending and, what they considered to be, irresponsibility. Scott's response was to desist, not from the work, but from writing about it. The crisis over the war with Mlozi, the threat of Portuguese invasion and the campaign to gain some kind of British Protection for the area, afforded plenty of other topics about which to write and keep the FMC busy.

The next extant letter from Scotland about the church, is an enthusiastic letter from Dr McMurtrie, thanking Scott for the photograph of the now completed and dedicated church.[10] The Committee's anger over the

---

[7] The daughter of Joseph Booth, radical missionary, patron and friend of John Chilembwe. (See Shepperson and Price, *independent African*.)

[8] E.B. Langworthy, *This Africa was Mine*, (Sterling: Sterling Tract Co., 1952), p. 44.

[9] McMurtrie to D.C. Scott, 20 December 1888, Convenor's Letter Book, M.1.

[10] McMurtrie to D.C. Scott, 22 July 1891, Convenor's Letter Book, M.1.

completion of this tremendous project without their authority, indeed against their expressed wish, was turned to praise by Scott's very success. The measure of his success was that the *Illustrated London News* chose to feature the new building in an article, as did other less eminent illustrated magazines. This extraordinary building with its blend of Moorish and Byzantine features together with those of medieval European, is a visual representation of Scott's concept of the future of the Church in Africa, and the goal towards the achievement of which the energies of the mission were to be concentrated.

He had a deep historical sense through which he saw the Church as a living organism existing down the ages, changing and adapting itself to suit the varying circumstances it faced. It was the fullness of this tradition that he wished for Africa, indeed that he held to be Africa's due. A really African Church could only find its own identity if it were allowed to grow in relation to that whole tradition, not if restrained by one single strand of that tradition. This understanding was closely related to his firm belief in the role of the Church as the catalyst in the growth of civilization, which we have already considered. So he wrote of the missionary:

> Unless he cut himself from all that is human and declare himself an ascetic, or unless he fall below the appreciation of culture, he must perforce take an interest in and develop the people around him to the best of his ability. He does not produce a non-native product, he only brings a civilisation before the native spirit as its inheritance and its right, to allow the native spirit not merely to develop a native Christianity, but to become a conscious member of the Catholic Church of Cluist.[11]

In the midst of the controversy of 1894-97 with the General Assembly of the Church of Scotland about the form the Church was taking in the Shire Highlands, he wrote a series of articles in the mission magazine under the general heading "The Native Church", where he explicitly developed his ideas. These ideas had always determined his activities and there are many earlier references to them in his writings. One of these, in 1893, could almost be a commentary on the imagery of his newly built Blantyre Church:

---

[11] *LWBCA* December 1893.

> One feels here what people at home can never feel, the force of a Christianity which has not been troubled by Greek and Roman schism, which knows nothing of Protestants and Papists, and which seems to us above them all broader than them all. In the breadth of nature here in Africa, one looks for the notes of a triumphant unity of the faith and at no very distant date.[12]

Like so much else that D.C. Scott said and did, this must also have produced a "state of shock" in his Scottish readers, since at that time in Scotland, relationships between the differing Presbyterian groups were difficult enough without the introduction of the idea of unity with the other denominational streams within Christianity.

Scott firmly believed that the task of the mission was to produce a Church that would be African. This could only be if the whole wealth of the Christian past was brought before the African people, from which they then could select the materials for their own building. This .was the duty laid upon European Christianity: indeed, Scott saw it as something that was owed to Africa. Scott said:

> Our purpose we lay down as the foundation of all our work that we are building the African Church - not Scotch or English - but African. Rather we should say the African portion of the "one Catholik and Apostolik Church". The African has a part to play in the Church of Christ universal. His character and his influence have still to be reckoned with. In the early days of Christianity, the African was a leader in Christian life and thought, while the Church of North Africa sent its representative to take part in the great Church Councils. We Christian nations of Europe are the heirs to those ages and of the labours of those men. Our debt is consequently to be paid back to the new-born African races of today.[13]

After the dedication of Blantyre Church, D.C. Scott continued the shaping of both the worship and the organisation of the Christian community in the Shire Highlands along these lines. Up till then there had been services of worship in English and Nyanja in the tiny wattle-and-daub church. The main emphasis of work in Nyanja had, however, been evangelistic services, very often in the open air. Scott did not discontinue the usual

---

[12] *LWBCA* May 1894.

[13] *LWBCA* April 1895.

afternoon service in the English language, nor the evangelistic meetings, but he decided that primary service of worship for the Blantyre congregation should be the morning service in Nyanja, to which European Christians were to be invited and to which they were expected to come. Nyanja prayer-books and hymnals were provided for their aid.

> The all important communion of native and European in one worship before God will elevate all who take part; and the founding of the Native Church in this land will be fostered by a Civilisation Christian in deed as well as in name...[14]

Scott had been planning this move for some time. In March 1890 he had written to his friend James Robertson, the minister of Whittinghame:

> I have proposed a native church for Europeans and natives in the native language for Sunday morning service - and am just waiting to see it gather shape and approval and definite promise of success. I have of course a native liturgy and would use this slightly altered - keeping the big villagers' meetings evangelistic ... one of the chief works of the mission is to keep the Europeans true to the vows of Christian civilisation, the Church must be a European-Native Church.[15]

This liturgy already existed in Yao as well as in Nyanja and had been introduced as the form of worship at Domasi.[16] The institution of the united morning service was followed by the insistence that the communion services, whether in English or Nyanja must be open to all Christians of whatever race. He saw this as:

> The overt act of union of Native and European Christianity here as one body in Christ, one can hardly over-estimate the import of such an act.[17]

The response from the side of those Europeans who were Protestant Christians, was clearly unsatisfactory to him, because again and again he was forced to repeat his exhortation to come to communion.

---

[14] *LWBCA* May 1891.
[15] D.C. Scott to Robertson, 17 March 1890, EUL Ms. 717/10.
[16] *LWBCA* June 1890.
[17] *LWBCA* May 1891.

D.C. Scott's policy on this issue was contrary to the tradition of most denominations. In areas of white settlement outside Europe, chaplains (separate both from the mission and the native church) were usually provided for the European communities. Indeed, the Church of Scotland continued to do this in many other areas of her concern into the middle of the twentieth century. Scott's understanding of the Christian mission, and his high estimate of the role of Africans in the Church and his respect for African ways, could not allow him to visualize such a procedure. He specifically opposed the whole chaplaincy policy, when in December 1891 he wrote:

> We are working here for the unity of the Church, European and African. It has been the aim of the mission during all these past years to bring and keep together the two parts of the Church - native and foreign. It would be a great blow to the Church of Christ should there arise in the future such severance as we confess exists in the Colony between the native and the European portions of it. Both portions will greatly increase together - not side by side, but as one.... In God's great wisdom the native may be saved without us, we doubt it we here can be saved without the native.[18]

For Scott there could be no apartheid, there could be no Christian pursuit of a doctrine of "separate but equal". His firm belief in the necessary unity of the Church was a belief which he held over against racialism as well as denominationalism. This attitude of Scott carried into the smallest matters. The fact that throughout the 1890s the births, deaths and marriages of Christians in Blantyre were listed in the issues of the mission magazine simply by alphabetical order, with no reference to race, was a small but significant reflection of Scott's sincerity.

In all of this he was backed by Dr Bowie, Willie Scott and his right-hand man, Alexander Hetherwick. For example, in July 1893, Hetherwick married Mrs Fenwick, the widow of the notorious ex-missionary and trader. After Fenwick's death she had stayed on in the Shire Highlands and had gained an appointment with the mission to help with the training of girls. The Hetherwicks' wedding day was also the great day for two of the newly baptised young men, who married two of the mission

---

[18] *LWBCA* December 1891.

girls. That evening all three couples presided over a huge, open-air marriage feast, which was attended by the friends of the three couples, Scots and Africans together.[19] However, as his constant exhortations to attend worship, and his reiterated explanations of his aims, indicate that Scott's policy did not meet with much enthusiasm from local whites. Indeed, it soon became clear that even several members of the staff of the mission shared neither his views on the nature and worship of the church, nor his views on the role of African people in it.

This group of missionaries found ready support among settlers who disliked Scott for his opposition to the possible ceding of the Protectorate to the British South Africa Company; disliked him because he "spoiled the niggers", as well as for the pattern of church life that he was trying to create. Before discussing their opposition, which led to a formal Commission of Enquiry by the General Assembly (the second in the short history of the mission), the African response to Scott's work must be considered.

During 1888-1889 there was recorded the beginning of a definite movement of people living on and around the mission at Blantyre to ask for baptism. Thus the year 1891 did not mark the beginning or ending of a stage in the growth of the Christian community, but the fourth year of an increasing movement. The impact of education on village society has already been noted. This spreading of literacy into the villages, both around Blantyre and Domasi and, to a lesser extent, around Chiradzulu, would seem to have been a vital factor in this movement. By January 1891 the first edition of the Gospels in Yao and a hymnal in Nyanja had been sold out.[20] The singing of these hymns in the villages, some set to African tunes, had a profound effect in propagating Christian ideas and views among the people.[21]

---

[19] Even a cursory glance at the contemporary writings of whites in South Africa or Rhodesia (e.g. the books of F.C. Selous) is enough to highlight the different nature of the relationship between the races reflected here from that common in Southern Africa at the time.

[20] *LWBCA* January 1891.

[21] A knowledge of these hymns was very widespread. In a survey conducted in 1960 by the author on the reasons for people entering the Church, the outline of

What was an essential accompaniment to the spread of literature and the dispersal through the villages of people who had learned to read during a stay on the mission as scholars or employees of some sort, was the village preaching of teachers and senior schoolboys. In April 1891 it was reported that the teachers and scholars of Blantyre were holding regular Sunday services in fifteen neighbouring villages.[22] Around Domasi a similar campaign, though on a smaller scale, was carried out. These visits were not simple "hit and run" affairs. Those who went out, often accompanied by catechumens who were thus initiated into the propagation of their new faith, even before baptism, were usually asked to stay and eat at the village. They then had to take part in long discussions on the meaning of what they had been preaching - a salutary experience for any preacher - as well as having to answer questions about missionaries.[23] Informants, in describing these visits, have emphasized that the questions about missionaries were as important as the questions about doctrines or ideas.

D.C. Scott was known to a number of people because of his appearance in many *milandu* and because of his part in protecting people during the last great raid of the Ngoni. However, people were keen to know more of him and his companions. If they could be trusted as men, perhaps their teaching could also be trusted. The coming of the Boma and the increase in the numbers of European planters meant that the old world was being badly shaken for a large number of people. Perhaps Scott and his people could provide a help in dealing with this new world of the Boma with its demands for taxes and of the planters with their demands for work at

---

the Christian message conveyed through hymns, especially those sung at funerals and other public events, was a very significant factor. This was confirmed as being of long standing by informants.

[22] *LWBCA* April 1891.

[23] The Reverend James Poya Nthimba and Mr Lewis Bandawe, M.B.E., who were both schoolboys on the mission at this time, described these expeditions in interviews with the writer. They both insisted that the discussions in the villages after the formal evangelistic meetings were over, were of fundamental importance in accounting for the sharp increase in the number of people asking for baptism.

the most inconvenient times of the year. He was the one representative of this new world that they knew and could approach.[24]

In this situation, the personal attitudes of D.C. Scott and the little band of missionaries around him were vital. His belief in the great potential of Africa and Africans, his daring theological flights into glimpses of Africa as a recrucified Lamb of God,[25] led him into a long controversy with the Administration. They also led him into a position of high esteem and affection among many African people. He had shown the Africans who worked or lived at Blantyre or Domasi that he believed and trusted in them; he had shown many chiefs that he respected them as men. Already on Hetherwick's last leave, Joseph Bismarck had been left in sole charge at Domasi; again, Nacho took over Chiradzulu on the departure of Cleland for Mulanje in 1889. In the 1880s Scott had built up a devoted following among the young men who lived on the mission and it was they who now influenced others, who, in turn, passed on what they learned. In this way a ripple effect outwards from Blantyre was created.

Scott set out from the beginning to create an African Church, a Church that he hoped would be free from racial as well as denominational divisions. Some of the measures he took have been discussed above. But what was peculiarly African in what he set out to do? From the opening of the Blantyre church until he left Malawi family in 1898 a rapid growth of the Christian Church took place. Around Blantyre, school and church buildings began to appear in an ever-widening circle; the same thing happened at Domasi, Zomba[26] and Mulanje. New centres of work staffed by Africans were set up among the Ngoni in September 1893,[27] and in Lomweland in 1897.[28] In 1891 there were thirty Africans in communicant membership of the Presbyterian Church. By 1897, at the end of the

---

[24] This paraphrase is based on information gained in interviews with Mr Bandawe, Mr Nthimba and the Reverend Harry Matecheta.

[25] See Chapter 5, p. 127.

[26] The mission there was taken over from the Buchanan brothers when the last of them died in 1896.

[27] *LWBCA* September 1893.

[28] *LWBCA* August 1897, reports on the work of four schools in Lomweland which were well attended.

decade of expansion, presided over by Scott but carried out primarily through African agency, there was a communicant membership of four hundred with more than four thousand people regularly worshipping in church and attending "catechumen" or "hearers" classes.

However, these facts need not mean that there was anything particularly African about the nature of the growing Church. Such expansion might only be African in the sense that African people made up the numbers, but their presence need not have in any way affected policy, worship, organisation or authority in the Church. Scott insisted that he wanted to create a Church that would be genuinely an African part of the one Catholic Church. He certainly produced a response in African people, but how did he attempt to help the new Church not only to be African in membership, but also in its nature? His desire to grant responsibility to Africans was an essential beginning to such a development.

The trust he placed in Bismarck, Rondau and Nacho, and the key part the Sunday visits to the villages played in his scheme of work were all indications of the way Scott saw the future growth of the Church. He soon went further in the granting of responsibility in the affairs of the mission to Africans; in September 1893, two women missionaries, Miss Bell and Miss Alice Werner went to join Harry Matecheta, the teacher-evangelist who had already begun the new work at Panthumbi among the Ngoni of Chikuse.[29] The response from Scotland to this move was one of great unease. Dr McMurtrie[30] said that the Foreign Mission Committee was unhappy about the ladies being in the care of an African. He went on to point out that the Women's Committee for Foreign Mission, whose servants the ladies were, had already insisted that they should not serve anywhere except where they would be under the care of an ordained or medical missionary. The good ladies of the committee objected to artisan missionaries, let alone African evangelists, as companions for their staff.

To be of any permanent significance, this move towards the sharing of responsibility with African Christians would have to be institutionalized in some way. The usual pattern in Protestant missionary circles at that time was that, soon after the work was undertaken, a Mission Council was

---

[29] *LWBCA* September 1893.

[30] McMurtrie to D.C. Scott, 1 February 1894, Convenors Letter Book, M.1.

constituted. This type of council, which usually met quarterly, was responsible to the home committee for the work of the mission.

Although in some areas an indigenous system of church courts at the Kirk Session or Presbytery level was set up, the Mission Council was always the real source of both power and authority. This was because it controlled the larger resources, usually including all the buildings, whether schools or churches. The teachers and evangelists were also usually paid by the Council, so that although pastors might be paid by the local people, the local sessions and presbytery had little or no control over the major element in the staff and property of the churches in their area. The Christian community was thus often made up in a dual form of mission and indigenous Church, two separate institutions, inter-locking through the members of a Mission Council who served on the church courts.

Scott called together a Mission Council on September 10, 1889; but he saw this body as an annual meeting for stocktaking on the work done, as well as for transmitting requests and ideas to the authorities in Scotland. He saw it primarily as an advisory body to him as head of the Mission. There was no question of its meeting quarterly to oversee the work of the mission.

The alternative way which Scott wished to follow was one that would have got round the church/mission dichotomy, and moved rapidly towards a self-governing, self-propagating African Church. At the third Mission Council held in July 1891, Dr Willie Scott had called for the selection of men to train as ministers and had offered himself as their teacher. His brother did not make any moves in this direction immediately but the next year he selected seven men to be deacons, men of proven worth and experience from among the mission teachers and evangelists. By the term "deacon", Scott did not mean what is meant normally in Presbyterian Churches: that is, a layman chosen by the congregation to look after property and money. Scott "ordained" his deacons and saw them as having taken the first step towards a full ordination to the ministry of Word and Sacrament. In a long and very theological article in the September number of the Blantyre *Life and Work,* he explained that this ordination was:

> We believe the same ordination as of a minister only that it is limited in intent to obedient discipleship, the noviciate of those who approach the holy in the sanctification of the secular.[31]

These men were John Chipuliko, Mungo Chisuse, Thomas Mpeni,[32] James Kamlinje, James Mwembe, Harry Kambwiri Matecheta and John Gray Kufa. They received two periods of instruction a day, as well as doing their ordinary work as teachers or printers. Their curriculum included History, Geography and English, as well as theological and biblical subjects, and was of a high school level. In November 1894, these seven were ordained and another seven began training. How did these men fit into Scott's scheme?

The once-a-year meeting of the Council was no effective authority for the work of the mission, and despite some reference to a Kirk Session to be made up of lay missionaries made by Dr McMurtrie to Scott, no such body had been set up. Therefore, in effect, D.C. Scott had been in sole charge of the work of the mission during the previous thirteen years. Now that the African Church was growing, he did not wish to rule that body as he ruled the mission. He began to use the seven deacons as a Kirk Session.[33]

They met regularly to discuss church problems. They met not only to talk but to function as a body for exercising Church discipline. Kirk Sessions in Scotland had exercised this authority during the 17th and 18th centuries, but the practice had lapsed. It was revived in most mission fields in some form or another. The form Scott chose fitted very well into the *mlandu* tradition of all the peoples of Malawi, a tradition of which, we have seen, Scott thought very highly. The informal discussions he had with these men in the past when they were senior pupils on the mission, now grew naturally, aa they achieved responsibility, into the meetings of a chiefs court where cases were heard and policy discussed. The traditions of the Kirk Session and that of the chief always acting in conjunction with his headmen and elders, readily blended.

---

[31] *LWBCA* September 1895.

[32] Son of the Makololo chief, Masea.

[33] *LWBCA*, October 1894.

However, since Scott saw these men as ministers in training, his court would be better likened to that of a bishop's in the early Church, where the bishop worked with a group of presbyters who often served outlying churches. The parallel became more close in 1895 when each deacon was given responsibility for the life and work of the mission and church in particular groups of villages around Blantyre. Scott had shown already, in sending Harry Matecheta to Panthumbi with Miss Bell and Miss Werner, how far he was willing to go in attempting to set up an African leadership with real power and authority. Of this new leadership he was trying to build, Scott wrote:

> We must beware of woodenness in our development of African life. To attempt to force on Africa the details of church life and organisation at home is, we believe, fatal to true growth. African life must be met in its own way and it will grow on its own lines. No one who understands the problem before him would dream for a moment of employing the same evangelistic methods in this country as one would do at home. Neither can we expect the native church life will move in the grooves cut out for it elsewhere. We have said it again and again, we repeat it, doubtless ad nauseam, but the African has got his own gifts of Life and Work to present to the Church Catholic.[34]

In the realm of the possible integration of African ways into the life of the new church, so that it might begin to be African in the way Scott wished, he and his deacons took several small but very important steps. These steps were made in the realm of dancing, drumming and African music; that very realm which African writers of the 1950s and 1960s have emphasized as being of such great significance to African culture.

Drumming and dancing were commonly banned by the Protestant missions of the latter part of the 19th century in Africa, not only for Christians, but for all who were in any way associated with the mission. From the beginning Scott took a different attitude, one confirmed by his deacons. He held that drumming was not sinful; neither was dancing, though it was decided that certain dances should not be performed by Christians or adherents of the mission. The forbidden dances were those with strong sexual associations, especially the *unyago* dances, the dances

---

[34] *LWBCA* September 1895.

of Yao female initiation. The attitude in Blantyre was not simply one of tolerance towards selected dances, but went further. It was an attitude of encouragement of this form of African self-expression. It was a regular custom of D.C. Scott to call out the boarders from their dormitories on a moonlight night and personally preside over the kind of drumming and dancing that would have been normal in their home villages on such an occasion.[35] This attitude dovetailed into an attempt to translate hymns in such a way that they fitted traditional African music.[36] African music has often been found objectionable by Christian missionaries and still in the 1960s in Malawi, African Christians of theologically conservative churches, well taught by the missionaries of their youth, objected to these tunes as unseemly. They sometimes called them *nyimbo za chamba,* literally "marihuana hymns". This was because of the profound affect of their rhythm on those present, when they were sung repetitively over a long period of time, as they often were in Malawi church life.

Marriage customs and funeral customs are areas of life vital to any society. In this much more difficult sphere, Scott tried to create a situation that might enable practices to develop which were both African and Christian. Clearly he had to oppose not only for Christians but for all, the practice of slaying handsome young people to accompany a chief or other important man to the grave.[37] But many other old funeral customs were established as Christian during this period when the Church was, in effect, being ruled by Scott and his deacons' court. For example, at a funeral the corpse was carried out of the house and a short service of prayers and hymn-singing took place, then the mourners carried their friend to the grave. At the grave, after the brief prayer of committal, two

---

[35] Information gained from interviews with the Reverend Harry Matecheta and Mr Bandawe.

[36] The majority of these tunes were not included in the Union hymnal in Nyanja of 1914, *Nyimbo za Mulungu,* because of protests as to their unseemliness by missionaries of the Zambezi Mission and the South Africa General Mission.

[37] Details of this custom were related to the writer by Mr J.F. Sangala, church elder and founder of the Nyasaland African National Congress as a modern political party, and by various headmen in the Chief Kwataine area of Ntcheu District.

men entered it to receive the body, whether in a coffin or wrapped in the traditional clothes, placing it in a niche cut in the side of the grave, or carefully and gently packing the earth round it till it was covered if no niche was cut. Then the mourners took turns in filling the grave. During the procession to the grave and while the work at the grave went on, people sang hymns - this activity at a Christian funeral taking the place of the dancing and singing in the non-Christian form. It had been traditional to say a word about the person at the grave, either before it was filled in or at the end of the work. In the Christian form this was allowed but also a short exposition of a biblical text accompanied it.

This pattern was not planned by Scott but grew up with his blessing. The first European to be buried in this way was the greatly loved John Bowie, D.C. Scott's brother-in-law, whom the people specially asked to bury in their own way as an expression of their love for him.[38]

Among the Ngoni of Ntcheu, members of the ruling Maseko clan and their ministers of the Ngozo clan had to be buried sitting in an upright position. When members of these clans became Christians, as the work begun by Harry Matecheta developed, this custom was also integrated into the Blantyre funeral practices.[39] It became customary in the Blantyre churches to return to the grave after a period of months in order to erect a cross and have a short service. This also was a Christian form of an older ritual. There is no direct evidence in any of the records of the mission before 1914 of when this began. However, there exists an interesting article by D.C. Scott, written while he was staying at Domasi where he witnessed a ceremony at Malemia's grave:

> An offering of beer was poured out. It is the anniversary of the old chiefs death. The custom so far from being in our mind reprehensible, gave us beautiful illustrations of the chalice of the body filled with the wine of the blood of life, and of our Saviour's

---

[38] W. Robertson, *The Martyrs of Blantyre,* (London: John Nisbet & Co., 1892), p. 101. Robertson records that the African people "asked to dig his grave". Matecheta said that they buried him according to their own ways.

[39] On describing such a burial to a senior African pastor from another territory, the present writer was thus rebuked, "Why do you tolerate these ways of darkness still?"

> blood poured out without the chalice being broken. Missionaries lose much by failing to understand the frequent beauty and even naturalness of heathen customs.[40]

It was this attitude of mind in Scott that gave people the chance to cultivate a new way that was still linked to the old.

Marriage was also dealt with reasonably successfully, in that the traditional marriage pattern was accepted as valid, the church adding the wedding service as a church blessing of the natural contract. This meant that the traditional idea, that marriage was as much a matter of the families as for the individuals concerned, was preserved. To such an extent was this preserved that at hearings of marriage disputes in the Kirk Session, the *ankhoswe*[41] had - and still have - to be present as well as the married pair. One essential possibility of traditional marriage was rejected: that was polygamy. In this matter Scott was certain that there was no possibility of adaptation, though he did recognize that the matter was not simple. In connection with the attraction of Islam for the people, the month after Scott left for home family, his colleague, H.E. Scott wrote with signs of real uneasiness:

> We have known many cases where natives have been desirous of attaching themselves to the church, but because they would have to put away some of their wives, they preferred to stay outside. It is a great hardship, we know, and among the churches it has long been a matter of controversy.[42]

D.C. Scott and his deacons had taken the basic decision along these lines in 1894.[43]

There was one complete blind spot in Scott's approach to this subject of indigenization of the Church; and there now seems to be no way of finding out what the thoughts of his deacons were on the matter. This was the socially vital custom of initiation, both of boys and girls, into

---

[40] *LWBCA*, January 1895.

[41] The representatives, one from each family, who have special responsibility for the marriage, not only the initial arrangements, but throughout its duration.

[42] *LWBCA* April 1898.

[43] *LWBCA* October 1894.

adulthood. Because of the ritual defloration of the girls by the *fisi*,[44] Scott insisted that Christians could take no part in these ceremonies and indeed asked the Administration to make them illegal.[45] This was a profound misunderstanding of their importance in traditional society, although it should be noted that Scott did comment in the mission magazine that he thought they had been originally good customs, but he felt they were now corrupt.[46] Also in the matter of witchcraft and sorcery - *ufiti,* he misjudged the situation, insisting that it was a dying belief. But he did begin to attempt to create a form of prayers to clear people of accusations of witchcraft.[47] This custom did not become firmly established and so the Church grew up without any formal way of dealing with a deep social and psychological need among its members. He misjudged the reality and persistence of this whole complex of beliefs associated with *ufiti.*

In a number of other less radical ways Scott also attempted to let the Church grow so as to express both the dignity of individual Africans and to give an African quality to its Christianity. People were not forced to take new names on their being baptised but could retain their old African names.[48] In many Protestant missions elsewhere in Africa, new names were demanded, names which had to be biblical or worse "Christian", which in effect meant European. The Roman Catholic Church, when it began in Malawi, insisted on saints names being chosen by candidates for baptism and this continued into the 1950s.

Again, no one was pressured into becoming Christian. Indeed, it was laid down that no one was even to be asked to come forward for baptism;

---

[44] Literally, "a hyena". In this custom an old man, chosen and paid by the parents for the ceremony, where his role is to perform a ritual sex act with each of the girls undergoing initiation.

[45] *LWBCA* October 1894.

[46] *Ibid*

[47] *LWBCA* February 1891.

[48] A careful count of the Baptismal lists published in *LWBCA* between 1888 and 1898 shows 30% of the people kept their African names without any foreign additions whatsoever.

the initiative had to come from the person himself.[49] Related to this basic approach, and of vital importance to real indigenization, was a very practical decision with regard to the nature of the expansion of the Church which was taken during this period. It was decided that no new building, whether a school or a church - the one structure often doing service as both - should be paid for by mission funds. If people in a village wanted such a building, they had to erect it themselves. In this way the new expanding systems of schools and churches spreading out from Blantyre, Domasi, Zomba and Mulanje, was seen by the people as truly theirs. Undoubtedly financial stringency helped the mission's consistent adherence to this policy, but for Scott it was a matter of principle and not simply a pragmatic decision. How well people responded to this approach can be seen in that, at Panthumbi where Matecheta began work in 1893, a year later Paul Matenje, the head teacher, could report that he was starting the erection of a brick school building.[50] Thus the new churches were truly the peoples', not the possession of any outside body or group.

In the area of worship Scott also hoped to see new African forms develop. The open-air evangelistic services, and the daily services for mission staff at the different centres, all took the common Scottish form of hymns combined with free prayer and the expounding of a reading from the Bible. However, as has been noted, on Sundays a form of prayers was used. These prayers were culled from the whole heritage of Christian prayer and translated into Nyanja. They were responsive. Scott said that this practice acted out the doctrine of the priesthood of all believers; but it *was* also the basic pattern of the liturgical aspects of public events in traditional Malawi society. In Malawi most singing was antiphonal, and antiphonal chanting of greetings and slogans was an important part of any public function.[51] This fitted in well with Scott's

---

[49] *LWBCA*, February 1893.

[50] *LWBCA*, September 1894.

[51] This was still so in the 1950s and 1960s in Zambia and Malawi, where all political rallies began with long warming-up sessions of antiphonal chanting. Also during their speeches some politicians would break the flow of words by initiating another burst of such chanting, e.g., *Kwacha - Kwacha, Ufulu - Ufulu, Chitaganya - Zi, Kamuzu - Moto*, or *Kaunda - Moto*.

thinking, which had clearly been influenced by the ideas of the Scoto-Catholic movement expressed through the Church Service Society.[52] However, he was no slavish member of that Society, and he insisted that he presented free and liturgical prayer to the people to educate them so that they, in the end, could develop their own forms free from the "isms" of Europe.

> There is no need of sowing sectarianism in the heart of this broadminded, broad church, practical people - and the relief to get away from the necessity of 'isms' even of introspective Augustinianism and Westernism is very great.[53]

This "Westernism" of which he wrote, to his friend Robertson of Whittinghame, was not of the West in the mid-twentieth century sense, but the whole "Western" tradition of Christianity both Protestant and Catholic.

Almost from the beginning of this period, Scott began to meet an increasing opposition to the work he had set himself to do. This did not come from Africans or from the nature of African society, the source of the frustration and tension in the lives of many of his contemporaries in other missions in Africa. The opposition, which played a large part in the break down of his health in 1897, came from fellow Scots, some of them planters, some colleagues on the staff and others in Scotland, both inside and outside the Foreign Mission Committee of his Church. This was so serious as to create another crisis that came near to repeating the tragic dismissals of 1881.

The first signs of real trouble appeared when Hetherwick arrived back in Scotland on furlough in October 1893. He was handed a series of questions that had been raised with the FMC as to the ways of worship of the Blantyre Mission. The source of the unhappiness in certain circles in Scotland was the attitude adopted by Scott to worship undoubtedly lay partly with what he wrote himself in the Blantyre magazine. The magazine was to some degree circulated in Scotland, and some of its articles were reproduced in the home *magazine, Life and Work and*

---

[52] One of the books his deacons were given was the *Euchologion,* the service book compiled by the Society.

[53] D.C. Scott to Robertson, 16 December 1893, EUL Ms. 717/10.

Missionary Record. Disquiet in Scotland was given focus by R.S. Hynde, a teacher sent to Domasi in 1888. He was a close friend of Dr Rankin of Muthill, whose recommendation about Blantyre's future made when the General Assembly's Commissioner to the Shire Highlands, was so blithely ignored by D.C. Scott. Hynde seems to have been temperamentally unsuited to work with Hetherwick.[54] However, this only became a serious threat to the continuance of the work along the lines for which Scott hoped when Hynde appealed to Rankin, not against Hetherwick as a difficult colleague, but against Scott, as a ritualist who had ceased to be true to the standards of the Church to which he owed allegiance. McMurtrie wrote to Scott that Dr Archibald Scott of St. George's, Edinburgh, Convenor of the FMC was very disturbed by the situation. Dr A. Scott wished McMurtrie to warn the Blantyre staff that

> the mission is being keenly observed, not always by friendly eyes, for anything that savours of ritualism. Criticism from Mr Primmer is of no consequence and ought to be left unanswered. But remember that most of the supporters of the mission are low church in doctrine and practice ... anything which gives offence to good persons is to be avoided. Otherwise the mission will be greatly injured, and the difficulties which we at home have (already great enough) in raising money for the mission will be much increased.[55]

The letter then ominously turned to the terrible financial situation, saying that the Treasurer of the FMC would be writing separately about it. In fact, it was McMurtrie himself who sent out a special letter on finance to each individual missionary in the employ of the FMC outlining the drastic nature of the financial situation and demanding their co-operation in cutting expense.[56]

---

[54] Hynde worked directly with Hetherwick at Domasi after his appointment in 1888. There are hints of tension in McMurtrie's letters to them both in the two following years, but there was no overt break recorded in the records. But Scott's point in his handwritten comments on the General Assembly Commission's report in the Blantyre Council Minutes of May 5, 1897, that he had hardly ever even met Mr Hynde during his tour of service with the mission, would also indicate that the initial breakdown in relations was with Hetherwick.

[55] McMurtrie to D.C. Scott, 15 June 1893, Convenor's Letter Book, M.1.

[56] McMurtrie to all missionaries, 12 July 1893, Convenor's Letter Book, M.1.

It must be remembered that 1893 was also a year when the Blantyre Mission was immersed in controversy with the Administration and the campaign to prevent any possible take-over of the region by the British South Africa Company. The FMC was then completely weighed down with problems about Blantyre. Financially they were struggling to make ends meet, while Blantyre was trying to press home vigorously new opportunities for work and development which implied increased expenditure. On top of this, the political actions and the theology of the missionaries made the task even more difficult; thus, the FMC felt justified in reproving them. If ever there was a time not to "rock the boat", this was it. D.C. Scott, however, did not see the situation in that way and continued to pursue his course. His controversies with government, and his campaigns against Rhodes' British South Africa Company must be seen as the background to this new, ecclesiastical controversy.

The year 1891 saw a change in the situation of the mission which made R.S. Hynde's charges more serious than they would have been otherwise. Until that year the main body of the staff were men who could be thought of as D.C. Scott's own staff. Indeed they were almost his clan. The deaths of Cleland, Henderson and Bowie left vacancies that were filled by two men who were not relations of Scott nor men chosen and influenced by him. From the beginning the new men disliked what they found in the Shire Highlands and were open to any invitation to become an opposition party to D.C. Scott. These two men, Dr George Robertson and the Reverend Adam Currie, were joined at Mulanje where they had been posted on arrival, by a teacher, H.D. Herd, who adopted their attitude to affairs in general.

From the viewpoint of missions in Africa current at that time, it was not surprising that they should have been taken aback by what they found. In the Shire Highlands there did not exist the usual missionary democracy of a Mission Council ruling the work through its quarterly or six-monthly meetings. Instead, they found one man as effective head of all the work, acting as a superintendent or bishop. The Council did meet annually, but this was little more than a token to comply with FMC regulations.

What was probably more shocking to them, given the views on race questions that they expressed in other contexts, was that this same mission "bishop", presided over the new born African Church with the aid of a consultative body of African deacons. This was an informal arrangement at first, but was formalized by Scott after the first deacons had been ordained at the end of their training in November 1894.[57] There was more consultation with this African group than with fellow missionaries in a formal context.

This situation had worked well when the main body of the staff were those who had some relationship to Scott, and, indeed, were in the Shire Highlands primarily because of him, but the new missionaries did not accept his leadership because they were of a slavish mentality. John Bowie had been a brilliant Harley Street physician before following his brother-in-law to Africa. Willie Scott, an outstanding athlete, David's own brother, was of a very independent and radical spirit. In his last years as a medical and divinity student at Edinburgh University he had lived in a little rented room in the Cowgate. There he had led a club for young men, not of the "deserving" poor, the usual object of Victorian charity and social concern, but for the young toughs whom twentieth-century social workers would call "unclubables". His thoughts about the Church of Scotland were recorded by one of his friends:

> He was terribly dissatisfied with the Church life as it showed itself throughout the city. He had no sympathy with the system that is too general in all the Presbyterian churches in Edinburgh, which forces the minister to devote most of his time to his congregation and leave the "mission hall" to an assistant.[58]

Alexander Hetherwick, who had turned aside a post-graduate scholarship to Cambridge in order to go to Blantyre, was brilliant and aggressive; he was nobody's "yes-man". They, along with Henderson, H.E. Scott, James Reid, John McIlwain and the others, accepted D.C. Scott's leadership.

However, D.C. Scott was not in the position of being able to choose his staff. He had only done so up till then because the dearth of candidates had meant that those attracted by him were the only people available. Such groups tend to inspire very strong reactions, either of admiration or

---

[57] *LWBCA* October 1894.

[58] W.H. Rankine, *A Hero of the Dark Continent,* (Edinburgh: Blackwood, 1897), p. 79.

aversion. Currie, Robertson and Herd just did not feel part of the Scott "clan", and this only made worse the fact that there were real differences of opinion between them, and no formal arena for discussing these apart from the annual meeting of the Council.

These differences appeared at the first Council they attended in November 1892. They petitioned that a woman missionary be posted to Mulanje as a companion for Mrs Currie. Indeed, Currie had sent his apology for his absence from the meeting since Mrs Currie could not be left without a "white man" as her companion.[59] This was hardly received with sympathy. Mrs MacDonald and Mrs Scott had both lived through situations of far greater strain and danger in the past, and no special provision was needed to be made for them. In fact this incident was an example of the very profound differences between the new Mulanje staff and the rest of the missionaries with regard to their racial attitudes. D.C. Scott published their regular reports in the mission magazine, but on two occasions he took the very severe step of adding editorial notes sharply disagreeing with the content of the Mulanje piece. On one occasion he disagreed with their report on the ability and potential of African school children;[60] the other time he not only disagreed with, but publicly condemned their reported action in taking one of their boarders to court in a case of theft. Scott added to their report this paragraph:

> We are glad that there are courts of justice and would not hesitate to use them, but the course pursued in this case does not seem to us a missionary use of the courts of justice towards those whom we have taken from the village and set ourselves to train. We have inserted the account because it had become a public mission action, but we cannot let it pass as if we had any sympathy with the proceedings.[61]

This was harsh; but the stage had been reached by then when Scott could no longer communicate with the Mulanje men. There was a barrier which prevented him exercising his usual technique of personal, friendly talks with each individual about their work and the situation in general.

---

[59] Minutes of Meeting on 9 November 1892, Blantyre Mission Council Minute Book, Volume 1.
[60] *LWBCA* July 1894.
[61] *LWBCA* October 1893.

The Mulanje staff did not see Africans as D.C. Scott saw them; they did not establish the kind of relations with local people that so many of the others had done. Thus, when there were rumours of an attack by the Yao chief Mkanda on all Europeans in the district, they did not have the kind of African contacts that would have let them know of its truth or falsehood. As a result of the rumour in May 1893 they abandoned the mission and sought refuge with the Boma from an attack that never came. This was infuriating for D.C. Scott and the others, who were busy pleading with the Protectorate authorities not to assume that Yao chiefs were enemies and a constant threat. In October 1893 Mkanda did finally lead an attack on the British in the Mulanje area. Again the Mulanje missionaries fled, this time leaving guns which were later used by Mkanda's men against the forces of the Protectorate. This was the last straw for Scott, who bluntly condemned their conduct as cowardly in the columns of his magazine.[62]

Relations could not really have been worse it seemed; but worse they did become, because Robertson and Herd then joined with Hynde and those Scots planters whom Hynde had got to support him in criticism of Scott's and Hetherwick's liturgical practices. How much the local Scots planters opposed D.C. Scott over his conduct of public worship for liturgical reasons, and how much because of his stand against the British South Africa Company, and his insistence on there being one Church, not two, in the Shire Highlands, it is now impossible to know for certain. However, an examination of the charges and evidence submitted to the General Assembly's Commission of Enquiry in 1897, points to race feeling being a strong element in the situation. Scott's refusal to provide a chaplaincy service for whites clearly rankled, as did his insistence on communion, whether celebrated in English or Nyanja, being open to both races.

The importance given to the African deacons also rankled. This was made explicit in an article by Hynde entitled "Mulanje Mission" in the April edition of his newspaper in 1896.[63] Referring to the absence of European staff at Mulanje - Herd was being invalided home, Robertson had

---

[62] *LWBCA* December 1893.

[63] In 1896 Hynde started a planters newspaper called *The Central African Planter,* which later became *The Central African Times.*

become the European community's doctor in Blantyre, and Currie had already resigned - he commented:

> This we would have thought would have been a capital opportunity to test the capabilities of those deacons about whom we have read so much in the pages of the mission magazine.... It, of course, can't be done.... The fact is, no native can, or will for years to come, be able to fulfil even in a moderate degree, the place of a European.[64]

As we have seen, stations had been worked in the past by African Christians, and, indeed, the whole breakthrough which was creating the large numbers entering church "class" at that very period was the result of the work of African Christians. Within a few months of this article, Scott' &deacons were to open up five schools and dispensaries in a new field in Portuguese Lomweland.

The same issue of Hynde's paper, *The Central African Planter,* had a front page article by Herd. It was headed, "The Capabilities of the Native", and was clearly meant as a refutation of all that D.C. Scott and others had been saying in the columns of *Life and Work in British Central Africa,* about the capabilities of Africans. Herd's article was full of the usual epithets, "lazy", "rascally" and "stupid"; but it concentrated on the moral capability of the African and concluded, "the native is an object for contempt from a moral point of view."[65] There was also a mention of "High Churchism" in Hynde's article, which was followed up the next month by an unsigned letter to the editor that was a long diatribe against Scott. The writer insisted that people in Scotland would refuse to give anything at all to support the system Scott had instituted, though the main, specific accusations made were that there was a procession into church each Sunday, that prayers were read and that the sermon was of an "essay type".

From 1893 a constant stream of criticism of Scott's leadership of the Blantyre Mission reached the Foreign Mission Committee. Because of Hynde's close relations with Dr Rankin of Muthill these complaints got both publicity in the press and an airing in church circles. The FMC was particularly vulnerable because of yet another crisis in the finances of the

---

[64] *The Central African Planter,* vol. 1, no. 8, April 1896.
[65] *Ibid*

Committee. Accusations and rumours of Anglican practices at Blantyre engendered a further diminution of funds. A paragraph from a letter McMurtrie wrote to Scott in March 1894 is typical of complaints of the FMC officials:

> That ritualism cry has cost us hundreds of pounds and much labour. The choir is turning to the East and anything else that people lay hold of are nothing to you and me. But they terribly increase my already heavy burden, and they withdraw contributions from Dr Scott. I hoped to hear from you a good while ago that you had put any such occasion of offence out of the way.[66]

This pressure resulted in a real threat to Scott's position. Edinburgh now wished to know all the details of what he did in church, of what he taught his deacons, and to answer the autocracy charges, they demanded that the Mission Council should operate on a regular basis.

Scott tried to evade having to respond to these demands. This was undoubtedly because he knew many of the FMC would not like what they learned, but primarily it was because he rejected in principle the idea of detailed control from Edinburgh and the making of Mission Council the source of authority in the field. In April 1894 in the first paragraphs of the mission magazine he summed up his position:

> We are true to our responsibilities, both as regards those who send us, whether that be the standards of our Church or those unwritten laws of love and faith of the people, and as regards those to whom we are sent. We only ask for the LIBERTY necessary for the fulfilment of responsibilities, seeing we are held responsible for failure or success; we MIGHT HAVE FAILED in ANY of the CRISIS TIMES through which we have passed.[67]

However, it was this very liberty which, as Stephen Neill points out, had been taken away largely from the missionaries in Asia and Africa in that era. Detailed interference with the way he was to conduct the work and even what he was to say and publish now began to press in on David Clement Scott. Dr Scott of St. George's, who was under pressure in

---

[66] McMurtrie to D.C. Scott, 10 March 1894, Convenor's Letter Book, M.1.

[67] *LWBCA* April 1894. The capital letters are Scott's.

Edinburgh, began to put D.C. Scott under similar pressure. Typical of FMC attitudes was a letter from him saying:

> I do not understand your paragraphs as to the future Church in Africa, and I have found it difficult to explain your position to friends of the mission here. They feel by writing such things you are playing into the hands of those who allege that your aim is to form the mission after an Episcopal form not a Presbyterian type; You would put yourself right with all such who hitherto have been strong friends of the mission, if you showed yourself active in carrying out the instructions of the Committee as to the formation of a Session. You surely have among the European lay missionaries materials for a good eldership ... and were you provided with a proper Session you would find yourself a much stronger minister.[68]

Scott's deacons' court was not a "proper session" presumably, and the racial orientation even of someone as well intentioned as Dr Scott of St George's is seen in this and in his assertion of how D.C. Scott was to be a stronger minister. He appeared to need to be a stronger minister in Edinburgh eyes, yet in terms of the growth of an indigenous church, he had presided over a development much greater than in any other mission of the Church of Scotland. Indeed, at times during the 1890s the number of baptisms at Blantyre was greater than all the other missions of the Kirk put together, excluding the mission in the Punjab. Where was Scott's failure with the African people he had been sent to serve? His failure was that he had aroused the antagonism of some Scottish residents of the Shire Highlands and had not gained the sympathy and understanding of some of his Scottish colleagues.

It was while he was under this kind of pressure from Scotland that D.C. Scott suffered a great personal blow. While visiting Domasi with his wife who was ill at the time, the station was threatened by Kawinga who had revolted against the British authorities in Zomba. In contrast to the behaviour of his Mulanje critics, but in line with everything he had done in the past, Scott and his wife stayed on with their Domasi hosts. After all, had not Scott gone out to talk with Ngoni regiments in the midst of a major raid, when there was not a British force within a thousand miles to give aid? Kawinga came very near to taking the station at Domasi.

---

[68] Dr A. Scott to D.C. Scott, 4 December 1896, Convenor's Letter Book, M.3.

Hearing of the danger a group of Blantyre teachers and senior school boys set off to help Scott and his wife. They arrived in time to carry their friend's dying wife back to Blantyre. In the subsequent campaign against Kawinga, Willie Scott acted as a non-combatant medical officer. He became ill during that time and died also. Scott suffered the terrible blow of losing both his wife and brother in the same month - March 1895.

This blow was too much for Scott, and he decided to return to Scotland to recuperate. Hetherwick was now left in charge and attempted to continue things along D.C. Scott's lines. This led to a final head-on clash with Robertson who refused to take orders from Hetherwick. In the end the FMC asked, in November 1895, for Robertson's resignation because he refused to obey their telegram ordering him back to his post at Mulanje. He then became doctor to the European community in Blantyre. Wordsworth Poole, the Administration medical officer, cynical as ever, suspected that he had been angling for this job anyway.[69] Hetherwick continued as best he could Scott's pattern of work, even to the much complained about "non-essentials" in worship. These were the things that most infuriated some of the home supporters of the mission and created a real problem for poor McMurtrie. Hetherwick was formally ordered to send the exact details of his communion service home for inspection and this satisfied the officials.[70] They were still unhappy about the way things were being run, and they insisted that the Mission Council should meet regularly.[71] Hetherwick's explanation of the ideal administration of Blantyre, with Scott as superintendent, was dismissed as impossible by Dr Scott of St. George's, and never reached the agenda of the FMC as far as the records show. However, from the way that the FMC treated the rest of Scott's ideas, it probably would not have been successful in any case.[72] Unfortunately, Hetherwick also continued the Scott tradition of not being a good book-keeper, and this was almost the last straw for the officials in Edinburgh. They were under tremendous pressure to clear the Foreign Mission debt and had to instruct

---

[69] Gelfand, *Doctor on Lake Nyasa,* p. 32.

[70] Dr A Scott to Hetherwick, 1 January 1896, Convenor's Letter Book, M.3.

[71] Ibid

[72] Dr A Scott to Hetherwick, 15 July 1895, Convenor's Letter Book, M.3.

missionaries in the field in the most extreme terms in order to curtail expenditure. Because of Scott's continued refusal to cut back on the work, though he and his colleagues, Scottish and African, did give a month's salary to help clear the debt (a gesture which had few parallels in any other field or in Scotland), Blantyre was singled out for a special letter.' It was signed by all the officials of the FMC and ended ominously,

> If in Africa retrenchment is impossible with the present staff working on present lines, we shall be forced to limit the present area of effort, recall some of the staff and curtail the operations of the mission.[73]

In July 1896, D.C. Scott was back in Blantyre at the end of his sick leave, which had included a trip to Australia. He-returned with a new wife and a D.D.[74], awarded him by Edinburgh University at the Graduation ceremonies of that year. This was not the beginning of a new act, but the last scene of the old. Scott still refused to form any Kirk Session of the kind requested by the authorities in Scotland, insisting that his deacons' court was the effective body judicative in the new African Church. He still ignored the request for a detailed defence of his conduct of worship and the training of his deacons in the worship of the church. Further, instead of planning a radical retrenchment, he laid before Mission Council an elaborate plan for the future of Blantyre, which the Council accepted and sent to Edinburgh.[75]

This envisaged new work was to be started on the lower Shire, in Lomweland, and in northern Zambezia. Each of the new stations was to have a staff consisting of a minister, doctor, deaconess, carpenter and teacher. Blantyre was to be the headquarters of this system and the educational work there was to be advanced as rapidly as possible to University level. The Mission Council was to be an annual meeting again, but one with authority which would be exercised between meetings, by the Head of Mission. This official was to be primarily responsible to the Council and to the African Church as it grew, but not to the FMC in any direct way. New missionaries were to sign articles accepting this form of organisation.

---

[73] FMC to Hetherwick, 24 October 1895, Convenor's Letter Book, M.2.

[74] Doctor of Divinity.

[75] Minutes of 10 Febrary 1897, Blantyre Council Minute Book, vol. 1.

This was a defiant gesture. The Church of Scotland was just not able to produce the men or money necessary for the task, and was certainly in no mood to accept any structure of authority independent of the detailed control of the FMC. Indeed, at this time the Committee was under severe criticism for the freedom they had already allowed Scott.[76] At the time the Council was meeting and drawing up this last of

Scott's schemes for the work in Malawi, a new Commission of Enquiry into the working of the Blantyre Mission was holding its hearings in Edinburgh. In January 1897 the pressure of the criticisms of the Blantyre Mission, especially against D.C. Scott, had proved irresistible and a Commission was appointed to enquire into these charges and to report to the General Assembly through the Foreign Mission Committee.[77] Dr Rankin of Muthill, Dr George Robertson and R.S. Hynde formally laid the complaints.

The Commission added to these several other allegations against the Mission which had been made in letters to the press by these same three men. Three of these charges were directed against the FMC but the principal allegation was against the Blantyre Mission, and claimed that the Mission was an autocracy because there was no Session; that it was Anglicanising and therefore distasteful to the Scottish Community; that *Life and Work in British Central Africa* was a badly conducted periodical; and that the mission was not effective as a missionary enterprise.[78] The Commission sat in Edinburgh and heard evidence there only.

The Commission formally exonerated the Blantyre Mission of these charges, making their report public in March, well before the meeting of the Assembly in May. However, they were unhappy about the way the mission had been working, and *The Scotsman, in* its editorial comment summed up their long and very full report not unfairly by saying:

---

[76] For example, *The Scotsman,* 25 March 1897, second editorial.

[77] It was made up of five distinguished men, headed by Sir Charles Dalrymple, M.P.

[78] *Assembly Reports,* 1897, East Africa Mission, Report of Committee of Enquiry into Complaints against the mission, pp. 148-177. D.C. Scott's hand-written comments on the report are to be found in the Blantyre Council Minute Book, vol. 1, Minutes of the Meeting of 19 May 1897.

> The verdict ... as respects Dr D.C. Scott and Mr Hetherwick might be summed up as "Not Guilty; but don't do it again". Each head of complaint was set aside as unproved, yet it was followed by a reproof or censure in each case.... The broad facts remain that the FMC have allowed this important mission to get sadly out of hand, so that its heads were permitted to do practically what was right in their own eyes, in the matter of expenditure, of organisation, of ritual and of local policy and management.[79]

There was no doubt about this: the real issue was that D.C. Scott believed that this kind of freedom was right and necessary for the sort of mission in Africa; people in Scotland did not.

The FMC really agreed with *The Scotsman;* for some time they had been insisting in practice on detailed control. After the report was approved by the Assembly they insisted all the more firmly. D.C. Scott was now to face the extreme humiliation of detailed criticism on how, and even what, he was to preach from his pulpit in Blantyre. This came in a letter from Dr A. Scott, provoked by some of his published sermons.[80] He was also strongly urged to alter his whole policy with regard to the editorship of Blantyre's *Life and Work*.[81] In the complaints made to the Commission, in the subsequent letters to D.C. Scott, both from Dr A. Scott and Dr McMurtrie, as well as in Dr Rankin's letters to the press,[82] there is not one mention of African people, of the remarkable growth of the Church among them, nor any hint that their opinions were relevant to the points at issue. This is the other part of the barrier between the Church in Scotland and the main body of the missionaries in Blantyre. It is most clearly highlighted when the response of the officials in Edinburgh to Hetherwick's complaints about Dr Robertson are considered. Hetherwick complained that he "was anti-African, anti-mission and anti-Christian."[83] This was an intemperate way of expressing what D.C. Scott in his columns of *LWBCA,* had already made clear that he felt. Dr A. Scott, in reply said, that he felt the Robertson was certainly "deficient in sympathy for the African" and

---

[79] *The Scotsman,* 25 March 1897, second editorial.

[80] Dr A Scott to D.C. Scott, 9 November 1897, Convenor's Letter Book, M.3.

[81] McMurtrie to D.C. Scott, 23 July 1897, Convenor's Letter Book, M.3.

[82] *The Scotsman,* 25 March and 27 April 1897.

[83] Dr A Scott to Hetherwick, 9 August 1895, Convenor's Letter Book, M.2.

"dwelt on their faults", but he was still a good Christian and could become a good missionary if handled properly.[84] This is the attitude that we have already seen as only too common in Africa: that of not liking Africans, but staying on to "convert" them. It was intolerable to D.C. Scott and those who believed in his ideas. To be anti-African was to be anti-Christian and anti-mission, in his understanding of Christianity and its mission.

The fact that the findings of the Commission were published before he had seen them, that the report was essentially condemnatory, although officially exonerating him,[85] combined with the insistence on detailed supervision even of what he preached, was too much for Scott. His health was not fully recovered. The strain of the work and this dismal prospect of serving a Church that did not understand much of what he dreamed of, and did not like what little it did comprehend, all contrived to bring on another breakdown of his health. He resigned from Blantyre Mission for health reasons and in January 1898 he left Blantyre for the last time. In October 1907 Mungo Chisuse wrote an obituary of D.C. Scott when the news of his death at Kikuyu, Kenya, where he subsequently went in mission service, reached Blantyre. In it Chisuse said that for the older generation, pagan and Christian, Blantyre Mission was "pa Scott", (translated: "Scott's Place"); he said that the people were amazed to hear of his death because they had mourned him since 1898.[86]

This was not just African rhetoric. In January 1898, David Clement Scott was dead in effect, because his vision for the development of the Christian Church and the British Central Africa Protectorate had no longer any direct relevance to either. The secondary level education that was being carried out at Blantyre did not survive for long.[87] Scott's plans for

---

[84] Ibid

[85] As *The Scotsman* editorial correctly pointed out.

[86] *LWBCA* September/October 1907.

[87] According to Mr Bandawe and the Reverends Harry Matecheta and James Poya Nthimba, work at a secondary school level was carried out from about 1892 or 1893 until just before the First World War. This was begun with Scott's deacons, then with trainee teachers, then trainee hospital assistants, but it was never formalised into a high school as such. This sort of instruction did not reappear after the War.

the future work of the mission and for a university were not even taken seriously enough by the officials in Edinburgh to find a place for them on the Agenda of the FMC[88] His dream of an African Church, free from Western sectarianism, was apparently stifled by men who could only see the Church grow in terms of Scottish Presbyterianism.

One last consolation he received before he departed was the advance of the Church into Lomweland. At the January meeting of the Mission Council, the last with D.C. Scott in the chair, James Reid reported that he had left four of Scott's deacons in Lomweland. Each of them was building a school in the village where he had been received; and one, John Gray Kufa,[89] had also started a small dispensary. This was no elaborate structure with expatriate staff as had been envisaged in the Plan of Development, but perhaps it was better since it was locally staffed and financed; proof of the real success of Scott's work and confirmation of his trust in African ability.

---

[88] Minutes of October 1897, Blantyre Council Minute Book, vol. 1. This contains a formal protest that although enough copies of their Plan of Development had been sent home for distribution to all members of the General Assembly, only members of the FMC had received copies, and the FMC had not discussed the document.

[89] The first African in Zambezia to be trained as a Hospital Assistant.

Chapter 7: Growth of the Church, 1989-1914: Hetherwick as Leader

In his biography of Hetherwick, W.P. Livingstone said,

> Hetherwick had been so much in control at Blantyre that when he became head of the mission in 1898 there was little occasion for overhauling the organisation.[1]

Whatever Livingstone meant by that first clause of this sentence, the second part missed the mark completely. Hetherwick did not overhaul the organisation; but it certainly did not continue as before. The overhaul was done by the authorities in Edinburgh. D.C. Scott's bid for independence from detailed control from outside the Protectorate, his attempt to have no institutionalized authority except that which grew up in the African Church on the foundation of his chosen deacons, had failed. A Mission Council meeting quarterly and detailed control and supervision of the work by the Foreign Mission Committee did constitute an overhauled machine. Edinburgh soon reminded Hetherwick and the Council of the new situation. Hetherwick had enquired about the possibility of setting up a Presbytery. Dr A. Scott replied that this might be possible but only after Kirk Sessions were established. He had in the past made it clear that he saw the lay missionaries being the core of the sessions. He went on most significantly,

> Two things must be postulated as essential: 1) our Church in Africa is to develop according to the constitution of the Church of Scotland, and 2) if there be no Kirk Session there can be no Presbytery.[2]

In contrast to the language of *Life and Work in British Central Africa,* the Church in Africa is not "Christ's Church", nor is it "the African portion of the Church Catholic", but it is "our Church". It is not to be a Church free from Western divisions, but to be according to "the constitution of the Church of Scotland". Apparently, not even the alternative forms of Presbyterianism can take were to be open to it. This was the death of D.C. Scott's vision with a vengeance.

---

[1] Livingstone, *A Prince of Missionaries,* p. 95.

[2] Dr A Scott to Hetherwick, 30 November 1898, Convenor's Letter Book, M.3.

However, Hetherwick did make one major change in the situation, contrary to the wishes of D.C. Scott and without any pressure from Scotland to explain it. This was the dismissal of Dr Neil Macvicar. Macvicar had come out to Blantyre to replace Dr Willie Scott in March 1896. He had only been appointed by the FMC after intense pressure by D.C. Scott and Hetherwick. This brilliant young doctor (he had won the gold medal in some of his classes at Edinburgh) had a passionate desire to serve in Africa. But he had serious doubts about the doctrines of the Resurrection and the Trinity as they were currently taught, as well as about the Virgin Birth. He had applied for service with Zambezi Industrial Mission,[3] perhaps thinking that their inter-denominational character would mean that they were willing to allow more freedom in these matters than a denominational society. They rejected him, saying he would need a missionary to himself.[4] He then applied to the Foreign Mission Committee of the Church of Scotland. Dr A. Scott was impressed by him, as was D.C. Scott; and they, together with Hetherwick, pressed for his appointment. The FMC was loath to appoint him unless he could assent to the Confession of Faith in all matters. After much negotiation and discussion he was appointed as Medical Officer, expressly forbidden to teach on any religious matters.[5] On first arrival at Blantyre he stayed in the manse with D.C. Scott and fell completely under his spell. He developed the work of the hospital enormously, getting the first brick built wards built. He also began training Africans to be Hospital Assistants of the standard that would enable them to run rural dispensaries. He became Secretary of the Mission Council when that body was pushed into life in 1897. It is perhaps significant that this happened while Hetherwick was on leave.

---

[3] Founded by Joseph Booth in 1892. See Shepperson and Price, *Independent African,* Chapter 2.

[4] R.H.W. Shepherd, *A South African Medical Pioneer,* (Lovedale: Lovedale Press, 1952), p. 17.

[5] This must really have caused poor McMurtrie to despair. The same Blantyre missionaries who attacked that pillar of Scottish Presbyterianism, George Robertson, as anti-Christian, were now seeking the appointment of a man who could not accept the Creed.

Soon after his return to Blantyre, Hetherwick and Macvicar came to be on bad terms. In Council, Hetherwick stood very much on outraged dignity because certain important letters from Scotland about the appointment of a new missionary, E.D. Bowman, had gone to Macvicar and not to him.[6] For reasons that cannot be dis-covered from the records, the Foreign Mission Committee also seemed to begin to treat him unpleasantly. He received a letter saying that he could not receive the full doctor's salary of three hundred pounds a year unless he could assent to the Creed.[7] Despite all this he went on leave in 1900 and did deputation work in Scotland for the FMC, which would indicate just how inconsistent that Committee could appear to be. The FMC then refused, in February 1901, to allow him to return to Blantyre. The Mission Council had requested that this ban be imposed because of Macvicar's continuing religious doubts.[8] A suggestion that he should serve at Kikuyu in Kenya was then turned down by the FMC which went on to dismiss him from its service by a huge majority. D.C. Scott, who was a member of the Committee at that time, insisted that his opposition to this should be recorded in the Minutes.

Apart from Macvicar's own testimony about persistent tension with Hetherwick,[9] there is no explanation in the records as to why Hetherwick, who had backed D.C. Scott over Macvicar's appointment, should have initiated his dismissal. There is no doubt that Hetherwick was an abrasive character, who readily clashed with many different kinds of people. Although Robertson and D.C. Scott had disagreed profoundly, it was when Hetherwick was in charge that relations broke down completely. Hynde's initial troubles were with him, and later the Reverend J. Melville

[6] Meeting of 4 July 1899, Blantyre Council Minute Book, vol. 1.

[7] There is no record of such a letter in the Convenor's Letter Books now in the National Library of Scotland. However, not all the letters were recorded in that way. It might have been written by the Treasurer, Moffat, whose correspondence is not preserved. The reference to the letter is in Shepherd, *A South African Medical Pioneer*, p. 61.

[8] Meeting of 9 January 1901, Blantyre Council Minute Book, vol. 1.

[9] Shepherd, *A South African Medical Pioneer*, pp. 60-65.

Anderson and J.F. Alexander had their troubles with him also.[10] But in the case of Macvicar it is perhaps not insignificant that he was such a passionate admirer of D.C. Scott. Indeed, it was he who had persuaded Scott to publish the sermons that Dr A. Scott and others in Scotland had found so objectionable. He said with regard to his difficulties over the faith:

> It does me a lot of good to listen to Dr Scott's sermons. No preacher has influenced me to anything like the same extent ... if this generation fails to appreciate Dr Scott's genius, the next will.[11]

Whatever the reasons, it is important to note that, soon after their parting, D.C. Scott and his right-hand man Hetherwick could be as radically opposed as they were over the worth of Neil Macvicar as a missionary.

In strictly ecclesiastical matters, however, the difference between Hetherwick and D.C. Scott were not so obvious as in Church/state relations, which were considered in the last chapter. The Church of Scotland had created a new situation in which Hetherwick now had to work. The key change was the fact of the new importance of the Mission Council and its quarterly meetings. Once inaugurated as an important institution, the Council grew in importance. In 1896 D.C. Scott was resisting its establishment in the new form, but once formed, by 1904 it was demanding fuller authority from the FMC. There is more logic in this than in many such apparently "empire-building" claims. The meetings of the Council were costing £112 per annum. In the chronically bad state of the Foreign Mission Committee's funds this high cost could only be justified if there was effective work to be done. The Council claimed there was not. They felt that far too much still had to go finally to the Committee in Edinburgh.[12] This claim seems amply confirmed when only the next year, Edinburgh was cabling Blantyre on the details of the posting and the work to be done by one of the artisan missionaries.[13]

---

[10] Blantyre Mission Council Minute Book. The years 1902, 1904 and 1912 reflect periods when Hetherwick clashed with these men.

[11] Shepherd, *A South African Medical Pioneer*, p. 66.

[12] Meeting of 13 October 1904, Blantyre Council Minute Book, vol. 1.

[13] Meeting of 15 January 1905, Blantyre Council Minute Book, vol. 1.

This struggle for more authority in the field and more independence was almost the direct opposite of the apparently similar bid for independence made by D.C. Scott, who wanted freedom for itself. Blantyre was now going along the conventional lines of most Protestant missions of the time. The Mission Council, in effect a white oligarchy, controlled the major financial resources in the field, paying for African teachers and evangelists (that is, for most of the full-time staff), and controlling their posting and work. Neither the Kirk Sessions, formed in 1900,[14] nor the Presbytery founded in 1903,[15] had any authority over these vital matters. Even the matter of the directions in which the Church should expand appeared on the Agenda of the Mission Council.

As was also typical, the Council began to show strong tendencies towards introversion. A great deal of the time of the Council meetings between 1900 and 1914 was taken up over petty internal matters, and over squabbles between missionaries.[16] Despite this, however, Hetherwick did manage to preserve a surprising amount of what Scott had built up. The stations in Lomweland and Ngoniland, held by Scott's deacons, were maintained, and good reports of their work appeared in most numbers of the mission magazine from 1898 until August 1900 when it was reported that the Portuguese had forced the abandonment of the stations in Lomwe-land. In the three years of their existence six schools and a dispensary had been run by the men, and a stream of able young boys were sent to Blantyre for further education.[17] The most outstanding achievement was perhaps that of Wilson Mwepeta who translated the Gospel of St Mark into Lomwe.

---

[14] Meeting of 11 July 1900, Blantyre Council Minute Book, vol. 1.

[15] *LWBCA* February 1903.

[16] For example, the quarrel between Dr Bell-Walker and Rev. J.M. Anderson. Meeting of 25 July 1904, Blantyre Council Minute Book, vol. 1. The Rev. J.F. Alexander's insistence on housing of the appropriate status if posted to Blantyre, Meeting of 7 August 1912; Ibid

[17] Among them was Lewis Bandawe, who did two years of schooling under John Gray Kufa. The latter persuaded Bandawe's father to let the boy go to Blantyre to be educated further.

The nature of the Blantyre Mission Jubilee celebrations of September 1901, which took the form of a general conference of African elders from all over the Protectorate, must also have gladdened Scott's heart. Mungo Chisuse and Yuriya Chatonda of Livingstonia planted trees on the site of Scott's original wattle-and-daub church.[18] The papers at the conference were all delivered by Africans and free discussion followed. One of the papers, that on dancing, was read by Charles Domingo, the most brilliant of Robert Laws' students, who was to become the first African Licentiate in Malawi in 1903.[19] This gathering of the African leadership of the whole country was very much in the Scott tradition.

Hetherwick was still quite sure that only African agency could spread the Gospel effectively in Africa. So the reliance on the preaching and teaching of African Christians, and even of catechumens, was maintained. The African Church continued to grow. More and more people crowded into the "class". This catechumenate, except on Blantyre Mission itself, was always taught by Africans. More and more villages built for themselves wattle-and-daub buildings to act as school and church. Having shown this initiative, they then received a teacher/evangelist to work with them.

The setting up of Presbytery in 1904 was the signal for the establishment of a series of parishes. These were full ecclesiastical units with their own Kirk Session to oversee their Christian life. Chiractzulu and Panthumbi were created in 1904, and in 1906 a positive wave of new parishes came into being. In the Blantyre area, Nsoni, Lunzu and Soche reached this status; Kasonga and Msondole in the Domasi area, and Matiti was the daughter parish of Zomba. This so inspired the Reverend J.D. McCallum, a Scots minister acting as locum for Hetherwick during his furlough, that he reported that he believed that African evangelism was so effective in the Shire Highlands that the Christian Church there would soon be independent and self-governing.[20] At the end of that year, Machemba

---

[18] *LWBCA* October/December 1901.

[19] The Presbyterian equivalent to the Anglican or Roman Catholic deacon, a status usually only held for a year or two at the most, before ordination to the ministry of Word and Sacrament.

[20] *LWBCA* July 1906.

parish was formed in Mulanje, the most backward and the least developed area served by the mission.

This whole new structure was African except for the minister, who was an irregular visitor anyway. The teacher/evangelist, and the local elders were responsible for the creation of these parishes and for their day-to-day oversight when created. So many of these men were D.C. Scott's old deacons, or had been pupils of his. It was in these parishes that the ways of doing things, of integrating the new with the old, that he had encouraged, now continued. J.D. McCallum, who was a perceptive observer, wrote:

> The village church has a peculiar interest for the student of African Christianity. Here he finds the church of Christ developing, naturally, apart, or largely apart, from the presence of European missionaries. When he asks what the African Church of the future - that Church when her own sons have become sole guides - will be like, he finds the answer in the Christian life and devotion of these village communities.[21]

At the second Missionary Conference held at Blantyre in 1904, Laws and his brilliant new colleague, Donald Fraser, gave a paper on evangelism. They attacked the idea of a European pastorate as both expensive and ineffective.[22] They saw the role of the European minister as "episcopus perhaps, teacher certainly." Hetherwick wrote an article in the edition of the mission magazine which reported the conference, vigorously supporting them. However, all three emphasized regular and careful supervision by the missionary[23] - which was not quite what McCallum had said - and perhaps to the benefit of the local churches due to the constant shortage of missionary staff, the Blantyre African Church leaders had a good deal more freedom than Hetherwick intended or Laws thought ideal. The movement of growth went on steadily and by 1914 Blantyre Presbytery contained twenty parishes, six thousand, five

---

[21] *LWBCA* October 1906.

[22] *LWBCA* October/November 1904.

[23] *LWBCA* March/June 1908.

hundred Christians in full communion, four thousand catechumen and schools with eleven thousand young people under instniction.[24]

The growth of a vigorous African Church at village level was Scott's epitaph. It was the one area where his ideas did not suffer a major setback in the years following his departure. The very size of this network of parishes with their many centres of worship and instruction, prevented a rigid supervision by the missionary staff which was always small. Whether the members of the Mission Council believed in this amount of freedom in the life of the church was not really very important, because they were never in any position to exercise a detailed supervision. Hetherwick does seem to have believed in the maintenance of this tradition of Scott: that a Church created by African evangelists should have some freedom to develop in its own way, and certainly his most congenial colleague, the Reverend Robert Napier did believe so.

This very able young man, the first to join the Blantyre staff from Glasgow University, arrived in 1909 and was preaching his first sermon in Nyanja only three months after his arrival. He went on many journeys in the villages around Luchenza church on the Phalombe Plain and also on the Shire at Chikwawa. There he entered into village life thoroughly, sleeping in an African house and eating with the people.[25] His relationship with the school boarders in the new Henry Henderson Institute at Blantyre was very close. They came to his house for discussions as the deacons had done in the past with D.C. Scott.[26] Most others of the staff, except the veterans like John McIlwain and Miss Beck, did not have this kind of relationship, nor did they seem to want it.

The new staffs understanding of their role, especially the ministers and the large number of women missionaries - a new factor in the situation - may help to account for the fact that in the other areas of Scott's concern, the unity of the Church and its freedom both from outside control and from racialism, his ideas were almost extinguished. For the

---

[24] *Assembly Reports* 1914, FMC Report, Nyasaland Section, 158-175.

[25] A. Hetherwick, (ed.), *Robert He/her Napier of Nyasaland*, (Edinburgh: Blackwood, 1925), p. 51.

[26] *Ibid*, p. 37. This was also confirmed by James Poya Nthimba who was a boarder at that time, and by Lewis Bandawe who was by then a teacher.

majority of the new staff, as we shall see in the following chapter, missionary control of affairs through the institution of a Mission Council was the natural way forward.

It was at the 1904 Mission Conference that the first definite discussions on the matter of church union took place. Scott had planned and dreamed and written about the one church in British Central Africa.[27] These ideas had never really been brought to any practical application in relation to other Christian groups until 1897, when he approached the Zambezi and Nyasa Industrial Missions. They simply turned him down, bewildered more than anything else.[28] However, in 1902, Mission Council asked the General Assembly for permission to enter into negotiations with the Presbytery formed by the Livingstonia Mission, with the intention of forming the one church. At the 1904 conference, Laws and Fraser brought large numbers of their people with them; so again, as in 1901, African church leaders from the north and south were able to meet. Laws and Hetherwick had some serious talks on the issue of union. Before the conference, Hetherwick had outlined his ideas to Laws in a very long, and obviously carefully prepared letter.[29] In it he wrote:

> Missionaries who come Out from the Home Church must throw in their lot with the church they are sent to here, and put themselves under the jurisdiction of the local church courts. There can be no half measures in the matter: the Home Church must learn to trust the good sense of their daughters in the foreign field ... the local church must be independent of the Home Church, that is my point.

At the time of writing Blantyre Presbytery had only just been set up and although independent of the Church of Scotland, its missionary members were not true members, because the court of final authority over each was his own home presbytery in Scotland. Hetherwick hoped that a synod formed by the two presbyteries could end this. He said in the letter that such a synod would be a supreme court for Europeans and Africans in all church matters.

---

[27] *LWBCA* May 1891 and June 1890.
[28] Meeting of 7 April 1897, Blantyre Council Minte Book, vol. 1.
[29] Hetherwick to Laws, 9 August 1904, Hetherwick Files, Mal Arch.

His outline was in some ways as radical as anything of D.C. Scott,[30] and is significantly different from Dr Laws' proposals in this vital area of ecclesiastical independence. Laws had written:

> In matters of Church discipline, status and the like, the European missionary is to be responsible to the Church sending him out.[31]

However, point number three in the scheme outlined to Laws in Hetherwick's reply, is the one where he is ominously in complete agreement with Laws:

> (3) That the connection with the Home Church should be by means of Mission Council ... and should be concerned with all affairs of finance that deal with home funds ... the church taking cognisance only of those funds that are the product of local church liberality, and are to be dealt with by the Sessions, Presbytery etc.[32]

When the very different economic circumstances of the two sources of funds are measured this third paragraph casts a very different light on his programme: especially when it is borne in mind that large government grants came to be awarded to church schools in later decades, and that these grants were made the responsibility of the Mission Council.

In this same letter the final paragraph was a plaintive one about the difficulties of church unity racially. Hetherwick said that he had always wanted Scott's ideal, one church of both races, and abhorred what he saw in the south:

> I want to see ONE church in Central Africa. I have fought for this in Blantyre here - latterly it has become more difficult with the greater variety of European elements in the country ... still we-are one, and if the church is from the beginning laid down on true lines, I think the race feeling in church affairs will not prevail as they have done in the south.

---

[30] Especially when it is considered that it was not until August 1959 at Mulanje that the Church of Scotland Missionary ministers entered fully into the ecclesiastical structure of the CCAP.

[31] Laws to Hetherwick, 21 June 1904, Hetherwick Files, Mal Arch.

[32] Hetherwick to Laws, 9 August 1904, Hetherwick Files, Mal Arch.

After the discussions at the Blantyre Missionary Conference most of the negotiations had to be carried on by letter, transport difficulties being an insuperable barrier to frequent and regular meetings.

These negotiations by correspondence were enlivened by Donald Fraser of Loudon who raised again D.C. Scott's idea of a single united Protestant Church. His ideas were debated in Blantyre Presbytery, which according to Hetherwick saw them as a basis of some sort of Federation, but not for a united church.[33] They were not very seriously regarded by his fellow missionaries in the north, any more than Scott's ideas had been received by the Zambezi Mission or the FMC in the past.[34] Of Fraser's ideas Ehnslie[35] wrote to Hetherwick,

> Mr Fraser's scheme was one of those pious wishes for the unity of all branches of the Christian Church which everyone has in common ... I am not hopeful about it, nor am I desirous of sacrificing Presbytery and think we should go on with our Presbyterian union.[36]

Although more personally sympathetic, Hetherwick basically agreed. He wrote to Fraser:

> As to Union, I say, let us at Blantyre and you of Livingstonia and if possible the Dutch,[37] make our union ourselves and the other will follow ... we must not let this conference pass without our two Presbyteries getting together, whether the others do or no.[38]

At the third Missionary Conference held at Mvera[39] in 1910, the two presbyteries of Blantyre and Livingstonia formally decided to unite and

---

[33] Hetherwick to Fraser, 4 April 1909, Hetherwick Files, Mal Arch.

[34] ZIM to D.C. Scott recorded in full at meeting of 7 April 1897, Blantyre Council Minute Book, vol. 1.

[35] Elmslie was the most senior of the Livingstonia missionaries after Laws.

[36] Elmslie to Hetherwick, 21 July 1908, Hetherwick Files, Mal Arch.

[37] A Dutch Reformed Mission from the Cape Synod of that Church came to the aid of Livingstonia Mission in 1888. In 1896 the whole of what is now the Central Region except for Ntcheu was held to be their area by their fellow Presbyterians. Now the CCAP Nkhoma Synod.

[38] Hetherwick to Fraser, 8 November 1909, Hetherwick Files, Mal Arch.

[39] The central station of the Dutch Reformed Church Mission.

form the one synod, that of the Church of Central Africa Presbyterian. However, it was not until 1914 that the slow process was completed of getting the agreement of the Church of Scotland and the, by then, United Free Church of Scotland,[40] to this union.

The two General Assemblies meeting in Edinburgh finally agreed in May 1914 to the entry of the two presbyteries in the field into the new union. Everyone in the field and at the Assemblies, which passed the resolutions unanimously, rejoiced at this accomplishment. Hetherwick expressed no qualms in any letter that survives in collections in Scotland or Malawi, yet a significant change appeared in the final constitution of 1914, which was not present in his initial plan worked out and sent to Laws in 1904. There he had insisted on the fact that the new Church should mean that the missionaries would cease to have their Scottish presbyteries as the final ecclesiastical authority over them, but would be full members of the local Church. He insisted that "there can be no half measures", yet paragraph six of the "Terms of Union" read thus:

> 6) That the European members of Presbytery shall continue in their present relations to the Home Churches.

The outbreak of the First World War prevented the holding of the first meeting of the new synod, the inauguration of which will be considered later.

What must be noted now is the decline from the original concept to the actual achievement. D.C. Scott started with the view that the one African portion of the Church Catholic was the goal of their activities; a Church free in the very widest sense from bondage to the West. The imposition of the administrative structure of the Mission Council and the insistence of detailed control from Edinburgh cut this dream down in scope. However, in 1904 Hetherwick was still calling for a local Church, free from the home Church, which would have ecclesiastical authority over the missionaries. The 1914 document is the union of an African Presbyterian Church, in which the missionaries play a leading role but which has no authority whatsoever over these missionaries.

---

[40] The United Presbyterian Church and the Free Church of Scotland united in 1901.

The other aspect of the unity of the Church that D.C. Scott had insisted upon, and with which Hetherwick had passionately agreed, was its racial oneness. In his definitive letter to Dr Laws in August 1904 he insisted that this oneness had always been "on my heart". He had complained, though, that this was more and more difficult to maintain. It was a matter to be maintained, not created, because, as we have seen, Scott had always held English and Nyanja services to which people of all races were expected to come. Especially at the services of Communion, he had insisted that both races had to partake together.[41] This had never been well received by the European population, the growth of which around Blantyre led to increasingly explicit racial feelings being expressed and more insistence on separation in social life.

When the arrival of R.H. Napier in Blantyre enabled Hetherwick to begin a regular course of preparation for the ministry of the Church, it was not the fourteen deacons who Scott had trained that were brought forward, but only two, Harry Kambwiri Matecheta and Stephen Kundedia. By this time the missionary ministers, J. Melville Anderson, J.F. Alexander, J.A. Smith, E.D. Bowman and James Reid were no longer involved in village society like the men of the last decades of the previous century. Until the arrival of Napier, James Reid was the only one who would wrap himself up in a blanket and sleep on a mat in a village house.[42] Indeed, Bowman was an explicit upholder of the Afrikaaner doctrine of African development. For him, African ways were best when they meant that Africans should not share European culture. Later in his career he was quite open in his rejection of the Blantyre pattern of education, insisting that it should be geared more to village needs. Education should have been primarily in Nyanja, not in English, it had been hitherto far too Anglicizing in character.

This group of missionaries did not have the trust in African leadership that D.C. Scott did. Of the fourteen men trained by Scott, only Matecheta and Kundecha were now to be trusted fully. Exactly what European opinion was like in general during these years can be gauged from an editorial by R.S. Hynde in his newspaper. This was in connection with the

---

[41] *LWBCA* May 1891.

[42] This is according to Lewis Bandawe and James Poya Nthimba

discussion of the possible ordination of Africans to the eldership and to the ministry, which took place at the Livingstonia Missionary Conference of 1900. The editorial opposed ordination of "natives" as elders or pastors, because it implied some sort of equality and this was totally wrong:

> It is utterly wrong to teach any native he is as good as the white man because he is not. If he were, he would be on a level with the white man, but it is because he is inferior that he is under the white man.[43]

The editorial continued that the training of African leaders was no part of the task of the mission, and commented on the return of John Chilembwe[44] to the country with his "travesty of Christianity".

The next year the Editor went even further. He insisted, in a long editorial headed "Ethiopianism",[45] that any African left to preach unsupervised was a danger - as many as three hundred Blantyre Christians preached and taught in the villages on most Sundays - and that the American negro was a savage when not closely supervised. Indeed, although he agreed that lynching was a bad thing, it was very easy to see how Americans were provoked into it.

It is no wonder therefore that in 1904 Hetherwick complained to Laws about the difficulty of maintaining the racial oneness of the Church. Indeed, by that year he had already made a decision, fatal to any successful maintenance of racial unity. Until Scott left in 1898 there was one congregation at Blantyre with services in both languages and open to all. But in 1901 two congregations were formed in Blantyre, one European, the other "native". Multiracial services were no longer normal, but occurred only on special occasions. It was at this time that a European Kirk Session, as well as an African, came into being.[46] Al Zomba the same thing occurred later, but there is no reference in the records to

---

[43] *The Central African Times,* September 1, 1900.

[44] John Chilembwe was a Yao lad taken to the USA by Joseph Booth. He returned an ordained Baptist minister. His Christianity was conventional and no travesty. His story is fully told in Shepperson and Price, *Independent African.*

[45] *The Central African Times,* 25 May 1901.

[46] Hetherwick to Arthur, Kikuyu, Kenya, 5 October 1916, Hetherwick Files, Mal Arch.

the exact date. Later Hetherwick was to say that this separation was for the good of the African elders.

> The native session meet by themselves apart from the Europeans ... the whole conduct of the session is thus laid on the native members. We have found this absolutely necessary as the tendency of the native is to throw the responsibilities ... onto the shoulders of the Europeans.[47]

No comment need be made on this, except to recall D.C. Scott's belief that racial unity at the Communion table was essential, and his words, already quoted elsewhere, are:

> In God's great wisdom the native may be saved without us, we doubt if we here can be saved without the native.[48]

W.P. Livingstone in his adulatory biography of Hetherwick says of this matter:

> Dr. Hetherwick's hope for the unity in Blantyre of the religious life had not been realised. Theoretically the European and native congregations were one, with a single session, but in practice they formed two self-contained bodies and held separate communions.[49]

What Livingstone failed to mention, or perhaps did not know, was that this unity had already existed from 1881 until the turn of the century when Hetherwick had allowed the split to occur.

Perhaps because of the new staff the mission was receiving, or perhaps in order to keep Europeans coming to church at all and to prevent another wave of complaints by whites to Edinburgh as in 1894-97, there was no alternative. But the story is of a unity that had real existence and then was lost, not that of a unity that was aimed at but not achieved as Livingstone implied. A more positive note can be struck about the hopes for better relations, if not union, among all the Protestant bodies in the Protectorate. At the Mvera Missionary Conference in 1910, attended by the representatives of the Livingstonia and Blantyre Missions, the Dutch Reformed Mission, the Zambezi Industrial Mission, the Nyasa Industrial

---

[47] Ibid

[48] *LWBCA* June 1890.

[49] Livingstone, *A Prince of Missionaries,* pp. 177-178.

Mission, the Baptist Industrial Mission and the South African General Mission, these bodies agreed to form a Federated Board of Missions. This would consult over things such as education, Bible translation and other matters of common interest. Its bases of agreement were:

1. The Holy Scriptures to be the only rule of life and faith.
2. The Apostles Creed.
3. The two Sacraments: Baptism and Holy Communion.
4. The recognition of each other's church membership and church discipline.
5. The same standard of religious knowledge for membership.[50]

The Universities' Mission was not able to take part in this Board.

This new body accepted the Nyanja New Testament produced by a United Board of Translators set up by the conference of 1900 which had been headed by William Murray of Mvera. They now also backed the translation of the Old Testament by the same group, so that there would be one accepted Union version of the Bible in Nyanja. They also set about the preparation of a Union hymnal. This was completed

in 1914. Hetherwick, however, liked the African tunes used so widely in the Blantyre churches, lamenting:

> Some of my fellow missionaries are not of the same opinion as to their worth, so they are few in number. It means a great deal to the Christian Church when the old war chants are put to Christian use in the service of the Lord's house.[51]

The freedom of the vigorous congregations of the Blantyre Presbytery, however, enabled these African tunes to survive. When no missionary was present, which meant most of the time, they were the tunes usually sung.[52]

---

[50] p. Bolink, *Towards Church Union in Zambia,* (Franeker: T. Weber, 1967), p. 193.

[51] Hethenvick to Morrison Bryce, 28 January 1914, Hethenvick Files, Mal Arch.

[52] They still were the tunes usually sung in the parishes served by the author between 1958 and 1965.

The setting up of the Federated Board of Mission, with their mutual recognition of each other's integrity, was a help towards ending the clashes that had taken place between the Blantyre Mission and some of the other missions. Livingstonia and the Dutch Reformed Church Mission were not bothered in this way because the missions which came into the Protectorate in the 1890s mostly settled in the south. Blantyre had experienced most difficulties with the Zambezi Industrial Mission, but there had also been awkwardness at times with the Nyasa Mission. The squabbles that had from time to time in the past taken place over encroaching on one another's areas or bribing away teachers by offering higher wages, were now at an end. However, they had not dominated the relationships between the missions, which had been predominantly amicable. The notable exception was the Universities' Mission to Central Africa.

Until the mid-nineties relations between Blantyre and the UMCA had been the most cordial of the inter-mission relationships. Bishop Smythies and Bishop Hines had often preached at Blantyre church, and had celebrated the Eucharist on the broad veranda of Blantyre manse for the few Anglican communicants in the area. However, the UMCA refused to attend any of the three missionary conferences of 1900, 1904 or 1910. They took no part in the United Board of Translators and, of course, did not join the Federated Board of Missions. Before 1900, although no formal comity agreement had been entered into with Blantyre, one had worked in practice.

After 1900, this was ignored entirely and most tensions in the years leading up to the First World War were between Blantyre and the UMC.A, and not with the other missions, whose initial relations with Blantyre had not been good.

Although John Chilembwe was not asked to the Mvera Conference relations between his Providence Industrial Mission and the Blantyre Mission were cordial. When he was unwell, especially with some persistent eye trouble, he went to the Scottish mission doctors. At least once he stayed for a few days at Domasi Mission for treatment.[53] The

---

[53] The Reverend Augustine Ndalama told of this stay and pointed out his room in the old manse, then being dismantled, at Domasi in November 1958.

most interesting contact in the Blantyre records is a letter from him to Dr Hetherwick about the problems of what to do with partners in a polygamous marriage who desired baptism. The letter began with the greeting, "Dear Father in Christ", and ends with the following:

> How are you dealing with such cases? (of polygamists wishing baptism) I determined to know nothing but the right way and principles of the gospel of Christ. For here are many persons of that kind, and yet seeking to know God. I shall be very thankful if you can take time to explain this to me, so that I may know what to do. Excuse me for the trouble, Your Son in Christ, John Chilembwe.[54]

Hetherwick wrote a careful and cordial reply, explaining the position adopted by the Blantyre Presbytery on that matter.

However, the maintenance of cordial relations is very far from being one body. It was one body that D.C. Scott had wished the Church to be. A body which would surmount what Scott believed were the irrelevant - for Africa at least - denominational ties of Europe and the racialism of Europe. Under the leadership of Hetherwick these hopes faded. Despite the growth and free dynamism of the village churches of the Blantyre Presbytery, within Blantyre itself there was also a declension. The authority of the Mission Council and the separateness of the new missionaries from the African people made a situation very different from what had seemed possible to David Clement Scott and his deacons twenty years before.

---

[54] John Chilembwe's letter to Hethenvia, 1 June 1909, Hethenvick Files, Mal Arch.

Chapter 8: The War and the Beginning of a New Day

The war of 1914-18 was not seen at the time by the peoples of the Nyasaland Protectorate as the end of an era and the beginning of a new stage in the history of Africa. It was seen by them more as a diversion which checked developments that had been planned, or as a chaotic threat to what had become accustomed ways.

As far as the Presbyterian Church and its Scottish and Afrikaaner missionaries were concerned, the War was a serious interruption in their slow but steady progress towards Church union. It checked any hope of an increase in Government aid to education, a prize that had been gained in principle, but had not yet been of great practical value. It was a serious threat to the growth of the Church among the people because so many of the church staff, both European and African were called into service by the Imperial Government. The War was also the setting and partly the cause of the rising of Africans against the Protectorate led by John Chilembwe.[1] The aftermath of this rebellion then presented the Presbyterian Church with the biggest threat to the continuance of its work since the days of Mlozi and Serpa Pinto. When all this has been said, it still remains to add that the War was also a positive aid to the development in the Presbyteries of Blantyre and Livingstonia of the already existing strong elements of African initiative and leadership.[2]

It was noted in the last chapter that the Church in the area served by the Blantyre Mission grew rapidly as a result of the work of the village evangelists and teachers, along with the village church elders. Supervision was not close because of the shortage of staff, as well as the Blantyre tradition of encouraging African initiative. The missionary supervision of the work in the villages from 1914 to 1926, the end of the

---

[1] A very full discussion of the rising and its implications is to be found in Shepperson and Price, *Independent African*.

[2] See M. Wright, *German Missions in Tanganyika, 1891-1941: Lutherans and Moravians in the Southern Highlands,* (Oxford: Clarendon Press, 1971), chapter 7, for a description of the Initiative of Malawi evangelists and teachers in the Langenburg (Tukuyu) area of what is now Tanzania during the years 1917 to 1926.

period under discussion, was even less than before. Many staff were conscripted into Government service because of the War, and when the fight was over they had to get home leave that was due to them. In addition, some of the small European staff had to help with the work in the Iringa area of German East Africa when it was cleared of German troops and its German missionaries.[3]

The work of church and school went on apace, and was almost solely in the hands of the kind of men that D.C. Scott had intended it should be: the "new men" of African society, Christian and literate. They did all the teaching in the "hearers" and "catechumen" classes, and it was they who had to make a host of small decisions about what was or was not permissible for Christians in terms of many customary forms of behaviour. It was in this way that the movement of the indigenization of Christianity that has already been discussed continued. Just how successful these "new men" were can be gauged from two reports by missionaries.

The first was by Robert Napier, who, after a period of service with the army at Karonga, spent a long leave getting on with his work in the village churches around Chiradzulu and Luchenza. In January 1915 he stayed at Nsoni and held services in the new brick church, built entirely by Africans with African funds.

> Nsoni Church is beautiful in its simplicity, with Gothic windows at the west end; rising there far higher than any native house, and built of durable brick, it reminds me of the ancient cathedrals that rose among the clustering houses of wood - houses which have long since fallen - leaving the sacred building still standing. The native chief of the builders, called Paul, has put up two churches, repaired a third, has ideas about decoration, and longs for stained glass.[4]

---

[3] The work in the Irlnga district of Tanganyika, although staffed by Scots and Africans from Blantyre, was kept administratively separate by the authorities in Edinburgh. It is therefore not an integral part of this study, but has been fully dealt with by Wright, *German Missions in Tanganyika, 1891-1941*, chapter 7.

[4] A letter from Napier to his family in Hetherwick, *Robert He/her Napier in Nyasaland*, p. 91.

The second report is that made in 1918 by James Reid to the General Assembly of the Church of Scotland. The year 1918 was the most taxing year for the mission in terms of the use of its staff by the Government for war work; but he reported:

> Had there been a retrograde movement all round this year, we would not have been surprised; had we even held our own, we would have been thankful; but that in every department of our work there should be progress to report fills us with such joy and great hope for the future.[5]

The fact that what regular supervision there was during the war years was done by Hetherwick himself, James Reid and Robert Napier, was a positive encouragement to the tendencies towards African initiative and indigenization. Hetherwick and Reid still had in them some real residue of the views of their old chief, D.C. Scott, and the new man Napier was one who would have been thoroughly at home with the original "Scott clan". His report of a journey by bicycle from Mangochi to Blantyre had the ring of the earlier days of the Mission about it.

> Hiring a cycle, I rode south till I met my own machine which I had wired for, and that night I spent in a chiefs house. He entertained me to tea and sweet biscuits, while I gave him a slice of bread and jam.[6]

This acceptance of simple village hospitality, a characteristic of the mission pioneers, was not again a characteristic of missionary behaviour until the Second World War and after. More significant is his report of a journey to catechize and baptize the folk trained by the village elders and teachers near Lake Chirwa.

> The local Christians have put up a well-built church which I am to open tomorrow. At this point the narrative broke off, for a deputation waited on to ask if I approved of a little dancing. The folk were quite jolly in anticipation of opening a church and wanted to 'make a joyful noise'. I told them that if they chose nice dances and didn't go on too long, it was all right. I went to see the fun.... After watching, I sat round the fire with some lads and had songs. I gave

---

[5] *Assembly Reports,* 1918, FMC Report, Nyasaland Section, p. 84.
[6] Hetherwick, *Robert Helfer Napier in Nyasaland,* p. 98.

them some of ours, there being no critical audience, and they sang a few of their's.[7]

This was the kind of relationship that had marked out D.C. Scott in the affection of Africans. It did the same for Napier. Of this relationship Lewis Bandawe said:

> The very first missionaries, especially D.C. Scott and his brother really did get on with the people - they slept on *mphasa* in the houses and ate what the people gave them. My father-in-law, Mr Joseph Bismarck had many stories about this ... Napier was the missionary whom I saw and knew who was like that. He above the others really loved and was one with the people. Wherever he went he simply slept where space was offered and ate whatever was going, like the first ones. Whenever there was any tension or difficulty with teachers or other staff it was he who resolved it.[8]

Had he lived what the result of this very positive revival of the D.C. Scott tradition might have been on the history of Blantyre can only be speculation. Some time in January 1918 in Mozambique, where he had gone with a group of Blantyre deacons and teachers as an unarmed scouting party for the Allied Forces, Napier was killed by a patrol of von Lettow's troops.[9]

This was a tragedy for the Blantyre Mission because it left it with no one who had the easy, close, intimate relations with the villagers or the new elite of teachers and pastors which Napier had maintained. Informants were clear that none of the other staff was anti-African as Dr Robertson

---

[7] *Ibid*, p. 106.

[8] Transcribed and translated from a tape recording of an interview with Lewis Bandawe on January 9, 1964.

[9] Napier's instructions were to try to locate the German forces who were moving in areas of Portuguese East Africa which had not effectively been, administered by the Portuguese and were, in effect, unknown and uncharted. However, Napier, from his Lomweland Mission experience, knew the Portuguese well; he also knew the war was nearly over for the German army no longer had a base, so he saw his mission to be at least partly one of shielding the African population from Portuguese vengeance. He constantly warned the people against any apparent co-operation with the German *askari* for this reason. See Hetherwick, *Robert Heflier Napier in Nyasaland,* pp. 130-135.

or Herd had been, but still between men like J.F. Alexander or E.D. Bowman and the teacher or villager there was a distance not bridged by any form of intimacy.[10]

The vigour of the local African leadership of the Church was added to in 1916 when three more African ministers were ordained. These were Harry Mtuwa, Joseph Kaunde and Thomas Maseya, who had been trained by Robert Napier as had Harry Matecheta and Stephen Kundecha.

The continuing shortage of European staff allowed this vigorous growth to go on in a very free and independent way. The fruits of this were that Blantyre Presbytery, by 1926, had nearly 20,000 church members, with 5,800 in the catechumenate; there were also 326 schools and 16,000 children under instruction. That year Hetherwick reported to Scotland:

> The year has been marked by two things which indicate growth. The first of these was the erection of four new brick churches - a record for one year.... These churches are the result of the efforts of the church members and catechumens themselves, without any extraneous aid whatever.... The second item of note is the arrangement made by the Presbytery for the instruction, and afterwards for the ordination, of five new native ministers ... These men will all be supported, as the others have been, by the Central Fund of the native Church, which is maintained by the churches to whom they minister.[11]

The years from the outbreak of War until 1926 were years when no new departures took place, but the growth of the Church went on in the way in which it had been doing in the previous period. The natural culmination of this process was the meeting for the first time of a nation-wide Synod of the Presbyterian Church. Before this is considered, the

---

[10] J.P. Nthimba, Lewis Bandawe, Harry Matecheta and Lester Chopi, as well as J.A. Rodgers.

[11] Quoted in *Assembly Report* 1926, FMC Report, Nyasaland Section, pp. 282-3. In this connection it should be noted that as late as 1965 in many areas of India pastors of churches connected with the Church of Scotland were still being paid from Scottish sources.

dangerous threat to the work of the Presbyterian Church which emerged from the Chilembwe Rising must be considered.

As the classic authority on the Rising rightly points out, Hetherwick was as surprised by the rising as were most Europeans.[12] Yet, it must also be said that (as we have outlined in Chapter 5) the Blantyre Mission magazine, from 1891 up till almost the eve of the attack on the Livingstone Bruce Estates, had constantly warned of the dangers of the continuance of a system akin to serfdom in the European owned estates in the Southern Region of the country. This was the basic cause of bitterness on the part of the indigenous people of Malawi, and it is agreed by most authorities that it was a particularly unpleasant form of this relationship on the Bruce Estates that triggered off the Rising.[13] There were other reasons: unhappiness about the service of Africans in a European war,[14] and a general unhappiness about the status of the African in his own country, exemplified by the refusal of the Protectorate authorities to accept African evidence in court as being on a par with that given by a European.[15] In this connection the strength of European feeling on the issue of the equality of African and European in this matter is only too apparent in a letter Hetherwick received. Hetherwick had, in the tradition of the Blantyre Mission, accepted the word of some of the mission teachers against the word of a planter in some dispute. This "letting the side down" by Hetherwick provoked a startling response. The planter wrote and said he would attack him in the columns of *The Scotsman,* being unable to take him to court:

> as I have only to trust to nigger evidence as to the means you adopted and the endeavours you made to establish a case on the evidence of one of your lying, thieving and polygamous niggers.[16]

---

[12] Shepperson and Price, *Independent African,* p. 396.

[13] *Ibid,* pp. 223-228; and G.S. Mwase, *Strike a Blow and Die,* R.I. Rotberg, ed., (Cambridge: Harvard University Press), p. xxii.

[14] Letter from John Chilembwe to the *Nyasaland Times* quoted in full in Shepperson and Price, *Independent African,* pp. 234-235.

[15] Mwase, *Strike a Blow and Die,* p. 30.

[16] J.D. Wimpole to Hetherwick, 23 September 1908, Heth Corr, Mal Arch.

This letter was not untypical of the attitude of many whites in the Protectorate to the indigenous population. These generally bad race relations, the particularly harsh administration of the Livingstone Bruce Estates and anger at the involvement of the people of Malawi in the white man's war, were all factors in the rising.

John Chilembwe organised what was in fact a very small scale attack on the European rulers of Malawi. It began on January 23, 1915 and ended on February 4, when the body of a rebel was identified as John Chilembwe.[17] Short though it was, the affair caused a severe panic in the European community, all of whom in the Southern Province were ordered into lagers at the various Bomas. Afterwards, all who could be traced as having any connection with the rebels were sought out and punished. Many were ,hanged and many others lashed and condemned to various terms of imprisonment.

The enthusiasm among Europeans for the punishment of the offenders was intense and brought this rebuke from Hetherwick:

> I hear there were six further executions at Zomba on Monday and Zomba camera fiends were on the spot. I wonder what our countrymen and countrywomen are coming to these days. This whole affair is to them a "Roman Holiday" at Zomba.[18]

Hetherwick's immediate reaction was to press that the Enquiry into the affair which all seemed to agree was necessary, should specially enquire into African grievances. Before the meeting of the Blantyre Chamber of Agriculture and Commerce, he wrote to a friend about the paragraph he wished inserted into their petition to the Governor on this matter, and which he was going to move at their meeting. The paragraph read:

> Whether there are any grievances or other causes of discontent among the natives of the Protectorate which can be adduced as a factor in the question.[19]

---

[17] For the course of events in the rising see Shepperson and Price, *Independent African,* Ch. 6.

[18] Hetherwick to Metcalfe, 17 February 1915, Heth Corr, Mal Arch.

[19] Hetherwick to Metcalfe, 22 February 1915, Heth Corr, Mal Arch.

From his articles in the mission journal on the hardships of the *tengatenga,* his complaints about the virtual serfdom of many people on the European estates, it was a natural step to make this demand. However, it was also - or at least it could be construed as - a wise step, the first in the defence of the mission from the accusation that it was at fault; that all missions, but the Scottish missions in particular, were to blame for the rising.

The signs were certainly ominous as the Government took immediate action against the Churches of Christ missionaries and an independent African missionary, but this was, as it were, a prelude to the main piece.[20] This was an outburst from both the official and other European elements in Nyasaland expressing their basic distrust of the Scottish missions and their African churches. Hetherwick's biographer summed up the situation succinctly:

> A wave of racial hostility passed over the community. From the Governor downwards came condemnations of the missions and their work. Wild charges were made against the educated Native.[21]

It was the Scottish missions who had above all produced the educated African. Their schools far outnumbered those of the other missions; also the other missions frankly confessed to having a much more limited aim in their schools, simply that of creating church members able to read.[22] Distrust of the educated African was widespread throughout southern Africa and had not, until then, been so clearly expressed in Nyasaland, perhaps because of his usefulness in filling the middle-grade jobs in Government and industry which were filled elsewhere in East and South Africa by "poor whites", Coloureds or Indians.

Shepperson and Price describe very thoroughly the defence that the Scots put up. The first step was taken by Laws in the Legislative Council where he defended the missions from attack by the settler representatives. The second was at the meetings of the Commission of

---

[20] See Shepperson and Price, *Independent African,* Chapter 7, for a discussion of the treatment of these missionaries by the Nyasaland administration.

[21] Livingstone, *A Prince of Missionaries,* p. 155.

[22] Stokes, "Malawi Political Systems and the Introduction of Colonial Rule", Stokes and Brown, (eds.), *The Zambesian Past,* pp. 383-384.

Enquiry where Hetherwick gave evidence for over four hours. He took the initiative and attacked the Government for its lack of a positive policy of aid to education, pointing out that despite the African population paying comparatively heavy taxes, they got only 2d per child per annum back in education grants, compared with 15/9d in the Cape, or 13/5d in the more fairly comparable example of Basutoland.[23] He reached an emotional climax to his evidence in defending the African from the charge that he was becoming "cheeky" and no longer lifting his hat to Europeans. This issue of *Chotsa Chipewa*[24] went back to D.C. Scott's first deacons and his insistence that they were now civilized men. In the tradition of his old friend, Hetherwick asked that the Government use its influence to get Europeans to acknowledge the salutes:

> Then it will be known that instead of there being only one gentleman, two gentlemen have met.[25]

Meanwhile, the Scottish missionaries had alerted their respective Foreign Mission Committees that they were in some danger of action being taken to inhibit their work. They had every right to be wary, the race feeling that swept the European population was bound to affect them as the institutions which produced the majority of the very type of African so bitterly resented by the whites. Also, when the terms of reference of the Commission were announced they included an enquiry into missions and mission schools in general. This was particularly ominous, as the two non-official members of the Commission were Archdeacon Glossop of the UMCA, whose disassociation from the other missions we have already noted, and Metcalfe, the general manager of the British Central Africa Company. It was his chairman in the United Kingdom who had told Parliament that, "there is much reason for believing that the real trouble arose from the missionary schools."[26] Even more ominously, he had written to Hetherwick:

---

[23] Verbatim extracts of this speech are to be found in Livingstone, *A Prince of Missionaries*, pp. 156-7.

[24] "Take off your hat" in the 2nd person singular, which is the height of rudeness in Nyanja.

[25] Quoted in Shepperson and Price, *Independent African*, p. 367.

[26] Quoted in Shepperson and Price, *Independent African*, p. 363.

> I have heard nothing as to what happened at the Legco Meeting, but I am rather in agreement with Bruce's motion that all mission schools be closed unless under strict European supervision.[27]

The motion he referred to was the one that Laws had forced Bruce to withdraw, but it was still feared because it so clearly represented European thinking both on the part of officials and settlers.

The Commission made up of Glossop, Metcalfe and three officials was not going to blame the Government, the missionaries felt, and there was every indication that it would blame the missions, especially the Scots. This was confirmed by Metcalfe himself in a letter sent to Hetherwick and heavily marked as confidential and private. It was to do with the deliberations of the Commission preparatory to writing its report. Metcalfe said:

> I am certain this Enquiry will not be, nor is intended by Government that it should be, 'a complete and impartial' one.[28]

In May 1915, both Assemblies of the Scottish Churches concerned instructed their Foreign Mission Committees to co-operate over the task of ensuring the interests of the work of their missions in Nyasaland were not overlooked by the British Government. They had an entree with the Government, in that Steele-Maitland at the Colonial Office was a Church elder; the same kind of link had been vital in the crisis over Mlozi and the Portuguese when Lord Balfour had been their advocate with the Prime Minister, Lord Salisbury.

The preparations made to lobby the British Cabinet seemed well justified when the report of the Commission appeared. Its last sections (35-48) were on missions. Much in it annoyed the Scots, but two points were especially annoying and alarming. This was the attack on the trustworthiness of African teachers and leaders. The Commissioners felt they had to be tightly supervised by Europeans or evil consequences were inevitable. They then went on to insist that the Roman and Anglican missions were free from this danger. Although their sensibilities were sharply touched, and this resulted in many angry comments, the real

---

[27] Metcalfe to Hetherwick, 25 May 1915, Heth Corr, Mal Arch.
[28] Ibid

threat was that already raised by Livingstone Bruce in the Legislative Council - the demand for close supervision of African staff. If any kind of regulations ensued that insisted on such a pattern of work, then the development of the two new Presbyteries of the Church of Central Africa Presbyterian would have been effectively and permanently crippled. Their widespread work (Livingstonia had over 600 schools, more than all the other missions together) was based in principle on African initiative; and in practice the two Scottish missions had not the European staff to supervise closely anything other than a small fraction of their existing work.

Although the Governor prevented the Legislative Council from debating the Commission's report until he had received instructions from the British Government, a step which was very frustrating, the missionaries, though angry, were not unduly alarmed because the lobbying procedures that had been prepared were now in action and, as Hetherwick wrote to Laws,

> I have just time for a line in sending a copy of the correspondence as far as it has gone between our people and Steele-Maitland. think we are safe in his hands and those of Bonar Law.[29]

This was so; and no action was taken to bring in any regulations about mission churches or schools.

Relations between the Government and the settlers on the one hand and the missions and African churches on the other, did, however, remain strained. In so far as he had freedom of manoeuvre, the Governor did act along the lines of the ideas of the Commission vis-a-vis the missions. The most glaring example was over the churches and schools in the area of John Chilembwe's mission, whose church and schools had been destroyed by Government forces. The people there approached Hetherwick asking that the Blantyre Presbytery should set up a church and help restart schools in their area. This the Governor refused to allow, but he did not interfere with the expansion of Roman Catholic work from Nguludi Mission into the same area.[30] This was extremely annoying for

---

[29] Hetherwick to Laws, 3 January 1916, Heth Corr, Mal Arch.
[30] Hetherwick to Laws, 20 May 1916, Heth Corr, Mal Arch.

Hetherwick, but it was not a major problem. The real threat to their work did not materialize because the Nyasaland authorities never received any instructions from London to go ahead in the area of the control of African teachers and ministers.

The naked racial feelings that had been aroused did not quickly subside, nor did they cease to have an effect on the life of the community and Church in Malawi. The clearest impact of this on the work of the Blantyre Mission was on Scott and Hetherwick's aim of maintaining one Church which encompassed all Christians of all races. We have already noted the declension from one congregation worshipping and celebrating the Lord's Supper in both English and Nyanja services, to a situation where there was nominally one congregation at both Zomba and Blantyre, but congregations which were divided in practice into Europeans and native worshipping communities. This gulf widened in the decade after the rising and in 1926 Hetherwick accepted this bitter reality and began negotiations with the authorities in Edinburgh for the creation of a colonial congregation of the Church of Scotland with its own minister in Blantyre. This was to be a totally separate body because the other Presbyterian Christians of the area were members of the Blantyre Presbytery of the CCAP. This was an acknowledgment of the total defeat in the area of racial unity in the Church, which had been fundamental to the thinking of D.C. Scott and to Hetherwick himself.

After the actual flurry of the quarrel with the Government in 1916 over the report of the Commission on the Rising, relations with the Boma were tranquil, primarily because of the agreement over the need for unity in that time of emergency. However, with the War over, Hetherwick returned to his traditional role of critic of the Boma and defender of African rights. In Blantyre he was now alone. The other leading figures of the mission seemed to have no desire to fulfil such a role. But in the north there were still strong elements in the leadership of Livingstonia Mission with this concern: Robert Laws himself, Donald Fraser of Loudon, and the educationalist, T. Cullen Young.

The first issue that arose was the recurrent one of African rights over land. A Land Commission was set up by the Governor in 1920 on which Hetherwick was asked to serve. He kept in touch with the Livingstonia staff about these matters so that he would not be acting alone. His attitude was still the same as in the past. He wrote to Laws:

> We have the Land Commission sitting just now and it is taking two days out of my week ... which I can ill afford but it is a piece of work I can do for the natives of this country, and so I do not grudge the time.... The root principle that I go upon is that the land is the natives', and only such portions as can be spared within the next two generations are to be temporarily leased to Europeans and to natives for individual holdings.[31]

This Land Commission, like the other efforts before the War, produced no effective legislation; and so the problems associated with European estates were left to complicate life for the first post-Imperial Government in Malawi in the 1960s. This problem of the land was always associated with labour problems in Malawi and this particular controversy also took up Hetherwick's time and energy. During 1919 there was a long correspondence between Hetherwick and the Livingstonia leaders about Residents using their police to obtain forced labour for public works. In this they attempted to co-ordinate evidence with which to confront the Governor.[32] This problem was caught up with two others which received Hetherwick's concern. These were the tactics of the Government in dealing with tax defaulters, and the conduct of the police in general.

A letter from Cullen Young summed up both problems:

> No country will stand for ever what the village natives of this territory are being called upon to stand.... It (Government policy) is fostering a native class of official whose injustice to his fellows, whose methods of oppression and whose flagrant breaches of law are steadily adding to the account which we will be asked to pay. In the villages we are already feeling a growing estrangement and a dawning suspicion where once we imagined there existed something approaching friendship.... In every district violence is done to women whose husbands are absent at work or who are young widows.... In every district women are held hostage for defaulting relatives (in the

---

[31] Hetherwick to Laws, 8 October 1920, Heth Corr, Mal Arch.

[32] Hetherwick to Fraser, 8 June 1919, Fraser to Hetherwick, 8 August 1919 and 1 September 1919, Heth Corr, Mal Arch.

matter of taxes) and notwithstanding the fact that the woman so seized has paid her own hut tax.... Queues of these hostages follow the Government capitaos from village to village, rain or sun, with young children trailing behind.[33]

These were scenes that in British minds would typify the Portuguese colonial regime rather than any idea of their own colonial policy.[34] According to George Mwase, this kind of behaviour had been one of the grounds of Chilembwe's desire to rebel.[35] Hetherwick was able to get an interview with the Governor, the main burden of whose reply to Hetherwick seemed to consist of complaints about "the laziness of the native".[36] Hetherwick also began quietly to recommend to anyone who would listen that a properly educated police force would partly solve these problems. Such a force did come into being later.

Hetherwick and Laws also returned to the attack on the Government over their education policy and the use of funds gained from African taxation. The Rising Commission had recommended what the Scots had long pressed for: a Government Department of Education, and an increase in Government spending on schools. This had been begun but was still only a token. Indeed, the use of local funds to maintain the old type of administration which saw itself as having no social concern, other than that of maintaining law and order, still seemed the order of the day. Laws and Hetherwick campaigned about this in 1921. Hetherwick complained bitterly to Laws:

> It is too bad to go as much as £9,000 to increase salaries of the officials out of the native increase in revenue and only £5,000 for their educational wants.[37]

---

[33] T. Cullen Young to Hetherwick, 14 January 1919, Heth Con, Mal Arch.

[34] E.g., Norman MacLean's *Africa in Transformation,* (London: J. Nisbet, 1943) with its extraordinary claims of the special character of the British marking them out in contrast with lesser European types as ideal rulers of the "child" peoples of the world. Also Ogilvie's *Our Empire's Debt to Mission,* where similar ideas are expressed.

[35] Mwase, *Strike a Blow and Die,* p. 32.

[36] Hetherwick to Fraser, 26 June 1919, Heth Corr, Mal Arch.

[37] Hetherwick to Laws, 7 October 1921, Heth Corr, Mal Arch.

Indeed, the three or four years after the end of the War were exceedingly depressing. The enormous scale of the deaths resulting from *tengatenga* service with the army and from the influenza epidemic was followed by the return of some of the worst features of the pre-war colonial regime. However, three things brightened the scene for Hetherwick, now very conscious that his time of service was drawing to a close. These were also gleams of hope for the possibility of future development along the lines that D.C. Scott had laid down for both Church and community.

These three things were, first, the enunciation of the policy of trusteeship in the Kenya White Paper of 1923; second, the coming of the Phelp-Stokes Commission and the subsequent White Paper of 1925 on Education and Tropical Africa; and third, the union achieved, in the two meetings of 1924 and 1926, of the Church of Central Africa Presbyterian.

According to his biographer, W.P. Livingstone, Hetherwick felt that the emphasis of the Kenya White Paper and the following discussion with its emphasis on trusteeship and the moral duty of the metropolitan country to help positively the economic development of her dependencies, was what he had long wanted and what the mission had always stood for.[38] However, in his own book, *The Romance of Blantyre,* in commenting on the new attitude of the Imperial Government, he did sound a warning note. He pointed out how all of northern Zambezia (which humanitarians had long hoped that as a "Black Man's Country" would be helped to develop in its own way) was now faced with a vast increase in white population and influence from south of the Zambezi because of the beginnings of the Copper Belt development.[39]

There was less ambiguity about his enthusiasm for the Phelp-Stokes Commission and the subsequent developments towards a positive Government role in education; something, as has been seen, which the Blantyre Mission had pressed for since the beginning of the century. This was a major element in the sort of positive social concern on the part of the Government which Hetherwick held was its duty, and a just return for taxation.

---

[38] W.P. Livingstone, *A Prince of Missionaries,* pp. 179-180.
[39] Hetherwick, *The Romance of Blantyre,* pp. 235-237.

These two occasions for optimism were essentially pointed to the future. Their development lay ahead when he would no longer be a key figure in the Church and political life of Malawi. The third occasion for rejoicing was, however, the completion of something he had hoped for since his first days in Malawi: a united Church. He and his leader, D.C. Scott, had started with a vision of a united African Church embracing many if not all the denominational streams of the West. What emerged was something much less, a union of the Churches produced by the three Presbyterian missions in the country. Because of the War and its aftermath, it was only in 1924 that the union of the Presbyteries of Blantyre and Livingstonia took place. The ceremony was at Livingstonia during the Fourth General Missionary Conference in October 1924, exactly ten years after the date for which it had been planned. The business of the Synod was largely formal: the institution of the Synod, the election of its officers, and so on. One piece of important business was done however. This was the agreement to formalize negotiations which had been going on for some time with the Dutch Reformed Mission in the Central Province. These were completed in a very few meetings during the next two years.

Then, in 1926, during the celebrations of the Jubilee of the Blantyre Mission, the united Synod of the CCAP covering the whole of the Protectorate as well as areas in Zambia and Mozambique was instituted. Both Hetherwick and his biographer make these celebrations of the Jubilee and the setting up of the new Synod an emotional climax to their books.[40] But in some ways these meetings can be seen as symbolizing the defeat of much that the Blantyre Mission of Scott and Hetherwick had stood and worked for. As has already been noted, it was a union of Christians in the Reformed tradition only. Also, it was a federation and not a union. Each of the three Presbyteries maintained the real authority over the life and work of the Church in its area, and the Synod had little or no power of initiative. Thus, a very different style of life continued in the different Presbyteries, especially noticeable when the Dutch Reformed Presbytery of Nkhoma is compared with the other two. A strict racial separation was maintained in the Nkhoma area. A moralistic form of church life, furthermore, which condemned many African ways

---

[40] *Ibid,* pp. 253-255: and Livingstone, *A Prince of Missionaries,* pp. 184-188.

accepted by Blantyre was characteristic of the life of the Presbytery of Nkhoma. For example, drunkenness was a matter for church discipline in Blantyre, while to drink anything alcoholic at all meant exclusion from the Lord's Supper in the Nkhoma area.[41]

These differences were simply accepted. What was even more of a defeat for the early Blantyre vision was the fact that the missionaries were not full members of the CCAP. They retained membership of their Presbyteries in their home countries. A Mission Council existed in the area of all three Presbyteries. These Councils were completely independent of the CCAP and controlled the major budgetary resources as well as the posting and work of all missionaries. On top of all this, as we saw earlier, Hetherwick had been forced to accept racial division in the church at Blantyre with the negotiations for the setting up there of an independent "colonial" congregation of the Church of Scotland.

What is left to be said? Was D.C. Scott an unreal dreamer? Did all that he worked and hoped for die, except the bricks and timbers of his Blantyre Church?

The verdict seems to be that, despite appearances, life was still there, and a life of some real intensity. On the mission stations at Blantyre, Zomba, Domasi and Mulanje, there were the trappings of Mission Council authority, the attitude of many missionaries who saw themselves virtually as a sort of spiritual wing of the Empire,[42] the creation in the mid-1930s of a Blantyre Presbytery of the Church of Scotland which included all male missionaries which further confirmed the splitting of the Church on racial lines. All this obscured, but did not destroy the achievement of D.C. Scott, his "clan" and his deacons.

In the villages of Ntcheu and the Southern Province of the Nyasaland Protectorate, the CCAP went on growing along the lines described in this and the last chapter. African initiative was still the dominant factor there.

---

[41] Hetherwick to J. Pauw, 4 August 1910, Heth Corr, Mal Arch. Pauw had complained that most Blantyre men in his area, although regular churchgoers and otherwise good men, were regular drinkers, though not drunkards. They had to *be* barred from Communion as a result. Hetherwick replied that this was unacceptable to Blantyre.

[42] Ogilvie, *Our Empire's Debt to Missions.*

African music and Christianized African customs that have been described, continued to characterize the life of the Church.

The "new men" of African society who had been so much the concern of D.C. Scott, did not rule the Church or the nation; but they did dominate the village churches and they began, in the 1920s, to form Native Associations which were the roots of modern nationalism in Malawi. Unlike the north, where Donald Fraser and Robert Laws actively encouraged the formation of such bodies, and CCAP ministers, like the Reverend Yesaya Chibambo became officials of the movement, there was no official encouragement in Blantyre from the ministerial missionaries at least. However, the African teachers, pastors and other educated Christians did play their full part in this movement. In 1923 the Nyasaland (Southern Province) Native Association was founded. There also came into being Blantyre, Mulanje, Chiradzulu and Zomba Native Associations. All of these along with the associations in the other Provinces were the vehicles of expression and concern of these men who were the dynamic force in the church life of the Blantyre Presbytery of the CCAP. Van Velsen has characterized them thus:

> The Associations clearly bore the stamp of the 'new men' who founded and ran them. Meetings generally opened and closed with Christian prayer; office bearers were selected by vote; minutes were kept.... Each person contributed his own experience. Consequently one finds in the records a mixture of biblical and civil service phraseology.[43]

The first issues that they took up with Government were the same as those which Hetherwick, Cullen Young and Fraser had already raised: forced labour; the holding of women hostages in the matter of tax defaulting; and a plea for more Government concern for and activity in education.[44] This can be seen as a confirmation that the concerns of Hetherwick and Laws had not been out of touch with African feeling -

---

[43] Stokes, "Malawi Political Systems and the Introduction of Colonial Rule", Stokes and Brown, (eds.), *The Zambesian Past,* 381.

[44] *Ibid,* 382-384.

though the new missionaries of the 1920s and 1930s did become much more out of touch.[45]

D.C. Scott's deacons and teachers were the beginnings of a new Malawi. Unlike many other groups of "new men" produced by the missions in Africa, they were a conscious creation. Scott believed the future ought to be in their hands; he taught them to believe so themselves; he gave them independence and initiative at the village level. Also, to be fair to Hetherwick, in the crisis after the Chilembwe Rising, he and Laws defeated the threat of legislation which would have badly set back the development and growth of these new men and women in whom a new Malawi was growing.

The conscious development of such men and women and the careful fostering of their self confidence by David Clement Scott, and to a lesser degree by Hetherwick, marks the unique contribution of the Blantyre Mission to the political, social and religious life of Malawi. Given the realities of political and religious life in the late Victorian and Edwardian age, possibly most of D.C. Scott's detailed plans for the future were impossible to realize, but his influence was fundamental in the forming of a group of people who were the forerunners of a new Malawi and the creators in the village congregations of the CCAP, a genuinely African Church.

---

[45] My African informants were unanimous about this. The evidence of J. Allen Rodgers was the same, though he, through people like Levi Mumba and J.F. Sangala, did keep in touch with the Associations.

Table of Sources

The materials from which this study has been constructed did not readily fit the title bibliography; their heterogeneous nature also made their classification a problem to some degree. The most satisfactory solution to these difficulties seemed to be to follow the scheme used by Professor G.A. Shepperson and Dr Tom Price in *Independent African.*

Following their example I have divided the material simply into primary and secondary sources. Interviews and manuscript material were clearly primary, as were a number of printed reports of both the Government and the Church of Scotland. Along with contemporary periodicals, a number of printed books were considered primary material when their authors were eye-witnesses or participants in the events described. This criterion was applied even to books which were published after the close of the period studied.

With regard to the availability of primary material for the study of this period in the history of Malawi, the very nature of the section dealing with source material in A.J. Hanna's *The Beginnings of Nyasaland and North Eastern Rhodesia* necessitates some comment. There it states on page 270:

> The African Lakes Corporation assures me that it has not troubled to preserve the records of its predecessor, the African Lakes Company. A similar inability to recognize the importance of historical documents has been shown by the Church of Scotland, although printed minutes of its Foreign Mission Committee, and of the Free Church's Foreign Mission Committee, contain a few letters from missionaries in the field and a certain amount of other information.

In fact, whatever appeared to be the case in Scotland when Dr Hanna made his investigations - he did not investigate in Malawi at all - a mass of Church of Scotland and Free Church of Scotland material has been preserved by the now united Church of Scotland, and by the Blantyre and Livingstonia Missions in Malawi.

The bulk of the records of the Free Church and the Auld Kirk Foreign Mission Committee's archival material is now held in the National Library of Scotland, but there is also a significant collection in the University Library. In the National Archives of Malawi in Zomba, as well as in the

Synod offices at Blantyre and Livingstonia, there are also considerable quantities of material from the period. The Church of Scotland and Blantyre material is listed fully below; a full description of the Free Church and Livingstonia material can be found in the table of sources in John McCracken's *Politics and Christianity in Malawi, 1875 - 1940* (Cambridge: Cambridge University Press, 1977).

Primary Sources

Statements made as a result of interviews.

Apart from that with Mr Rodgers, interviews were conducted in Nyanja with men who were friends of the writer and with whom he had often chatted. The interviews were, therefore, not unnatural situations, but from the informants point of view, they were just talks with a friend. This was so even on the two occasions when a tape recorder was used.

- Bandawe, Lewis, M.B.E. (Pupil of John Gray Kufa in Lomweland; friend and later son-in-law of Joseph Bismarck; assistant to Robert Napier; in the last years of his life, chief interpreter of the Nyasaland High Court.)
- Chopi, Lester. (Pupil and clerk at Blantyre Mission at various times between 1910 and 1950, senior elder to Chief Kapeni.)
- Matecheta, the Reverend Harry Kambwiri. (D.C. Scott's deacon, first ordained minister of the Blantyre Presbytery of the Church of Central Africa, Presbyterian.)
- Nthimba, the Reverend James Poya. (Pupil and teacher in Blantyre from 1900.) Rodger, J. Allan. (Lay missionary at Blantyre and Zomba, 1924-1954.)

After the writer's Nyanja became fluent towards the end of 1959 until he left Malawi in May 1965, he talked on innumerable occasions with groups of African people, as well as with individuals, about the old days. These were mainly Yao people in the Chiradzulu district, Ngoni and Nthumba people in Ntcheu, as well as friends from all the many tribal groups of Malawi living in Blantyre. From them much was learned of the culture and tradition of the Malawi peoples and their views of the recent and distant past.

Manuscripts and other non-printed material.

Blantyre Mission Council.

The minute books of this body from 1887 until it was dissolved in 1958 are held in the offices of the Blantyre Synod of the CCAP. Minute Book I is the volume relevant to this study.

The Church of Scotland.

The Letter Books of the Convener of the Foreign Mission Committee.
These were consulted in the National Library of Scotland. The individual letters are referred to by date, the names of sender and recipient and the number of the letter book. This was the only classification possible when the writer consulted them. However, they have since been given National Library reference numbers. The citations in this work will still, however, enable them to be identified and located by an enquirer.

Treasurer's Letters.
A small collection of letters from the FMC Treasurer, Mr McLagan to Duff MacDonald covering the years 1878-1880 are to be found in the National Library listed as Mss 7541-7545.

The Foreign Office.

The correspondence included in FO 2 and in FO 84 are the main sources of material for the study of the official British presence in Malawi. Some reference to FO 83 was also necessary because of the role of the British South Africa Company in Malawi's affairs in the 1890s.

Hetherwick, Alexander.

A large series of box files containing all Hetherwick's correspondence from 1898 to 1928 is in the Malawi Archives. When studied by the writer they had not been re-classified in any way by the Archivist and so are referred to simply by the date and the names of recipient and the writer.

Moir, John.

The family correspondence of the joint head of the ALC in Malawi is now in the Library of Edinburgh University and is listed as files GEN. Ms. 717/11-13.

Morrison, F.J.

The diary kept by this employee of the African Lakes Company from 1882 to 1886 is in the Library of the University of Edinburgh.

Scott, David Clement.

A series of letters from D.C. Scott to his friend James Robertson, minister of Whittinghame, East Lothian, are in the Library of Edinburgh University. They are to be found in file: GEN. Ms. 717/10.

C. Printed material other than books

Newspapers

Central African News and Views, c. 1896.

The Central African Planter, (Songani, Zomba,) 1895-7.

The Central African Times, (Blantyre) 1899-1911.

The Nyasaland Times, (Blantyre) 1911-1926.

The Scotsman, (Edinburgh) The years 1888-1891 for the Scottish campaign for British intervention in Malawi, and 1896-97 for the attack on D.C. Scott's leadership of the Mission.

Periodicals

Church of Scotland Home and Foreign Mission Record (HMFR), later *Life and Work and Missionary Record*, 1874-1926.

Life and Work in British Central Africa, (LWBCA) later *Life and Work in Nyasaland*, 1888-1919. Neither the National Library nor Edinburgh University Library have a complete set but taken together the whole range is covered.

The Zambesi Industrial Mission, Occasional Papers, 1892-1918.

Pamphlets and Reports

Chirnside, Andrew, *The Blantyre Missionaries: Discreditable Disclosures*. (London: Ridgway, 1880).

Matecheta, H.K., *Blantyre Mission: Nkhani za Ciyambi Cace*. (Blantyre: Hetherwick Press, 1951).

Nyasaland Protectorate, *Report of the Commission appointed by His Excellency the Governor to inquire into the Various Matters and*

Questions concerned with the Native Rising within the Nyasaland Protectorate. (Zomba: Government Printer, 1916).

Report by Commissioner Johnston on the Trade 'and General Condition of the B.C.A. Protectorate, 1895-96. Cmd. Paper 8254.

Report of the Centenary Conference on Protestant Missions of the World. (London: James Nesbit, 1888).

Report on the First Three Years' Administration of the Eastern Portion of British Central Africa, 1894, Cmd. Paper 7504.

Reports on the Schemes of the Church to the General Assembly of the Church of Scotland. 1874-1926.

Waller, H., *Nyassaland: Great Britain's Case against Portugal*. (London: Stanford, 1890).

World Missionary Conference. *Reports of Commissions*. 9 Vols. (Edinburgh: Oliphant, Anderson & Ferrier, 1910).

D. Books

Buchanan, J., *The Shire Highlands as a Colony and a Mission*. (Edinburgh: Blackwood, 1885).

Drummond, H., *Tropical Africa*. (London: Hodder & Stoughton, 1888).

Foskett, R. (ed.), *The Zambesi Journal and Letters of Dr. Kirk*. (Edinburgh: Oliver & Boyd, 1966).

Fotheringham, L.M., *Adventures in Nyasaland*. (London: Sampson Low, 1891).

Gelfand, M. (ed.), *Doctor on Lake Nyasa, Being the Journal and Letters of Dr Wordsworth Poole, 1895-1897*. (Salisbury: privately printed, 1961).

Gamitto, A.P.C., *King Kazembe*. (trs. Ian Cunnison, Lisbon: Junta de Investigações do Ultramar, 1960).

Hetherwick, A., *The Romance of Blantyre*. (London: James Clarke & Co., nd., [1931]).

Hetherwick, A., *The Gospel and the African*. (Edinburgh: T & T Clark, 1932).

Hetherwick, A. (ed.), *Robert Hellier Napier in Nyasaland. Being his Letters to his Home Circle*. (Edinburgh: Blackwood, 1925).

Johnston, H.H., *British Central Africa*. (London: Methuen, 1897).

Johnston, H.H., *The Story of my Life*. (London: Chatto & Windus, 1923).

Langworthy, E.B., *This Africa was Mine*. (Stirling: Stirling Tract Co., 1952).

Livingstone, D. and G Livingstone, *Narrative of an Expedition to the Zambesi and its tributaries, and of the discoveries of Lakes Shirwa and Nyassa, 1858 - 1864*. (London: John Murray, 1865).

Lugard, F.D., *The Rise of our East African Empire*. (Edinburgh: Blackwood, 1893).

MacDonald, D., *Africana. 2 vols*. (Edinburgh: John Menzies & Co., 1881).

Moir, F.L.M., *After Livingstonia*. (London: Hodder & Stoughton, 1923).

Rankin, D.J., *The Zambesi Basin and Nyassaland*. (Edinburgh: Blackwood, 1893).

Rankine, W.H., *A Hero of the Dark Continent*. (Edinburgh: Blackwood, 1897).

Robertson, W., *The Martyrs of Blantyre*. (London, John Nisbet & Co., 1892).

Scott, D.C., *A Cyclopaedic Dictionary of the Mang'anja Language Spoken in British Central Africa*. (Edinburgh: Church of Scotland, 1892).

Secondary Sources

A. Periodicals

The Journal of African History (JAH)

Fagan, Brian, "Pre-European Ironworking in Central Africa with Special Reference to Northern Rhodesia," vol. 2, no. 1, 1961.

Saunderson, F.E., "The Development of Labour Migration from Nyasaland, 1891-1914," vol. 2, no. 1, 1961.

Marwick, M.G., "History and Tradition in East Central Africa through the eyes of the Northern Rhodesian Cewa," vol. 4, no. 3, 1963.

Lynch, H.R., "The Native Pastorate controversy and cultural ethno-centricity in Sierra Leone, 1871-1874," vol. 5, no. 3, 1964.

Oliver, R., "The Problem of Bantu Expansion," vol. 7, no. 1, 1965.

International Journal of African Historical Studies

Northrup, N., "The Migrations of the Yao and Kololo into Southern Malawi: Aspects of Migrations in 19th Century Africa", vol. 19, no. 1, 1986.

The Nyasaland (later Malawi) Journal

Pike, J.G., "A Pre-Colonial History of Malawi," vol. 18, no. 1, 1965.

Price, T., "Mbona's Water-Hole," vol. 6, no. 1, 1953.

Price, T., "The Meaning of Maneanja," vol. 16, no. 1, 1963.

Price, T., "Yao Origins," vol. 17, no. 2, 1964.

Rangeley, W.H.J., "Mbona - the Rain maker," vol. 6, no. 1, 1953.

Rangeley, W.H.J., "The Amachinga Yao," vol. 15, no. 2, 1962.

Rangeley, W.H.J., "The Arabs in Nyasaland," vol. 16, no. 2, 1963.

Religion in Malawi

Ross, K.R., "The Renewal of the State by the Church: The Case of the Public Affairs Committee in Malawi", vol. 5, 1995.

Transafrican Journal of History

Phiri, K.M., "Yao Intrusion into Southern Malawi, Nyanja Resistance and Colonial

Conquest, 1830-1900", vol. 13, 1984.

B. Books

Abdallah, Y.B., *The Yaos*. trs. and ed. M. Sanderson. (Zomba: Government Press, 1919).

Ajayi, J.F.A., *Christian Missions in Nigeria, 1841-1891*. (London: Longman, 1965).

Bandawe, L.M., *Memoirs of a Malawian,* (Blantyre: CLAIM, 1971).

Boeder, R.B., *Silent Majority: A History of the Lomwe*. (Pretoria: Africa Institute, 1985).

Bolink, P., *Towards Church Union in Zambia*. (Franker: T. Weber, 1967).

Cairns, H.A.C., *Prelude to Imperialism: British Reaction to Central African Society, 1840 - 1890*. (London: Routledge & Kegan Paul, 1965).

Chadwick, O., *MacKenzie's Grave*. (London: Hodder & Stoughton, 1959).

Chibambo, Y.M., *My Ngoni of Nyasaland*. (London: Lutterworth Press, 1942).

Duffy, J., *Portugal in Africa*. (Cambridge, MA: Harvard University Press, 1959).

Duffy, J., *A Question of Slavery*. (Oxford: Clarendon Press, 1967).

Fleming, J.R., *The Church of Scotland, 1843-1874*. (T&T Clark: Edinburgh, 1933)

Groves, C.P., *The Planting of Christianity in Africa*. 4 vols. (London: Lutterworth, 1948-1955).

Hanna, A.J., *The Beginnings of Nyasaland and North Eastern Rhodesia, 1859-1895*. (Oxford: Clarendon Press, 1956).

Latourette, K.S., *A History of the Expansion of Christianity*. 7 vols. (New York: Zondervan: 1937-1945).

Linden, I., *Catholics, Peasants and Chewa Resistance in Nyasaland 1889-1939*. (London: Heinneman, 1974).

Livingstone, W.P., *Laws of Livingstonia*. (London: Hodder and Stoughton, 1921). Livingstone, W.P., *A Prince of Missionaries*. (London: James Clarke, nd., 1931).

McCracken, J., *Politics and Christianity in Malawi, 1875-1940*. (Cambridge: Cambridge University Press, 1977).

MacLean, N., *Africa in Transition*. (London: J. Nisbet, 1943).

Mackay, P., *A Portrait of Malawi*. (Zomba: Government Press, 1964).

Mitchell, J.C., *The Yao Village*. (Manchester: The University Press, 1956).

Mufuka, K.N., *Mission and Politics in Malawi*, (Kingston, Ontario: The Limestone Press, 1977).

Mwase, G., *Strike a Blow and Die*, ed. Robert I. Rotberg, (Cambridge: Harvard University Press, 1968).

Ncozana, S.S., *Sangaya: A Leader in the Church of Central Africa Presbyterian*. (Blantyre: CLAIM, 1996).

Neill, S., *A History of Christian Missions*. (Harmondsworth: Penguin, 1964).

Nzunda, M.S. and K.R. Ross (eds.), *Church, Law and Political Transition in Malawi, 1992-94*. (Gweru, Zimbabwe: Mambo Press, 1995).

Oliver, R., *Sir Harry Johnston and the Scramble for Africa*. (London: Chatto & Windus, 1957).

Oliver, R., *The Missionary Factor in East Africa.* (London: Longmans, 1952).

Pachai, B. (ed.), *Early History of Malawi.* (London: Longman, 1972).

Perham, M., *The Diaries of Lord Lugard.* 4 vols., (London: Faber and Faber, 1959-1963).

Phiri, D.D., *James Frederick Sangala.* (Lilongwe: Longman, 1971).

Read, M., *Children of their Fathers.* (New Haven: Yale University Press, 1960).

Read, M., *The Ngoni of Nyasaland.* (London: Oxford University Press, 1956).

Robinson, R. and J. Gallagher, *Africa and the Victorians: the Official Mind of Imperialism.* (London: Macmillan, 1961).

Roome, W.J.W., *Can Africa be Won?* (London: SCM Press, 1927).

Rotberg, R.I., *The Rise of Nationalism in Central Africa.* (Cambridge: Harvard University Press, 1959).

Shepherd, R.W.H., *A South African Medical Pioneer.* (Lovedale, C.P.: Lovedale Press, 1952).

Shepperson, G., and T. Price, *Independent African.* (Edinburgh: The University Press, 1959).

Stokes, E., and G. Brown (eds.), *The Zambesian Past: Studies in Central African History.* (Manchester: The University Press, 1965).

Sundkler, B., *The Christian Ministry in Africa.* (London: SCM, 1960).

Temples, P., *Bantu Philosophy.* (Paris: Presence Africaine, 1959).

Tew, M., *Peoples of the Lake Nyasa Region.* (London: International African Institute, 1950).

Thompson, T.J., *Christianity in Northen Malawi: Donald Fraser's Missionary Methods and Ngoni Culture.* (Leiden: E.J. Brill, 1995).

White, L., *Magomero. Portrait of an African Village.* (Cambridge: Cambridge University Press, 1987).

Wills, A.J., *An Introduction to the History of Central Africa.* (London: Oxford University Press, 1964).

Wright, M., *Gdman Missions in Tanganyika 1891-1941: Lutherans and Moravians in the Southern Highlands.* (Oxford: Clarendon Press, 1971).

C. Theses and Papers

Alpers, E.A., "The Role of the Yao in the Development of Trade in East-Central Africa, 1698 -c.1850". (Unpublished London University Ph.D. thesis, 1966) Krisluiamurthy, B.S., "Land and Labour in Nyasaland, 1891-1914". (Unpublished London University Ph.D. thesis, 1964)

Ngwira, E.T., "The Life and Times of Hary Kambwiri Matecheta, 1870-1962". (Unpublished History Seminar Paper, Chancellor College, University of Malawi, 1973).

Index

Aberdeen 27, 36
African Lakes Company (ALC) 51, 92f, 95f, 98-101, 111-116, 118, 121f, 124f, 127, 130-133, 135-137, 142, 149, 174f, 179
African Mission Committee 21
Africana 21, 23, 50, 56f, 60-62, 67-69, 71f, 74, 76, 78, 83
Afrikaaner 236, 242
Afro-Americans 237
Agriculture, plantation 173-176, 180-182, 186f
Agriculture, traditional peasant 183, 186f
Ajayi, J.F.A. 155
Alexander, J.F. 227f, 236, 246
Algiers 98
Amangoche Yao 95
Anderson, J. Melville 227, 236
Anderson, Sir Percy 119, 133, 146
Anglican Missions 14, 16, 251
Anglicanism 216, 220, 228, 239f
Anglo-Indian official 148, 150
Anglo-Portuguese Convention 144
Anglo-Portuguese relations 141f
Ankhoswe 206
Annexation of land by planters 161, 176, 178
Anti-Slavery Expedition 161
Apartheid 84, 196
Artisans 23f, 39, 55, 60, 71, 82, 200, 227
Askari 142f, 161, 171, 245
Auld Kirk 17, 28, 51, 56, 78

Baganda 75
Baikie 138
Banda, Dr. Hastings Kamuzu 11
Bandawe 77
Bandawe, Lewis 12, 245
Bantu 91
Bantu Philosophy 91
Baptism 41, 108, 197f, 207, 217, 241
Baptist Industrial Mission 239
Beck, Janet 29, 34, 104, 168, 231
Bell, Miss 200, 203
Bell-Walker, Dr 228
Bemba 128f
Bentham, Jeremy 155
Bible 149, 208, 239
Bismarck, Joseph 78, 84, 87, 94, 103-105, 108, 199f, 245
Black, Dr 56
Blantyre Chamber of Agriculture 248
Blantyre Chamber of Commerce 171
Blantyre Mission: Nkhani ya Ciyambi Cace 52
Blantyre Presbytery 230, 232, 234, 239, 241, 246, 252f, 258f
Blantyre Synod 11-14
Bokwito, Tom 52-54, 56
Boma 138, 151, 154, 159f, 166-168, 170, 178, 184, 198, 214, 253
Bonar Law 252
Booth, Emily 192

Booth, Joseph 192, 225, 237
Borthwick, T.C. 43
Bowie, John 29, 34, 104f, 109, 167, 196, 205, 211f
Bowman, E.D. 226
British Broadcasting Coorporation 95
British Central Africa 150-153, 164, 169, 222, 232
British Central Africa Company 250
British Central Africa Gazette 153
British South Africa Company 142, 144f, 148, 197, 211, 214
Brooke, Rajah 137
Bruce Estates 247f
Bruce, Livingstone 251f
Bruce-Knight 83
Buchanan, John 15, 22, 57, 61f, 73, 87, 92, 98, 101f, 104, 106, 116, 126, 128f, 131f, 142-146, 162, 166, 199
Buganda 69
Burleigh, Lord 141
Burleigh, UK 134, 140
Bwalo 97
Bwanausi, Dr Augustine 11, 95
Byzantine architecture 109, 193
Cairns, H.A.C: 83f, 86, 160f
Cairo 137
Calico 143, 178, 181
Calvinism 32
Cameron, Comander 174
Cape Colony 52, 134, 150
Cape Maclear 52, 75, 77, 116
Cape Synod 153
Capital punishment 71, 76

Cash crops 116, 121, 179
Central Africa Company 174, 250
Central African Planter 214f
Central African Times 214
Central Region 68, 96, 151, 167, 175, 234
Chanting 208, 239
Chaplaincy 196, 214
Charteris, Professor 20, 25
Chewa 173
Chibambo, Yesaya 259
Chikumbu, Chief 68, 88f, 105f, 123, 158, 160, 173
Chikuse, Kaphatizika 101f, 109, 111, 118f, 160, 200
Chikuse, Makololo chief 118
Chikwawa 51, 54-56, 58, 231
Chilembwe Rising 101, 242f, 247-249, 253, 260
Chilembwe, John 84, 168, 188, 192, 237, 240-242, 247f, 252, 255, 260
China 35, 38, 43
Chinde 141f, 152, 174
Chinkolimbo 104
Chipatula 23, 81, 93, 100
Chipeta 90, 94, 173
Chipuliko, John 108, 202
Chiradzulu 53, 70, 88, 105f, 158, 197, 199, 243, 259
Chiradzulu Mountain 105
Chirnside, Andrew 69, 72-74, 76
Chiromo 142
Chisuse, Mungo 95
Chotsa Chipewa 250
Christie, Margaret 29

Church Missionary Society (CMS) 44-47, 64f, 77, 155, 191
Church of Central Africa Presbyterian (CCAP) 11f, 14, 233-235, 252f, 256-260
Church of Christ 85, 194, 196, 230
Church of Scotland 13, 17, 19-22, 24f, 27, 30, 32, 35f, 38, 40, 42-44, 47, 49, 58, 60, 62, 65f, 71f, 83, 122, 124, 131f, 134, 172, 191, 193, 196, 212, 217, 220, 224f, 227, 232f, 235, 244, 246, 253, 258
Church Service Society 209
Civil authority 64, 71, 74, 77, 149
Civil jurisdiction 14, 72-76, 91
Civil War US 181
Cleland, Robert 29, 34, 104-106, 109, 199, 211
Colonial Office 176, 251
Commerce 13, 17, 63, 80, 83, 113f, 117, 122, 133, 187
Commission of Enquiry 67, 78, 197, 214, 220, 250
Communion services 195
Congo 128
Copper Belt 256
Coutinho 144
Crime 70
Crown Colony 134, 159, 167
Crown Lands 161, 172, 174-176
Crusades 66
Culture 12, 14, 80, 83-85, 156f, 193, 203, 236
Currie, Adam 211, 213, 215
Currie, Mrs 213
Cuthbertson, John Nelson 113

Cyclopaedic Dictionary of the Mang'anja Language 85, 91, 104, 190
Dalrymple, Charles 220
Dancing 97, 203, 205, 229, 244
Dar-es-Salaam 13, 148
Deacons 97, 201-204, 206, 209, 212, 214-217, 219, 222-224, 228, 230f, 236, 241, 245, 250, 258, 260
Dean, Henry 87
Dedza 99, 179
Dennis, G. 43
Denominationalism 196
District Collectors 185
District Commissioners 182
Domasi 14, 29, 32, 34, 101-103, 105f, 110, 166, 195, 197-199, 205, 208, 210, 217, 229, 240, 258
Domingo, Charles 229
Downing Street 149
Dreams 107f, 170
Drumming 97, 203
Drummond, Henry 31f, 86
Duncan, Jonathan 22, 24, 29, 62, 87, 95, 103, 105
Dundee 27, 36
East Africa 35, 37, 51, 60, 64, 73, 111, 128, 139, 182f, 220, 243
East Africa Company 183
East Africa Mission 73, 220
Edinburgh 11f, 15, 20f, 27, 34, 36f, 39, 50, 70, 72, 74, 78f, 81, 84, 113, 122, 139f, 152, 155, 190, 210, 212, 216-221, 223-225, 227, 231, 235, 238, 243, 253

Edinburgh, University of 11, 212
Education 13, 56, 80, 82f, 92, 95, 104, 189, 197, 222, 228, 236, 239, 242, 250, 255f, 259
Education, Department of 255
Edwardian era 43f, 260
Elders 11f, 89f, 100, 202, 229f, 237f, 242, 244
Elton 112
Episcopal Church 20
Estates 177, 183f, 186, 188, 247, 249, 254
Euchologion 209
Evangelism 27, 43, 56, 95, 229f
Evangelists, African 200, 231
Federated Board of Missions 239f
Federation of Presbyterian Churches 163, 257
Federation of Rhodesia and Nyasaland 11
Fenwick, George 22-25, 55, 62, 64, 69f, 73, 82, 86, 93, 100, 118, 122, 196
Fenwick, Jose 103
Fenwick, Mrs 103, 196
First World War 19f, 43, 47, 182, 184, 222, 235, 240
Fisi 207
Fleming, J.R. 20, 27
Flogging 67, 72-74, 77
Foot, Captain 100f, 114f
Forbes, Major 144
Foreign Mission Comittee (FMC) 22, 24-26, 28, 30-47, 49, 60, 63, 65-67, 70-74, 78f, 81, 88, 92, 99, 104f, 109, 115, 124f, 131, 172, 190-192, 200, 209-211, 215-221, 223-227, 231, 234, 244, 246
Fort Lister Gap 89
Fotheringham, L. Monteith 128
Franco-Prussian War 94
Fraser, Donald 230, 234, 253, 259
Free Church of Scotland 17, 20, 50, 63, 121, 235
Frere Town, Kenya 64, 66, 77
Frere, Sir Bartle 49, 144
Funerals 20, 49, 103, 198, 204f
Gallagher, John 134f, 137, 139, 155, 157, 163
Gelfand, Michael 160, 218
Geneva 32
German missionaries 243
German occupation 128
Germany 44
Glasgow 21, 27, 36, 93, 121, 124, 231
Glasgow University 231
Glossop, Archdeacon 250f
Goodrich, Consul 115, 121, 162
Gordon 135
Goschen 163
Gowk 93
Groote Schuur 149
Guns 99, 115, 124, 168, 214
Hamilton, James 29, 103
Hamilton, UK 36
Hanna, A.J. 49, 54, 64, 70, 74f, 114, 128f, 132, 139, 145, 147, 152, 166
Harare 13
Harris, Rutherford 147f, 154

275

Hawes, Consul 115-132, 135, 139, 162
Hawick 20f, 49f
Henderson, Henry 17, 22, 24, 29, 51-58, 67, 71, 73, 87, 101f, 109, 167, 211f, 231
Henderson, Mrs 109
Henry Henderson Institute 231
Herd, H.D. 211, 213-215, 246
Herdman, J.L. 65
Hetherwick, Alexander 20, 29f, 34-36, 41, 49, 52, 54, 57f, 88-90, 94, 101-103, 105-107, 122-125, 133, 143, 149-151, 153f, 156, 158, 162, 165-168, 170-172, 175, 182-190, 196, 199, 209f, 212, 214, 218f, 221, 224-239, 241, 243-260
Hinkleman 118, 120, 124
HMS Stork 142
House of Commons 113
House of Nelson 155
Hymns 108, 197f, 204f, 208
Hynde, R.S. 171, 210f, 214f, 220, 226, 236
Ilala 127
Illustrated London News 193
Impi 102
Independence, political 13
India 22, 38, 43, 45, 49, 57f, 246
Induna 102, 128
Industrial Missions 81
Initiation rites 204, 206f
Inter-tribal warfare 63
Iringa 243
Ivory 100, 113, 128, 161

Jedburgh 49
Jesuit Mission 32
Johannesburg 185
Johnston, Harry 15, 28, 59, 89, 123, 129, 139-143, 145-154, 157-164, 166f, 169, 171-177, 179, 183f
Jubilee celebrations 229, 257
Jumbe 149
Kabaka 69
Kabula river 69
Kaferanjila, Rondau 87, 103f
Kainga 108
Kalaliche, Cedric 168
Kalimbuka, Chief 52, 54, 61, 78
Kamlinje, James 202
Kapeni, Chief 53-55, 78, 88f, 91, 115, 122f
Kapito, Henry Cowan 104
Karonga 126-133, 136, 142, 243
Kasisi 55, 89, 108, 120
Kasonga parish 229
Katangulu 106, 110
Katunga, Chief 81, 143
Kaunde, Joseph 246
Kawinga, Chief 32, 53, 68, 115f, 122, 125, 129, 160, 217f
Kenya 43, 64f, 166, 222, 226, 237, 256
Kenya White Paper 256
Kerr 83
Khartoum 135
Khonje, Dina 95
Kikuyu Mission 43, 166, 222, 226, 237
Kimberly 151, 173, 188

Kingsley, Mary 159
Kirk Sessions 30, 45, 202, 224, 228
Kirk, John 49
Kirkmicheal 57
Kongone 55
Kopakopa 128
Koyi, William 59, 61
Krapf, J.L. 65
Krishnamurthy, B.S. 173, 180
Kufa, John Gray 168, 202, 223, 228
Kundecha, Stephen 236, 246
Kuntaja 90f, 94, 115
Kurakura, John 98
Kwakwa River 55
Kwataine, Chief 204
Labour 15, 51, 88, 95f, 104, 171f, 174, 176f, 179-182, 184-187, 216, 254, 259
Labour Bureau 182
Lacustrine area 17
Ladies Committee for Foreign Missions 37
Lake Chirwa 101, 244
Lake Malawi/Nyasa 15, 22, 50f, 75, 114, 133, 137f, 160, 218
Lake Tanganyika 51, 112, 127f, 142
Land Commission 184, 253f
Land grants 174f, 183
Laws, Robert 55f, 59, 62, 67, 128, 229, 233, 236, 253, 259
Lay missionaries 29, 191, 202, 217, 224
Leghorn 138
Legislative Council of Nyasaland 171, 187-189, 249, 252
Lettow-Vorbeck, von 245

Life and Work and Missionary Record 210
Life and Work in British Central Africa 80, 84f, 95, 106, 108f, 125, 136-139, 141, 144-146, 150, 152, 156f, 160, 162, 164f, 168, 170-173, 179-183, 185, 188f, 193, 194-200, 202f, 206-208, 212-216, 220-222, 224, 228-230, 232, 236, 238
Likoma Cathedral 153
Likoma Island 128
Limbe 11, 52f
Lisbon 112, 134, 139, 143f
Lister, T.V. 114, 117f, 120, 123f, 126, 140, 146, 158, 162f
Literacy 197
Liturgy 195
Livingstone Bruce Estates 247f
Livingstone, David 14f, 19, 44, 49, 154
Livingstone, W.P. 53f, 62, 64f, 74, 140, 224, 238, 256
Livingstonia Mission 13, 52, 57, 77, 132, 185, 187, 232, 234, 253
Livingstonia Trading Company 51
Liwonde Barrage 52
Lobengula 134, 165
Lomwe 16, 228
Lomweland 29, 32, 41, 168, 199, 215, 219, 223, 228, 245
London Missionary Society 44-47, 127, 153, 191
Lopsa, Che 53
Lord Balfour 134f, 140, 251
Loudon 234, 253

Lovedale Institution 52, 57, 61, 104f, 225
Lozi 75
Luangwa 142
Luchenza 231, 243
Lunzu parish 229
Lusaka Conference 160
Macdonald, Duff 23, 25, 33, 50, 59, 62, 66, 74, 78f, 83
Macdonald, Mrs 59, 61, 213
Machinga Pass 52
Machinjili 112
Mackenzie, Bishop 52f
Macklin, Thornton 22, 24, 54f, 58f, 62f, 66f, 69f, 72-74, 76f, 88
Macrae, John 20-22, 25, 49-51, 58-60, 64-66, 74, 90
Macvicar, Neil 29, 167f, 225-227
Magomero 14, 16, 53f
Mahe 66
Makanjila 115, 120, 129, 160
Makololo 16, 23, 55, 68f, 73, 81, 89, 93, 100-102, 108, 118-120, 122, 125, 141-143, 145, 165, 173f, 176, 202
Makwangwala 100, 128f
Malawi Cabinet 95
Malemia 52, 61, 78, 101, 122, 166, 205
Malosa Mountain 101
Malota, Donald 104
Mandala 12, 93, 96, 104, 109f, 137, 143, 179
Mang'anja 15f, 85, 93, 174, 176, 190
Mangochi 14, 244

Manicaland 144
Maples, Archdeacon 153
Maravi 15
Marriage 197, 206, 241
Masea, Chief 202
Maseko clan 205
Maseko Ngoni 16, 68, 99, 101, 103, 111, 118, 123, 158, 164
Maseko, Chief 16
Maseya, Thomas 246
Mashona 165
Matapwiri, Chief 68
Matecheta, Harry Kwambwiri 13, 52-54, 89, 96f, 102, 199f, 202-205, 208, 222, 236, 246
Matenje, Paul 208
Mazaro 55
Mbame 51, 55
Mbelwa, Chief 61, 77, 128
Mccallum, J.D. 41, 229f
Mcilwain, John 29, 84, 98, 103, 167, 212, 231
Mclagan 58f, 66f, 70, 72, 74
Medical Missionaries 181, 200
Metcalfe, Charles 154, 248, 250f
Methodist Missionary Society 64
Middle Ages 66, 76
Milandu 90f, 198
Mill 155
Millen, Dr 103
Milne, William 22
Mines 184f, 188
Mission Advance Movement 31, 40, 43, 45f
Mission colonies 65, *see also* Christian colonies

Mission Council 185, 200f, 211, 213, 216, 218f, 223-228, 231-233, 235, 241, 258

Mission magazine 96, 108, 157, 163, 165, 169, 177-179, 181, 183, 186, 192f, 196, 207, 213, 215f, 228, 230, *see LWBCA*

Mission Sunday 30f

Missionary Auxiliary Committees 40

Mitochi 70, 72, 88, 105, 111, 122, 158, 160

Mkanda (Mkhanda) 89, 122, 165, 214

Mlandu 90f, 97, 118f, 158, 165, 202, *See also Milandu*

Mlozi 126-133, 137f, 142, 145, 160, 179, 192, 242, 251

Moir, Frederick 101

Moir, John 100, 149, 151

Monteith, Mr 101, 126-128

Moody and Sankey mission 20, 27

Morel, E.D. 159

Morrison, Frederick T. 93, 98-101, 103, 112, 115, 122, 156, 168, 188, 239

Moshweshwe 69

Mozambique 15, 32, 94, 112f, 117, 126f, 131, 138f, 142f, 145, 158, 180, 183, 245, 257

Mpama 78, 88, 91, 122

Mpeni, Thomas 202

Mphasa 245

Msalema 128

Msondole parish 229

Mtambo, Chief 76

Mtuwa, Harry 246

Mudi River 143

Mulanje 14, 32, 89, 101, 105f, 117, 123, 165, 173, 199, 208, 211, 213f, 217f, 230, 233, 258f

Mulanje Mountain 89, 101, 105

Mulunguzi 106, 110

Mumba, Levi 260

Murray, William 239

Muthill parish 72, 104, 210, 215, 220

Mvera 239

Mvera Conference 234, 238, 240

Mvula, James 98f

Mwepeta, Wilson 228

Namkango Hill 81

Napier, Robert 29, 167, 171, 231, 236, 243-246

Natal 16

Nationalism 107, 259

Native Associations 259

Native Commission (S. Africa) 189

Native Locations Ordinance 184

Ndebele 75, 134, 165

Ndirande 53, 94, 102, 110

Neill, Stephen 27, 190, 216

Netherlands 44

New Kirkpatrick 36

Ngabu 176

Ngoni 12, 16, 53, 61, 68, 77, 99f, 102, 111, 122f, 128, 164, 173, 179, 198-200, 205, 217

Ngoniland 29, 32, 175, 228

Ngozo clan 205

Nguludi Hill 53f, 103

Nguludi Mission 252

Ngunana, Shadrack 61

Nguni 61
Niger River Diocese 156
Nkhoma 234, 257
Nkhoma Presbytery 258
Nkhoma Synod 234
Nkhotakota 149, 175
Nkonde 127
Nkosi Chikuse 68
Nkosi Gomani 164
Nkosi Gomani II 102
Nkosi Mpezeni 164
Nkosikazi 102
North End War 133
Northern Region 167, 175
Nsoni 88f, 229, 243
Ntcheu 14, 16, 96, 99, 103, 151, 179, 204f, 234, 258
Ntcheu district 96
Ntcheu District 151, 204
Nthumbi 14
Ntimawanzako, Nacho 39, 78, 104, 199f
Ntithili, Mapas 69
Nyanja 12, 15, 28, 68f, 95, 98, 103, 106, 151, 171, 194f, 197, 204, 208, 214, 231, 236, 239, 250, 253
Nyasa Industrial Mission 232, 239
Nyasaland African National Congress 11f, 204
Nyimbo za chamba 204
Nyimbo za Mulungu 204
Oil Rivers Protectorate 159, 161
Old Livingstonia 116, 126
Oliver, Roland 64, 113, 128, 139, 142, 147-149, 152, 162f, 166, 171
O'Neill, Consul 112, 115, 126f, 130-132, 138f
One-party state 13
Oral Tradition 102
Ordination 191, 201f, 229, 237, 246
Our Empire's Debt to Missions 172, 258
Palmerstonian 138, 159
Panthumbi 200, 203, 208, 229
Paramount Chiefs 16, 69, 74, 89, 102, 118
Parliament, Malawi 52
Parliament, UK 71, 133, 250
Pauw, J. 258
Peden, Dr 29, 101, 103
Petrie 140
Phalombe Plain 105, 231
Phelp-Stokes Commission 256
Pilgrim's Progress 61
Plan of Development (FMC) 223
Planter 161, 166, 171, 173, 176-178, 180, 182f, 186f, 198, 209, 214, 247
Polwarth, Lord 51, 65
Polygamy 206
Poole, Wordsworth 160, 218
Portuguese 14, 30, 32, 41, 85, 87f, 95, 99, 101, 109, 111-114, 117, 119-121, 124f, 130, 132-136, 138-145, 147, 149, 164, 166, 192, 215, 228, 245, 251, 255
Portuguese East Africa 245

Prazero 113
Prazo 112f, 144
Prelude to Imperialism 83f, 86, 160f
Pringle, Alex 65, 72f, 81-83, 85, 92
Protectorate 11, 13f, 29-31, 109, 111, 124, 130, 134, 140, 147f, 150-154, 158f, 161, 164, 167, 171f, 174-177, 179-181, 184, 186, 188f, 197, 214, 222, 224, 229, 238, 240, 242, 247f, 257f
Providence Industrial Mission 240
Public Records Office 152
Quelimane 53, 89, 98, 100, 109, 114, 117, 133, 136
Race relations 179, 248
Racialism 196, 231, 241
Railway 180-182, 184
Ramakukan 16, 68, 100, 109, 118-120, 122, 124
Rand 176, 184
Rankin, D.J. 72f, 92, 104, 122, 141, 174, 210, 215, 220f
Rankine, Thomas 81, 85, 122, 133, 191, 212
Rhodes, Cecil 137, 141, 154
Rhodesia 11, 49, 54, 64, 70, 75, 114, 128f, 132, 139, 144f, 147f, 165f, 197
Ribe, Kenya 64, 77
Robertson, George 211, 220, 225
Robertson, James 23f, 32, 86, 92, 111, 146, 195
Robinson, Ronald 134f, 137, 139, 155, 157, 163
Rodgers, J. Allen 246, 260
Roman Catholic Church 207

Romance of Blantyre 49, 52, 54, 57f, 88, 102, 107, 143, 256
Rondau, Kagaso 78
Roseberry, Lord 122-124, 148, 159, 166, 174
Rotberg, Robert 12, 107, 247
Ruo River 133, 142-144
Salisbury, Lord 130f, 134f, 137, 139-141, 151, 251
Sangala, J.F. 12f, 204, 260
Sawelayera, Evangel 104
Sazuze, Kagaso 104
Scotland 14, 19-22, 25, 27-29, 31f, 34, 38-40, 44, 47, 49, 51, 53f, 60, 62f, 69, 72, 74, 76, 86, 91, 94, 99, 104, 109, 124f, 132f, 140, 146, 150, 155f, 192, 194, 200-202, 209, 215, 217-219, 221, 225-227, 232, 235, 246
Scotsman, The 92, 192, 220-222, 247
Scott, Archibald 34, 38, 46, 79, 210
Scott, David Clement 14, 20, 23-25, 27-30, 32, 34, 36-39, 46, 77-80, 84f, 91f, 95, 109, 111, 124, 133f, 137f, 140f, 146, 148f, 151, 154, 156-158, 166-168, 170f, 177, 179, 183, 189-192, 194-196, 198-200, 202, 204-206, 209-231, 233-236, 238, 241, 243-245, 250, 253, 256-260
Scott, Henry E. 29, 166
Scott, Mrs D.C. 88, 101, 103, 213
Scott, William A. 29, 167
Sebituane 69
Second Republic of Malawi 13
Second World War 244

Selous, F.C. 197
Serpa Pinto 142f, 147, 242
Seychelles 66
Shaka 16
Sharpe, Alfred 151
Shepperson, George 11f, 84, 192, 225, 237, 242, 247-250
Shire Highlands 14-16, 29, 38f, 52, 59, 61, 68, 81f, 92, 98-100, 103, 109, 111, 113, 118, 121, 125, 128, 131f, 134, 138, 140, 141, 143, 146, 149, 163, 172, 178, 182, 187, 193f, 196, 210-212, 214, 217, 229
Shire River 14-16, 29, 38f, 51-53, 57, 59, 61f, 68, 81f, 92f, 98-103, 109, 111, 113, 118, 121f, 125, 127f, 130-132, 134, 138, 140-144, 146, 149, 163f, 172, 174, 178, 182, 187, 193f, 196, 210-212, 214, 217, 219, 229, 231
Shire Valley 16, 29, 68, 81, 174
Sierra Leone Native Pastorate 156
Simons 66
Slave raiding 55, 75
Slavery 62-65, 74-77, 88, 124, 161, 178, 181
Slaves 53, 64, 66f, 75, 77f, 87f, 93f, 99, 113, 116, 125, 161f, 165, 179
Smith, J.A. 191, 236
Soche Mountain 53, 102
Soche parish 229
Sorcery 207
Sotho 16, 69
South Africa 142, 144f, 148, 180f, 184f, 197, 204, 211, 214, 249

South Africa General Mission 204
Southern Region 14, 68, 96, 98, 151, 158, 174, 247
St George's Church 217
St Micheal's and All Angels Church 109
St. Paul 87
Stalker, James 27
Steele-Maitland 251f
Steere, Bishop 83
Stevenson Road 127f
Stewart, James 20f, 52, 57, 59, 62, 65, 67, 69, 72, 75, 87
Stokes, Eric 12, 159, 167, 249, 259
Sunday Schools 33, 36
Sundkler, Bengt 107
Swahili 99, 115, 117, 125, 142, 149, 158, 164
Tanzania 65, 242
Tax Ordinance 186
Taxation 15, 165-167, 177f, 182, 255f
Temples, P. 91
Tenants 175, 178, 180, 183f, 188
Tengani 176
Tengatenga 177, 180-182, 186f-188, 249, 256
Thangata 184
The Beginnings of Nyasaland and North-Eastern Rhodesia 49, 152
Theft 70, 119, 213
Thefts 118
Thompson, Joseph 144
Thyolo 175
Tonga 77, 129, 145, 179
Tozer, Bishop 112

Traditional African Law 88, *see also* Milandu
Transport problems 180f
Transvaal 188
Treaties 121f, 124f, 145, 147, 174f
Tribalism 84
Tropical Africa 32
Ufiti 207
United Board of Translators 239f
United Presbyterian Church 20, 27, 56, 235
Universities' Mission to Central Africa 14, 27, 54, 112f, 129, 132, 240, 250
Unyago dance 203
Velsen, Van 259
Venn, Henry 154, 156
Victorian era 43f, 260
Walker, John 22-25, 55, 62, 64, 69f, 73
Walker, Miss 103
Waller, Horace 49, 113
Werner, Alice 200, 203
Wesleyans 77
West Africa 156
Westminster Abbey 20
Westminster Palace Hotel 146
White Paper on Education and Tropical Africa 256
Whitehall 125
Whittinghame 195, 209
Witchcraft 207
Women Missionaries 200, 231
Women's Committee for Foreign Mission 200
Wood, Julius 20
Yao 12, 15f, 24, 28, 52f, 57, 61, 68-70, 78, 88-90, 95, 99, 102, 111, 115, 117f, 122f, 145, 158-161, 164, 171, 173, 178, 195, 197, 204, 214, 237
Young, E.D. 17, 21f, 50-52, 62f, 77, 88, 113, 254, 259
Young, T. Cullen 253, 255
Zambezi 16, 20f, 55, 97, 101, 111-113, 122, 130, 133f, 136, 138f, 141f, 144, 151, 174, 180f, 192, 204, 225, 232, 234, 238, 240, 256
Zambezi expedition 16, 111
Zambezi Expedition 20, 113, 138f
Zambezi Industrial Mission 97, 225, 238, 240
Zambezia 16f, 20f, 37, 49, 95, 107, 111-113, 126-128, 134f, 139, 141, 145, 150, 157, 187, 219, 223, 256
Zambia 163, 208, 239, 257
Zanzibar 128
Zimbabwe 13, 180
Zomba 14, 23, 32, 52f, 61, 68, 81, 92, 98, 100-102, 104f, 116, 125, 152, 166, 176, 199, 208, 217, 229, 237, 248, 253, 258f
Zomba Mountain 53
Zulu 90, 137, 142f

www.ingramcontent.com/pod-product-compliance
Lightning Source LLC
Chambersburg PA
CBHW021657230426
43668CB00008B/649